CORPORATE REPUTATIONS

STRATEGIES FOR

DEVELOPING THE

CORPORATE BRAND

GRAHAME R. DOWLING

KOGAN
PAGE

First published in 1994 by Longman Professional Publishing, a division of Longman pty Limited, Longman House, Kings Gardens, 95 Coventry Street, Melbourne 3205, Australia

UK edition published in 1994 by Kogan Page Limited

Kogan Page Limited
120 Pentonville Road
London N1 9JN

British Library Cataloguing in Publication Data

A CIP record for this book is available from the British Library.

ISBN 0 7494 1436 7

Printed and bound in Great Britain by Biddles Ltd, Guildford and Kings Lynn

CORPORATE
REPUTATIONS

Contents

"I don't know who you are.
I don't know your company.
I don't know your company's product.
I don't know what your company stands for.
I don't know your company's customers.
I don't know your company's record.
I don't know your company's reputation.
Now—what was it you wanted to sell me?"

MORAL: Sales start **before** your salesman calls—with business publication advertising.

McGRAW-HILL MAGAZINES
BUSINESS • PROFESSIONAL • TECHNICAL

Preface

On the opposite page is one of the most famous industrial advertisements of all time. Many people refer to it as the 'McGraw-Hill ad'. It encapsulates much of the marketing task of most private and public sector organisations. The ad challenges the reader to answer two basic questions:

a What is the reputation that people hold of your organisation?
b What differentiates your organisation from your competitors?

If you can't answer these two questions quickly and in simple terms, then there is a good chance that your stakeholders (customers, employees, journalists, etc.) can't answer them either.

Another way to think about the McGraw-Hill ad is to ask yourself whether your organisation passes the IDU test. Is what your organisation does IMPORTANT to customers? Can your organisation really DELIVER a valuable product and/or service? Is what your organisation provides UNIQUE? If your organisation fails any aspect of the IDU test, then the task of marketing your products and services is harder than it should be.

This book focuses on helping managers build and sustain their organisation's most valuable marketing asset, namely, the reputation of the organisation held by different types of people. A good corporate reputation enhances the value of everything your organisation does and says. A bad reputation devalues your products and services, and it acts as a magnet which attracts further scorn. The management of your organisation's desired reputation is too important to be left to a public relations group. It is also too important to be assigned to the CEO. Reputation management is the responsibility of every employee.

As an internal stakeholder, you have the most to gain from a good corporate reputation, and the most to lose from a poor corporate reputation. The McGraw-Hill ad reflects the following quote attributed to the American essayist and poet Ralph Waldo Emerson:

What you are speaks so loud,
I can't hear what you say.

About the author

Grahame Dowling is an Associate Professor at the Australian Graduate School of Management. His teaching focuses on helping managers appreciate the role that marketing can play in providing better products and services for their customers. He believes that to appreciate customers' needs requires good market research, analysis and interpretation.

Grahame's major research interests focus on how companies can use their corporate reputation to improve customer service and other marketing activities. He also researches how people and business organisations adopt new ideas, products and services so that companies can design new products to enhance their acceptance in the marketplace.

Grahame is one of the few Australians currently studying business-to-business and professional services marketing. He has been a keynote speaker on these topics to academics and business people in Australia, Europe and North America and his research has been published in leading journals in each of these continents.

The Graduate School of Management encourages its faculty to spend time working with leading organisations to help them better serve their key stakeholders. In this role, Grahame is an active consultant with some of Australia's largest companies. Recent assignments include: studies of the corporate image of banks and telecommunications suppliers; calibrating advertising effectiveness; evaluating the quality of marketing research; guiding the development of a professional service marketing program; and numerous in-company executive briefings on various aspects of marketing.

Grahame is also the Associate Director of the Centre for Applied Marketing and of the Centre for Export Marketing at the Australian Graduate School of Management. His degrees are: BCom in Accounting and Dip Bus Stud (University of Newcastle), MCom and a PhD in Marketing (University of NSW).

Introduction

When a business sells its products and services to another business, or to end-user customers, its reputation can play an important part in supporting the company's marketing effort. World-class organisations like *BMW*, *IBM*, *McDonald's*, *Shell*, *Sony* and *Xerox* often use the name of the company as an integral part of each of their product names. Other corporate giants such as *Procter & Gamble* and *Unilever* choose not to advertise the association between the company and their brand names. Both strategies can be successful; however, the trend is for more good companies to use the equity in their name to help their marketing.

For organisations which deal with customers face-to-face, the management of their corporate reputation is more complex than for organisations which sell products to customers 'at arm's length'. The potential for things to go wrong in a real time service encounter is far higher than when a customer buys a product 'off the shelf' from a retailer. Hence, managing an organisation's reputation in a service-type situation requires ongoing internal marketing programs to ensure consistently high quality service encounters. As outlined later, the quality of the interaction between your organisation's employees and customers can have a big impact on your corporate reputation. Organisations which sell their products off the shelf tend to manage their reputations more through their external communications than do service organisations.

The central argument of this book is that if your organisation has a good reputation, it can always be used to support the organisation's business activities. If your organisation has a poor reputation, then it pays to fix it.

The management of your organisation's reputation is too important to be left to the marketing department or the corporate communications group. It is also too important to be handed over to a firm of corporate design consultants. Managing your company's desired reputation is the responsibility of senior management. Enhancing the company's reputation is the responsibility of every employee. For example, to the question of how many people were in the public relations department of his firm, an Australian CEO recently answered—'sixteen thousand', which is the total number of employees in the organisation.

The challenge to build a great reputation starts at the top of your organisation. The company's 'top team' moulds the overall culture in which a reputation is developed, and provides the leadership to ensure that this becomes a reality in the minds of those stakeholders who control your destiny. Corporate reputation building requires a long-term commitment to the ideas outlined in this book. However, the potential rewards for both the architects of change, and the organisation itself can be substantial.

On a personal level, our reputation is one of our most valuable assets. The same is true for any organisation. Just how valuable these reputations are is outlined in the early chapters of this book. To enhance this value, it is necessary to manage the factors which combine to create these reputations. As we look into the different types of information stakeholders use to form their reputations of your organisation, it becomes clear that advertising, name changes, and corporate signage are by themselves insufficient to create a good corporate reputation. The reputation people hold of your organisation is the net result of *all* its activities. In essence, reputation reflects performance.

Typically, reputations take a long time to form, and if they become strong and unique they can be quite difficult to change. This characteristic can be an asset to your organisation if its reputation is good, but it can be a crushing liability if it is bad. For example, government bureaucracies around the world tend to have a poor reputation. This then gets perpetuated in television programs such as *Yes Minister* and *Yes Prime Minister* (both from the UK), and in sayings such as 'you should be glad you don't get all the government you pay for'. Thus, the reputations of organisations are a long-term strategic asset or liability. In a highly competitive market it is better to be well armed with a good reputation, than have to rely solely on tactical manoeuvres.

This is not a book based on a series of in-depth studies of 'excellent' or 'winning' organisations. This was the approach adopted by Tom Peters and Robert Waterman in their best-selling business book *In Search of Excellence*. The companies they chose however, turned out to be unrepresentative of corporate USA, and many of the lessons they drew did not distinguish between good and bad performers. For example, as soon as we started to use these 'excellent' companies as benchmarks of good practice, many of them began to experience financial difficulty. (As I am writing this section, *IBM* just recorded one of the biggest losses in corporate history.)

Many of the companies selected by Peters and Waterman became the victims of their own success. Success created 'High Brand Equity' which in turn led to 'Corporate Arrogance'. This then resulted in what marketers affectionately call the 'Law of Fast Forgetting'. That is, these companies forgot what made them successful. Rather than try to pick a series of winners, the approach adopted here is to look at periods when various organisations have managed their corporate reputations well or poorly. When these short case histories are combined with various research studies, they provide a rich framework to enhance our understanding of how reputations are formed, and how they can be changed.

The overall approach adopted throughout this book is to integrate and synthesise the vast amount of material about corporate reputations into a descriptive theory. I'm a firm believer in the saying that 'there is nothing so practical as a good theory'. Every day most organisations rely on such theories to guide their operations. They are called corporate plans. These plans are created in exactly the same way that scientists create many of their theories, namely, by developing a series of hypotheses about what will work in a particular circumstance. The plan is then 'tested' by implementing it in the real world.

After reading this book you should know the types of information which need to be collected to manage your organisation's desired reputation, and the processes used to gather and disseminate this information throughout the organisation. In most organisations, the internal accounting and budgetary systems provide most types of information. They are designed to track the 'hard' inputs (for example, materials and labour) and outputs (such as sales) which define the financial status of the organisation. Other types of information such as market research and management experience tend not to be well integrated with formal accounting-based controls. Also, these types of information are not collected as often, nor given the same importance as financial information. To be blunt, most organisations can't manage their reputations because their current information systems don't integrate 'hard' and 'soft' information to focus on the relevant factors which shape stakeholder perceptions.

The design of new information systems starts by developing a good understanding of the set of activities which your organisation can use to manage its reputation. It is then up to the CEO and the top management team to commit to a program of reputation enhancement. The visible support of the CEO is crucial for both its symbolic value, and to ensure the implementation of activities across the organisation. Building your organisation's reputation into a strategic marketing asset requires developing a vision to guide business decisions and employee behaviour. It also requires aligning workplace incentives with this vision, and communicating it to outside stakeholders.

This book is organised into three broad sections. First, I develop an understanding of what corporate reputations are all about. In the management research literature there is some confusion about the concepts of corporate identity, corporate image, and corporate reputation. In the 'real world', managers tend to have a good feel for what is meant by the image or reputation of their organisation. By refining this understanding however, we can use it to build a stronger foundation for the second section of the book which focuses on the factors which combine to help shape your organisation's reputation.

The second section of the book identifies the factors which affect your corporate reputation. This is a task which many management teams struggle with. We see too many companies trying to change their reputations by telling (or yelling at) people about the company's virtues and aspirations, when what should be happening is some fundamental changes to corporate behaviour. Also, too many companies neglect the crucial role that employees play in the reputation formation process. By isolating the core set of factors which enhance or detract from your corporate reputation, the risk of spending a considerable amount of time and money for little or no effect is substantially reduced.

The final section of the book describes how to measure corporate reputations, and how to use these findings to guide the refurbishment of your organisation's desired reputation. If your reputation is to be used as a competitive weapon, then it is necessary to know what various groups of stakeholders think about the company, and about its competitors. It is also handy to know how stakeholders think an ideal company in your industry should behave. With this information, and the accumulated wisdom from the first two sections of the book, it is then easy to outline what to do to start the process of reputation change.

I have written this book for managers having either direct or indirect responsibility for managing their organisation's desired reputation. They will be concerned with the need to develop and protect the value of their organisation's reputation, because in the future it will be more important to own a market than to own a factory. The best way to own a market is to own the company and the 'brands' which dominate that market.

Finally, I would like to thank three of my academic colleagues who provided valuable comments on the draft chapters of this book: Phil Dawes (University of New Orleans), especially John Rossiter (Australian Graduate School of Management), and David Wilson (Penn State University). Also, thanks are expressed to all those CEOs and managers who talked so openly about how they manage the reputations of their organisations.

PART 1

Corporate
Reputations

CHAPTER 1

The Corporate Reputation Crisis

A crisis is creeping up on many companies and their managers are often unaware of it. It is the dilution of equity in their company's reputation. An organisation's reputation forms a basic platform from which it serves its customers, employees, and other stakeholders. CEOs whose names appear on the front of their building and professionals who have their names on the corporate letterhead know the value of a good reputation. They understand that an individual's most valuable marketing asset is his/her reputation. When the organisation has the same name as the founder or the partners, corporate reputations become a personal affair. For most employees, however, the link is not as strong.

During the 1980s, thousands of business enterprises around the world suffered a loss of reputation. Sometimes it was the result of an environmental disaster like the grounding of the *Exxon* corporation's oil tanker, the Exxon Valdez in Alaska. Sometimes it was caused by a lapse of ethical standards by managers who became greedy to make huge short-term profits for themselves and their companies. The aftermath of the

October 1987 collapse of world stock markets highlighted many such cases. Another cause was the deregulation of markets which revealed how many business enterprises struggled to come to grips with new market conditions. Classic examples of this were the banking industry in Australia and the domestic airline industry in the USA. Most often, however, reputation loss was caused by an inability to provide products and services which matched the expectations of customers.

That a crisis is occurring is a strong claim, but it is no exaggeration. Only a few companies and non-profit organisations tend to stand out in any market as making a unique contribution to business or society. Some that come to (my) mind are *Boeing*, *Club Méditerranée*, *Walt Disney Co.* (because of Disneyland), *McDonald's*, the *IBM* and *Apple* computer companies, the car manufacturers *BMW* and *Mercedes-Benz*, *Greenpeace*, *NASA*, and a few others. How many organisations can you recall that have really made a mark on our world? Even if you can list 100 organisations it still represents only a tiny fraction of all the organisations you have come in contact with or read about. That's not much of an impact is it?

Why has such a situation developed? And does it really matter whether your organisation has a distinct 'mean something' reputation? Answering the second question is easy. There are a lot of case studies and research findings which suggest that good corporate reputations are more valuable than bad ones. Some of these will be referred to later in this chapter. Answering the first question is more difficult. What can be said at this stage, however, is that the reasons for the developing crisis can be traced to three main factors.

First, most managers have only a fuzzy understanding of the quality of their organisation's reputation. While they may feel that business in general, and their company in particular, does not receive the social status it deserves, it is not clear what can be done to rectify this situation. This lack of a framework to understand how reputations are formed leads to the second problem—how to measure what various groups think of the company. Unless a clear picture can be drawn showing the current reputation of the organisation, it becomes almost impossible to agree about whether or not your organisation has a reputation problem. A wise old management guru once said that 'If you can't measure it, you can't manage it.' If it is difficult to pin down what a corporate reputation is, then it becomes doubly difficult to manage this strategic asset. This is the third factor which feeds the developing crisis. Research has shown that like most issues facing managers, this one is multifaceted. Hence, if you pull the wrong levers, or pull them in the wrong sequence, you can cause more harm than good.

The aim of this book is to provide you with the insight to manage one of your most potentially valuable strategic assets. The first step on this journey is a short trip into the history of advertising to find out what we really mean by the term corporate reputation. This is important because its outcome is to show that *no organisation has a reputation!* The acceptance of this idea is one of the keys to successful reputation management.

What are Corporate Reputations?

Many people create summary evaluations of products, companies, and countries as a way of thinking about them. Rather than weigh up the pros and cons of every attribute of a product as a 'rational economic person' might do, most people make choices on the basis of limited information. They also form summary evaluations, or stereotypes of people and professions. For example, many people are comfortable filling in the following types of sentences. In general, 'fast food is ....', 'accountants are .....', 'used-car salespeople are ....', 'Japan is ....', et cetera. These stereotypes can have a profound impact on our initial, and subsequent reactions to new ideas, products, and services. People also form stereotypes about organisations. For example, steel plants are noisy and dirty, libraries are quiet, hospitals are clean, and government instrumentalities are bureaucratic. Sometimes these stereotypes become the foundation for books, movies and TV series like *Dallas* in the oil industry, *LA Law*, and the popular UK comedy series about the workings of government, *Yes Minister* and *Yes Prime Minister*.

One of the world's most successful advertisers was the first person to commercially exploit these ideas. The name of this advertising genius was David Ogilvy. He is a founding father of modern advertising, and one of his main insights was that giving a product a 'personality' is a key factor for market success. His guiding principle was that consumers do not buy products, rather they buy products with a personality, namely 'brands'. Each of Ogilvy's successful brands embodied a distinct personality much like a stereotype represents a distinct type of person. This 'brand image' as it became known, was designed to fit the 'self-image' of the target consumer.[1] David Ogilvy's successful brands were those where there was a tight fit between the brand image and the target consumer's desired self-image.[2] This notion of self-image will be used to help understand the role and effectiveness of corporate image advertising in Chapter 6.

Ogilvy's idea that brands can have a personality or image reflects the fact that people buy many products and services not only for what such products or services can do, but also for what they mean to people and their reference groups. In marketing terminology, products and services offer the user both functional and psychological benefits. For example, some middle-aged men are thought to buy sports cars to provide transportation, and to reflect a desired self-image of youth and virility. Many clothing styles are also bought as visual signals to identify with a particular reference group, or to reflect the mood and emotions of the wearer. Products given symbolic meaning (or a distinct image in our terminology) help consumers choose among functionally similar offerings. Some advertisers are legendary in their ability to create these mental images in their advertising. For example, in a blind taste test many people can't tell the difference between a *Coke* and a *Pepsi*. However, put the brand name on the can and these same people often exhibit strong brand preferences.

The notion of brand image is easily generalised to companies and other types of organisations. One of the first times that this was demonstrated outside the field of advertising was by Pierre Martineau, who while doing research for the *Chicago Tribune* newspaper in the late 1950s, discovered that certain types of customers felt uncomfortable in particular retail stores.[3] What Martineau had stumbled across was the fact that sometimes the image of a retailer was not compatible with the perceived social status (or self-image) of the shopper. Since this time there has been much research on the impact of retailers' images on the patronage habits of consumers.[4]

If shoppers can form a distinct image of a retail store, then they can (and do) form images of other types of organisations like schools, hospitals, advertising agencies, and businesses. People also form images of countries. Often when the overall image of a country is favourable (such as Switzerland) marketers rent the image by using the words 'made in (country)' on their products or in their advertising. In the 1950s many people thought that products made in Japan were of inferior quality to those made in Western Europe, the UK, or the USA. In the 1990s, however, many people think that certain types of products made in Japan are of superior quality. Such country-of-origin effects can have an important influence on marketplace performance. For example, surveys consistently show that the Japanese electronics industry is much more highly regarded than the Australian electronics industry. Alternatively, Australian wool is the most highly regarded in the world.

The key idea to adopt from this section is that *different people hold different images of things* (countries, industries, companies and brands). One primary reason for this is that we all have different information about, and sometimes different experiences with these things. It is for this simple reason that your organisation does not have a single image or reputation—it has *many reputations*. It is therefore good to use the plural—reputations to remind yourself that different people hold different reputations of your organisation.

To avoid the problem of trying to cope with a different reputation for every person, you can cluster people into groups based on the similarity of their reputations. A useful, if somewhat crude way of doing this is to assume that different types of people will hold (slightly) different reputations of your organisation. These groups include customers, employees, third-party service agents (such as your advertising and market research agencies), public policy makers, and social critics (such as journalists). In essence, most organisations will have at least three or four distinct reputations—one for each major group who has some knowledge about the organisation. (Chapter 2 provides a useful framework for identifying which groups may have different reputations of your organisation.)

In order to deal effectively with the management of these various reputations it is necessary to clarify some terminology. In the following chapters, I use the terms '(corporate) reputation' and '(corporate) image' to capture the total beliefs and feelings that a person may hold about an organisation. This Gestalt (to use the German term for overall 'form' or 'shape') will be formed by individuals integrating all the information they have about the organisation. This may come from people's dealings with it, its communications to them, and the images they hold of its country of origin, industry, and the brands it sells. Like the

Corporate Identity: the symbols (such as logos, colour scheme) an organisation uses to identify itself to people. (See Chapter 7.)

Corporate Image: the total impression (beliefs and feelings) an entity (an organisation, country or brand) makes on the minds of people.

Corporate Reputation: the evaluation (respect, esteem, estimation) in which an organisation's image is held by people.

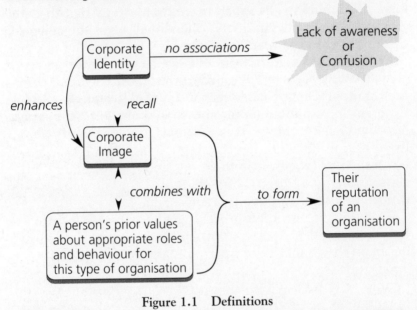

Figure 1.1   Definitions

German Gestalt, each organisation's reputation is likely to be more than the sum of the organisation's individual parts.

While the management literature uses the terms corporate image and corporate reputation interchangeably, it is useful to make a distinction between these two concepts. It is also important to clearly define a third concept, namely that of corporate identity. Figure 1.1 lists definitions for each of these three terms, and shows how people combine them to form a reputation for an organisation. In effect, people form reputations by comparing what they know about an organisation with the values they think are important for this type of organisation.

The top portion of Figure 1.1 shows that corporate identity can have three possible effects on corporate image.

1 If people make no association between the company and its identity symbols, then identity plays no useful role.

Alternatively, if there are inappropriate associations between the identity symbols and the company, then identity symbols cause confusion in the minds of people. In either case, identity is a problem for the organisation.

2 The organisation's identity symbols may help people recall images of the company. This can be the result of rote learning. For example, through years of advertising, the letters AMP have come to mean the *AMP Insurance* company for many Australians. In the UK, the symbol of an eagle standing on a star helps people recall the name *Eagle Star* (insurance).

3 The identity symbols enhance the organisation's image and/or reputation. For example, *Merrill Lynch*'s bull symbol, which signifies a rising stock market, may help (potential) investors associate positive feelings with this investment (brokerage) company.

If the total impression of a company (that is, its image) fits with the person's values about appropriate behaviour for that company, then the individual will form a good reputation of that company. For example, if people think that their bank should help them to manage their money, then a bank which shows people how to save interest payments by paying off their loan earlier will enhance its reputation. On the other hand, if the bank spends its advertising budget telling its customers how long it has been in business, as many such corporate campaigns do, then this is less likely to significantly improve its reputation. The role of the organisation's identity symbols is to help people recall their image, and to reinforce the image and reputation of the organisation.

Various seminars I have delivered to practising business people have convinced me that the term 'corporate reputation' has more intuitive meaning than the term 'corporate image'. It seems to make what is being talked about here more personal— because we know and care about our own personal reputations. Hence, extending this concern to the organisations we work for should be easier if we personalise our thinking. For the casual reader, it doesn't really matter if you use the terms interchangeably. Whatever you do though, don't equate corporate identity with either image or reputation. Corporate identity may or may not be perceived as contributing to corporate image: it all depends on what pieces of information and values these symbols connect with in the mind of your stakeholders.

Improving a Corporate Reputation

The first step in dealing with a reputation crisis is to recognise that it can be managed. Governments, industry associations, and business leaders must become proactive in their management of the wide range of dealings they have with their stakeholders. This can only occur if it is understood that reputations exist in the minds of key stakeholders, and not in the minds of managers. It is essential that the people responsible for image and reputation management get out from behind their desks and listen to these stakeholder groups. This is much more easily said than done, but it characterises all good market-oriented organisations. Research is the only reliable way to profile the reputations of your organisation. (See Chapter 9.)

One of the key questions that research can answer is whether your organisation has an awareness problem or a reputation problem. For example, when customers, potential employees, and other people think about your industry do they recall your company name? Do they recognise your organisation's identity symbols (such as logo, corporate colours)? Can they recall (seeing) your advertising? Do they confuse your organisation with another organisation? Do they know what products and services your company sells? Negative answers to any of these questions signal an awareness problem. This may be a deliberate strategy if you have decided to keep a low profile—but you pay a price. If few people know about your organisation, then it becomes harder to do business with certain groups. For example, the giant US packaged goods manufacturer *Procter & Gamble* has a policy of promoting its brands rather than the company. While brands such as *Pert* shampoo and *Pampers* disposable nappies have been very successful with Australian consumers, *Procter & Gamble* has not found it as easy as a high profile company like *IBM* in the staff recruitment area. The company's late entry into the Australian market (1985), and its lack of corporate advertising (in the business press) has meant that it is largely unknown among many potential employees.

The second step in dealing with a reputation crisis is to develop a framework identifying the major factors which combine to influence the reputations held of your organisation. In essence, your organisation's reputations are formed by what people are saying about it, and what the organisation does and says about itself. To fully understand these three factors it is necessary to identify the activities which influence every aspect of how a typical organisation communicates with both its internal and external stakeholders. Having identified these factors, the next step is to specify how they interact with each other to form the overall reputation of the organisation. A diagram of this overall process is shown in Figure 1.2 on p. 12.

Figure 1.2 shows the main factors which combine to create a corporate reputation. This diagram illustrates that simply changing the organisation's marketing communications is unlikely to have a major impact on the reputations held by employees or external groups. To achieve significant change in the way people think about your organisation usually requires changes to some very basic organisational activities, such as the work practices of front-line employees, product/service quality or the organisation's culture. Quick-fix solutions like changing the advertising or introducing a customer service training program are seldom effective by themselves. If other things your organisation does are not integrated to achieving a particular desired reputation, then external stakeholders will become cynical. Figure 1.3 on p. 13 illustrates how the German sports car manufacturer *Porsche* integrates some of the major reputation development factors to achieve its desired reputation, and a (substantial) price premium for its cars.

Chapters 3 to 8 of this book elaborate the major elements of Figure 1.2. By tackling each factor individually, you won't be overwhelmed by the complexity of the overall reputation management process. It is also possible to identify the specific factors which may be responsible for the strengths and weaknesses in your current reputations. The strengths can be used to gain more leverage for marketing and public relations activities, while the weak areas can be isolated for immediate attention. This type of analysis can lead to some quick improvements.

Given the potential complexity of the task of reputation management, it is worth pausing to assess whether trying to actively manage this strategic asset is really worth the effort. The answer to this question comes in two parts. First, it depends on how bad your current reputations really are, and how important they are to achieving financial success. Chapter 9 outlines how to answer this question in a quantitative (and scientific) way. At this point, however, if no market research is available, then your personal assessment, and those of fellow managers, is a good

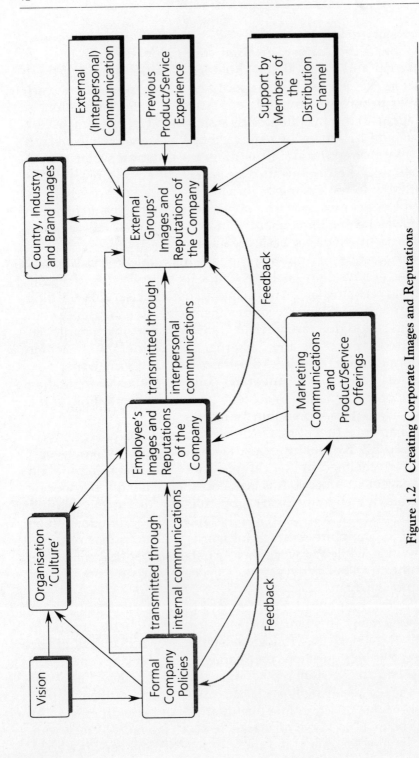

Figure 1.2   **Creating Corporate Images and Reputations**

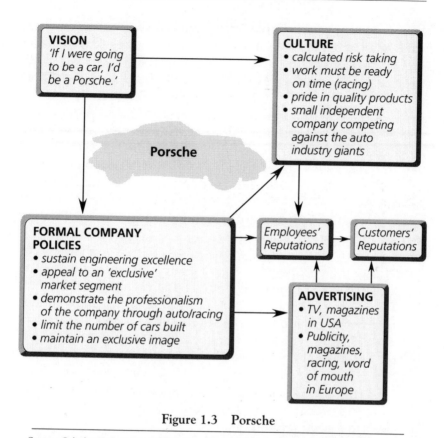

Figure 1.3 Porsche

Source: Schultz, P. & Cook, J. 1986, 'Porsche on Nichemanship', *Harvard Business Review*, March, pp. 98–106.

place to start. If your organisation's current reputations are poor then read on. If your reputations are good, then it is still worth reading this book to avoid falling into the trap of the *law of fast forgetting* mentioned in the preface. The second part of the answer to the question about the value of a good corporate reputation is outlined in the next section.

The Value of a Good Image and Reputation

Reputations are valuable to both the organisation and its stakeholders. Value to your organisation depends on how you use this marketing asset to generate excess returns from your products and services, and to signal about the organisation's strategy, future prospects, and employment opportunities to external groups. (See Table 1.1.) Value to internal and external stakeholders depends on how these people use their reputation of your organisation to help think about, and respond to its products and services. Hence, the potential value of a good reputation is significant. The remainder of this section reviews some of the research in economics, marketing, and psychology which seeks to establish the value of corporate reputations.[5] The discussion starts by focusing on how individuals use corporate reputations, as an understanding of this is necessary to fully appreciate how a corporation may use its reputations to advantage.

David Ogilvy's successful approach to giving products a personality, and then advertising the 'brand' rather than the product, provides a clue to how a company may use its reputation. If the organisation can create its own distinct personality, image, or position in people's minds, then it has differentiated itself from competitors. If this image fits the individual's values, then your organisation's reputation will be a good one. Also, research dealing with individuals' self-concepts suggests that people will respond more favourably to brands and companies they perceive to have an image which is consistent with their own self-concept. Hence, a 'good' corporate image is one that the target group of stakeholders can favourably relate to, and can use to form a good reputation.

When there is a tight fit between the organisation's image and an individual's self-concept, it is easier for a company to communicate with these people, and to form a '(commercial) relationship' with them. This attempt at relationship building is sometimes evident in a company's advertising. One widely used creative tactic in US television advertising is the on-camera spokesperson. Approximately one in three US advertisements use either:

- a celebrity (including company CEOs)
- a human or animated character
- people representing a particular lifestyle or the target audience
- a 'voice-over'.[6]

The way in which spokespersons work in advertisements is to personalise and endorse the message being presented. They also have been shown to 'boost' the effects of the advertising message.[7] For example, an advertisement which uses an unidentified dentist to say that he or she uses a certain brand of

Table 1.1

Introduction of the IBM PC

For a good illustration of the power of corporate image look at IBM's experience in the market for personal computers. When IBM entered the US market in August 1981, it seemed to be courting catastrophe. The original IBM PC offered no exciting technology and almost no proprietary features, e.g. most of the system's components came straight off the shelves of outside suppliers. Also, compared with other machines the PC looked overpriced. To sell it IBM used retail channels that viewed Big Blue as a threatening stranger. Apple Computer, the market leader at the time, was so far from being frightened that it ran cocky advertisements welcoming IBM to the world of personal computing.

By 1983, of course the IBM PC had become a smash hit, outselling Apple's computers, raking in nearly $2 billion in revenue for IBM, and entrenching itself as an industry standard. By launching a plain vanilla machine IBM made it easy for outsiders to design hardware and software to work with the PC. Thousands of companies did this which vastly enhanced the IBM PC's value to users.

But the biggest reason for IBM's success was its name. Decades of superior service had convinced business buyers, who were leery of personal computers and the upstart companies that sold them, that IBM was the safe choice. They knew that if the machines failed to perform as advertised IBM would stand behind them. Thus Apple and others ruefully discovered what mainframe computer companies had known all along: IBM often wins because of the 'FUD' factor—the fear, uncertainty, and doubt that assail corporate customers when they think of buying any computer gear that isn't blue. As those customers have been saying for nearly a quarter of a century, 'Nobody ever got fired for buying IBM.'

In fact, many corporations that bought IBM PCs later complained that they couldn't get good service and support because IBM had shuffled off those burdens onto the dealers who sold the machines. But the facts of the case were irrelevant. IBM had the 'unfair' advantage of its reputation.

Source: Davidow, W.H. & Uttal, B. 1989, *Total Customer Service: The Ultimate Weapon*, Harper & Row, New York, pp. 28–9.

toothbrush because it offers various benefits, is using the perceived status (reputation) of the expert to boost the credibility of the benefit claims. A tight fit between the characteristics of the spokesperson, the company advertised, and the target audience, will enhance advertising effectiveness.

Research in psychology has suggested that the images people create in their minds about an entity (such as brands, companies, countries) help them to think about that entity. These visual images or 'pictures in the mind's eye', help us encode, retrieve and manipulate information.[8] They are also thought to influence the way we evaluate problems, learn, assess probabilities, form intentions to respond to things, and generate feelings. In effect, they can act as a surrogate experience.[9] As a demonstration of the power of mental imagery, close your eyes and draw some pictures in your mind of Hawaii. (Like many people, my clearest images of Hawaii involve beach scenes. As I think more about the islands other images come to mind and are based on my travels there.) These visual images can have a powerful effect on the way we think and behave. Our first images of a company can influence our subsequent responses to the company. Sometimes, corporate identity symbols can trigger such mental images. If for no other reason than this, it is worthwhile understanding the images and reputations people have about your organisation.

To make this point a bit more concrete, consider the plight of the Swiss company *Nestlé* in the USA. Their research suggested that many people believe 'Nestlé makes the best ... (coffee) or (chocolate)?' *Nestlé USA* started an $8 million corporate advertising campaign in November 1992 to show that the world's largest food company makes a lot more than either coffee or chocolate. Using the slogan 'Nestlé makes the very best', the US advertising campaign set out to reposition *Nestlé*'s image to that of a 'warm, approachable, friendly' company which makes a range of leading brands such as *Quick, Taster's Choice* (coffee), *Carnation* and *Contadina* (pasta). It started a similar television campaign in Australia in 1993.

To fully develop the strategic value of its various images and reputations, an organisation must clearly identify the attributes different stakeholder groups use to describe it, and which of these are central to their values. Chapters 2 and 8 discuss many of these attributes. For now, however, the focus is on some research which indicates how organisations have been able to use their reputations to create wealth for shareholders.

Recent research reported in the corporate strategy literature argues that a good corporate reputation can lead to excess profits over those of other industry participants by:

- inhibiting the mobility of rival firms
- acting as a barrier to entry into markets

- signalling to consumers about the quality of the firm's products and possibly enabling the firm to charge higher prices
- attracting better job applicants
- enhancing access to capital markets
- attracting investors.[10]

These are a potent set of strategic benefits which may be derived from a good reputation. One such benefit is illustrated by two economists, Randolph Beatty and Jay Ritter, who found that US investment banks that had a good reputation earned a higher return when making initial equity issues for their clients.[11]

Corporate reputation-building activities are important for a firm when it operates in a market where competitors or customers have incomplete information about the organisation. Here, the company can use its reputation to credibly signal information about its future plans to uninformed competitors and customers in the market. For example, *IBM* has often used the competitive tactic of pre-announcing the release of a new computer in an attempt to get consumers to wait before they upgrade their hardware, and to devalue competitors' new product introductions. Also, companies which are uninformed about their competitors can use the reputations of these rivals to help them understand the true characteristics of their competitors. For example, a company such as *Procter & Gamble* may establish a reputation for aggressive price competition, and be able to use this reputation to 'lead' the pricing behaviour of other market participants.

A good corporate reputation can also have strategic value if it is used to add an extra element to the company's marketing mix, or to complement existing elements of the mix. A company's marketing mix is often referred to as the '4 Ps'—product, price, place (of distribution), and promotion (personal selling, advertising, sales promotion and public relations). For example, the *IBM* case history in Table 1.1 on p. 15 illustrates the power of a corporate reputation to enhance a new product marketing campaign. A good example of how a corporate reputation can enhance the operation of the personal selling element of the marketing mix is illustrated by a classic research study by Ted Levitt.[12] He tested whether salespeople who represented a prestigious chemical company (*Monsanto*) would be more successful than those representing a company with a moderate reputation (*Denver Chemical*) or a company with no established reputation (an anonymous company). He found that the better the company's reputation, the more likely the salesperson would be able to talk to a purchasing agent about a new product, and the more likely this new product would be adopted.

Two advertisers, Al Ries and Jack Trout, have illustrated that brand and company images can be used to position companies in customers' minds.[13] In this case, the company name can play an important role. For example, you would expect to buy fried chicken from *KFC* and pizza from *Pizza Hut*. Positioning can be thought of as a fifth P of the marketing mix. In the European automotive market, corporate image and positioning are being seen as key weapons to combat the lifting of quotas on Japanese cars. Many European car makers believe that the one valuable positioning attribute they have which the Japanese manufacturers can't emulate for some time is heritage. As a London-based advertising agency executive said: '*Lexus* and *Infiniti* are fantastic cars, but they lack class'.[14] Time will tell whether the heritage attribute of the European auto firm's images is more valuable to consumers than the Japanese image which is based on reliability, value for money, high specifications, and technical expertise. More examples of company positioning ideas are provided in Chapters 6 and 10.

For companies which sell products or services that are functionally equivalent, corporate reputation (and/or brand image) can be a major factor which influences consumer choice. Consider the following products: beer, cola soft drinks, petrol, washing powders. These are products where the brand image and reputation of the company providing them has become an important discriminating feature. Also, these factors give people a legitimate reason for preferring one brand over another. For example, petrol companies argue that their identities and images play an important part in generating sales (after site location and relative price are accounted for).

Image and reputation play a similarly important role where the consumer has difficulty in understanding the functional differences of a service prior to purchase (for example, business schools, legal services, and management consulting). In the (professional) service sector the reputation of the service provider may act to reduce the perceived risk associated with using the service. Also, in the fast growing direct marketing industry, the reputation of the company selling the products can act to significantly reduce consumers' perceived risk of using this mode of purchase.

Implicit examples of the value of a corporate reputation occur in the valuation of goodwill in a company's balance sheet, and in above average price/earnings (P/E) ratios of companies listed on the stock exchange. Another example occurs when an organisation is faced with a crisis. The case history of the *Johnson & Johnson* company and its pain relief drug *Tylenol* illustrates the value of a strong brand image and a strong company reputation. Capsules of *Tylenol* were contaminated with cyanide by an unknown person and the top-selling analgesic was withdrawn from the market. Market research showed a high level of confidence in both *Johnson & Johnson* and the *Tylenol* name, and this trust was used as the basis to relaunch the drug after the packaging had been redesigned to make it tamper-proof. Chapter 11 focuses on how to manage (salvage) your corporate reputation in a crisis.

Conclusion

This chapter argues that the reputations of many organisations are in crisis. We find relatively few organisations that have reputations for driving (or shaping) their markets, rather than being driven by them. To provide full strategic value, your organisation's reputations need to be designed to add value to your products and services. This is only possible if the major elements which combine to form these reputations in the minds of people can be identified. Figure 1.2 on p. 12 provides just such a blueprint.

A crucial point made in this chapter is that an organisation has many reputations. Different types of stakeholders will form their own distinct reputation of your organisation. This is an important insight because it suggests that the factors in Figure 1.2 may change their influence on the formation of the images and reputations of different people. Chapter 2 provides some examples of how this can occur.

Questions

1 Does your organisation have an awareness problem among key stakeholder groups (such as potential employees, journalists, retailers, or customers)?

2 Does your organisation's name really stand for something positive in the minds of key stakeholder groups? Does it add image and reputation value to your products and services?

3 Does your organisation's image fit with the values of your key stakeholder groups? Do you know what these key values are?

4 Does your organisation have a formal policy to guide the design and management of a desired reputation?

Developing your organisation's reputations into a strategic asset is not a job for the reactive type of manager. Many CEOs have known this for some time. Few, however, have been willing to implement all the changes necessary to create an organisation of distinction. It can be done—by proactive CEOs and management teams. The rest of this book shows how this can be achieved.

End Notes

1 David Ogilvy's book on his approach to advertising is worth reading. D. Ogilvy, *Ogilvy on Advertising*, Pan Books, London, 1983.

2 Our self-image is what we think of ourselves. In fact, we have two types of self-image. Our actual self-image—what we truly think of ourselves; and our ideal self-image—what we would like to be. These definitions of self-image are more compatible with the discipline of marketing than psychology.

3 P. Martineau, 'The personality of the retail store', *Harvard Business Review*, vol. 36, January–February 1958, pp. 47–55.

4 See various issues of the *Journal of Retailing*.

5 This section is based on part of the following paper: G.R. Dowling, 'Corporate image: meaning, measurement and management', *Australian Graduate School of Management*, Working Paper 88–005, 1985.

6 See J. Rossiter & L. Percy, *Advertising and Promotion Management*, McGraw-Hill, New York, 1987, Ch. 11; D. Aaker & J. Myers, *Advertising Management*, Prentice-Hall, Englewood Cliffs, 1987, Ch. 11.

7 ibid.

8 M. Marschark, et al., 'The role of imagery in memory: on shared and distinctive information', *Psychological Bulletin*, vol. 102, no. 1, 1987, pp. 28–41.

9 D. MacInnis & L. Price, 'The role of imagery in information processing', *The Journal of Consumer Research*, vol. 13, no. 4, 1987, pp. 473–91.

10 C. Fomburn & M. Shanley, 'What's in a name? Reputation building and corporate strategy', *Academy of Management Journal*, vol. 33, no. 2, 1990, pp. 233–58.

11 R. Beatty & J. Ritter, 'Investment banking, reputation and the underpricing of initial public offerings', *Journal of Financial Economics*, vol. 54, 1986, pp. 213–32.

12 T. Levitt, *Industrial Purchasing Behavior*, Harvard Graduate School of Business Administration, Boston, 1965.

13 A. Ries & J. Trout, *Positioning: The Battle for Your Mind*, McGraw-Hill, New York, 1981.

14 D. Kurylke, 'In Europe, image is key', *Advertising Age*, 30 March, 1992, S-52.

CHAPTER 2

Stakeholders

Each Group Holds a Different Reputation

Chapter 1 showed that an organisation does not have a single image or reputation—it has many of them. In fact, each person will hold a (slightly) different reputation of your organisation! This can present a daunting task if you try to manage all these separate reputations. A framework is needed to cluster people into various groups, each of which holds a similar reputation of your organisation. Chapter 1 referred to these people as *stakeholders*. Chapter 2 presents a framework to split stakeholders into a manageable number of groups which have a different reputation of your organisation. This partitioning is based on one of the fundamental organising principles of modern marketing—needs-based (market) segmentation.

Each of us is a bit different. We create our own identity and put our own imprint on the world. We have different experiences, needs and wants. These combine to cause us to see things slightly differently from other people around us. Psychologists have been studying these phenomena for as long as there have been psychologists. A simple piece of research which you can undertake to illustrate these claims is to talk to a range of people who have just come from the same: meeting, football match, movie, dinner party, or other interesting 'event'. Ask them to give you their personal impressions of what happened at this event, and how they felt about the overall experience. You won't have to talk to many people to discover that there were some quite different meetings and dinner parties going on!

The problem with so much individual diversity is that it stops you forming a single description of the organisation's reputation. This in turn, can make it difficult to convince other managers that it is possible to manage and shape these reputations. What we need is a simple approach to segment stakeholders into groups, and understand the basis for their different impressions of your organisation. It turns out that researchers who have been studying differences in consumer behaviour have uncovered the key to this problem.

Benefits and Solutions to Problems

Consumer researchers have known for some time that consumers only ever buy two types of things from your, or any other, organisation. These are:

1 Benefits, or
2 Solutions to their problems.

This simple assertion is true whether you are selling to (or serving) business organisations or individuals. It is an easily illustrated principle. For example, people do not buy drills and drill bits—they buy the ability to create holes of various diameters. Men and women don't buy cosmetics—they buy self-confidence and hope. Charles Revson of the *Revlon* cosmetics company once made the classic comment that: 'In the factory, we make cosmetics; and in the store we sell hope'. In a similar fashion, *Xerox* doesn't sell photocopiers—they market office productivity, and create the ability to communicate with other people.

It is not necessary to worry too much at this stage about whether your customers are buying benefits or solutions to their problems. What is necessary is that you don't try to sell a 'product' or its 'features', such as a 120 MB hard disk on a personal computer. Sell the benefit the consumer wants from the big hard disk, namely, the ability to gain immediate access to vast amounts of data and applications software. The only fine tuning of these ideas which is relevant to our discussion here, is to understand the mix of *functional* and *psychological* benefits, or problem solutions which customers will buy. This mix is well illustrated by what became known as the great cola war in the USA.

Pepsi often stated in its advertising that more people preferred the taste of *Pepsi* to *Coke*. That is, on one of the primary functional benefits of a soft drink, *Pepsi* was the winner. Yet for years *Coke* outsold *Pepsi* all over the world.[1] In the legends surrounding these blind taste tests, it was once claimed (probably by a *Pepsi* executive) that a senior *Coke* executive once mistook a *Pepsi* for a *Coke*! What gave *Coke* the sales edge? *Image* or the psychological benefit that their advertising developed over the years. Remember their famous slogan 'It's the real thing'. What a fantastic positioning statement. If *Coke* was 'the real thing' then *Pepsi* or any other cola must be inferior. In fact, this statement became so well established in the market that *7-UP* used it as a reference point to differentiate their soft drink. They called *7-UP* '*The* uncola'.[2]

In consumer and industrial markets, astute managers use the desired benefits, and/or solutions to problems of their customers as the basis for segmenting their markets. This is often referred to as 'needs' or 'benefit' or 'value' segmentation. Precision over terminology is not crucial here. What is important is that a person's needs will shape the benefits an organisation may offer, or the problems they may help the person to solve. If there is mutual benefit to be gained, then the person and the organisation may exchange something of value, such as money for products and services, or employment. Over time these exchanges may be instrumental in a person forming a relationship with the organisation. For example, a weak relationship may be reflected in the customer being loyal to a company's brands, while a stronger relationship may occur if the person is prepared to make favourable recommendations about these brands to other people.

The different relationships people have with an organisation will influence the amount and types of information they will receive about its activities. For example, shareholders and financial analysts are typically interested in indicators of financial and management performance. Other types of information such as the sponsorship of a sporting team, and the training and development of staff is of interest only to the extent that the effects of these factors can be linked to financial performance. On the other hand, journalists may show little interest in information about the day-to-day operations of an organisation. Their needs will often confine interest to extra-ordinary events such as those which occur in a crisis.

Managers in all areas of an organisation need to understand which groups of stakeholders are important to the successful operations of the organisation, and which people in these groups are likely to be opinion leaders. These are two separate issues. First, we should focus on the stakeholder groups, and then on the issue of opinion formation. The next two sections provide an interesting insight into which types of people will act as catalysts in the reputation formation process for your organisation.

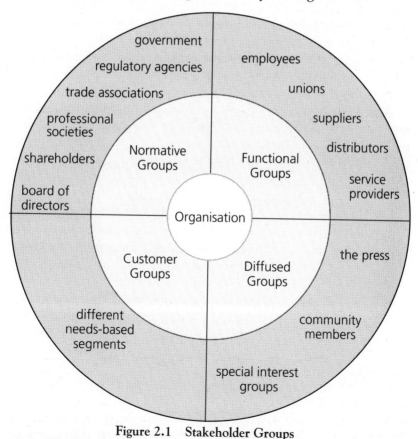

Figure 2.1   Stakeholder Groups

Groups of Stakeholders

Stakeholders are linked to your organisation in different ways. They may have different needs which the organisation can help fulfil, or your organisation may be subject to their surveillance. Some of these linkages will be much more important to your operational success than others. In order to define which groups will be most pertinent to your organisation, the following divisions (shown in Figure 2.1) can be useful:[3]

- normative groups
- functional groups
- diffused groups
- customer groups.

Normative groups provide the authority for your organisation to function and they set the general rules and regulations by which activities are carried out. Government departments, local councils, regulatory agencies (and laws such as Trade Practices legislation), and consumer and environmental groups may set limits on an organisation's scope and conduct of operations. A good example of two very powerful normative organisations are the international credit rating agencies *Standard & Poors* and *Moody's*. The treasury operations of international borrowers like governments can be severely affected by the credit ratings issued by these two organisations.

Normative groups also exist within organisations. For example, the needs of shareholders, and the governance of the board of directors sanction many of an organisation's activities. Other normative groups such as trade and industry associations and professional societies have less direct links with your organisation. They do, however, set normative guidelines for the activities of their members and they may act as a conduit for the dissemination of information to your employees.

Functional groups directly affect many of the day-to-day activities of your organisation. They facilitate operations and serving customers, and they are generally the most visible type of stakeholder group. Examples include: employees, unions, suppliers, distributors, retailers, and service providers such as postal and telecommunications organisations, advertising and market research agencies, legal services, and consultants.

By far the most important of these functional groups is employees. Work is a central part of the social, cultural, and economic life of most people. Paid employment provides income to sustain a person's quality of life. It also provides a significant part of an individual's identity which is important for self-esteem and social confidence. Being 'in work' and doing a particular type of job for a respected organisation can be extremely important for many people. These psychological aspects of work are often unappreciated by many managers. They can also have a direct impact on an organisation's reputations. For example, numerous surveys have shown that people who know someone who works for an organisation tend to regard that organisation more highly than similar people who don't know anyone working there.

Diffused groups are particular types of stakeholders who take an interest in your organisation when they are concerned about protecting the rights of other people. Issues which may raise the attention of these groups include: freedom of information, privacy of information, the environment, interests of minority groups, equal employment opportunity, child care in the workplace. Generally the most important of these groups is journalists. Their impact on shaping the public agenda and publicising specific issues is well known. Journalists can become friends or foe depending on how well the organisation understands the media, and the skills various people have acquired for dealing with journalists. A time of particular vulnerability for most organisations in their dealings with the media is during a crisis. Handling journalists badly can result in an incident developing into a crisis and the degradation of the reputations which people hold of the organisation. Chapter 11 deals with this important area.

Customer groups are arguably the single most important type of stakeholder. Non-marketers may wonder why customers are not referred to as a single group. A moment's reflection on the discussion in the previous section of this chapter provides the answer. Different types of customers will want different sets of benefits (and/or solutions to their problems) from your organisation. This means that to service these needs, your organisation will have to offer a tailored marketing mix (product, price, promotion, distribution, service level) to each different segment of customers. Professional marketers call this strategy 'target marketing'. In the context of corporate reputation management, it means that each of your organisation's target markets is likely to have a different reputation of the organisation.

We have now progressed from the position that everyone will hold a different reputation of your organisation to being able to classify stakeholders into four broad types. Within each type it is easy to identify particular groups of people whose relationship with the organisation may cause them to form a different reputation. This is a substantial improvement over much current thinking about corporate reputations. To substantiate this claim recall that the outer circle of Figure 2.1 on p. 25 lists more than fifteen different stakeholder groups. In a recent review of corporate advertising in the USA, it was found that most of the reputation-building advertising carried out by companies was directed at only two of these groups: 'the business and financial communities, and the customer'.[4] Now corporate advertising may not be a good way to communicate with all these groups; however, it will be applicable to more than two of them.

Too many managers still talk about *the* organisation's image or reputation (singular not plural). It is not uncommon to hear them say things like: 'we have a good image', or that 'our reputation allows our salespeople to get easy access to customers'. If you don't make explicit recognition of the fact that your organisation has many reputations, then it is impossible to reap the full value that this strategic asset can provide to improving operations. Also, any reputation-building advertising done by the organisation will have little relevance to any particular stakeholder group. As we will see in Chapter 6, advertisements aimed at everybody tend to be vague and meaningless and often ignored by many stakeholders.

Forming Stakeholder Reputations

Figure 1.2 in Chapter 1 (p. 12) showed the set of factors which influence the reputations that stakeholders have of your organisation. Because different stakeholder groups will each have a different reputation, it is necessary to modify this figure to reflect how the needs of these groups can alter the relative importance of the factors introduced in Figure 2.1. To illustrate this, consider how two of your organisation's most important groups: employees and customers form their reputations.

Figure 2.2 outlines the set of factors which are thought to influence the formation of employees' images and reputations of their organisation. The shading and darker lettering have been

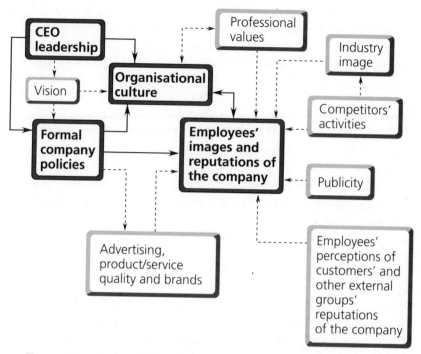

Figure 2.2 Factors Affecting an Employee's Corporate Image and Reputation

used to indicate the more significant factors. Likewise, unbroken arrows represent stronger relationships than broken arrows. Three new factors have been added to Figure 2.2 that are not in Figure 1.2. These are *CEO leadership, Professional values,* and *Competitors' activities.* Each is briefly outlined to round out the discussion presented in Chapter 1.

The upper left portion of Figure 2.2 introduces CEO leadership as an important determinant of vision, formal policies, and organisational culture. In the USA, Lee Iacocca is a good example of a high profile leader who embedded his vision into the *Chrysler* company's formal policies (and its advertising in which he often appeared). Such high profile leaders can have a dramatic effect on their organisation's culture and their employees' images and reputations. When they appear in company advertising they can also influence customers' reputations of the organisation. Developing the CEO into an attribute of the organisation, however, can be a high risk strategy especially at the time of succession to the leadership. This occurred when John Scully took over the *Apple* computer company from its founder Steve Jobs. It wasn't long before Steve Jobs left *Apple*. To avoid the problem of the CEO's style and values dominating the organisation, many organisations create a Vision Statement which is independent of any individual. Chapter 3 reviews the role of these statements in helping to form an organisation's reputations.

Research in sociology has shown that the values and ethical principles which people develop during their professional training can have a significant impact on their workplace attitudes and behaviour. Also, professional affiliations often provide people with professional authority in organisations, for example, the accountant and the in-house corporate lawyer. This authority, together with the codes of behaviour which various professions sanction, can be particularly strong for groups such as accountants, in-house advertising and market research groups, health workers and lawyers.[5] These professional values can affect the overall organisational culture and employees' reputations of their organisation. It has been suggested that identification with the company is a distinguishing characteristic of the Japanese, as opposed to many employees of Australian, European and US organisations who identify primarily with their job, profession or union.

Another factor which can affect employees' perceptions of their organisation and the industry in which they work is the actions of competitors. For example, when the Exxon Valdez oil tanker ran aground in Alaska and created one of the biggest environmental disasters of our time, every oil company's reputation probably suffered. In a similar way, every aeroplane crash degrades the reputation of the airline industry. Management of the overall image of an industry is often delegated to an industry association. The actions of individual organisations, however, are likely to be a more powerful determinant of industry image than statements from the industry's governing body.

Figure 2.3 outlines the set of factors which are thought to influence the formation of customers' reputations. The two new factors in this model not included in Figures 1.2 or 2.2 are service quality (which given the previous discussion also includes employees' images), and the images of intermediate service providers like retailers. Both of these factors are a direct outcome of the organisation's marketing strategy (discussed in Chapter 4), and they can have a significant effect on what customers think and feel about an organisation.

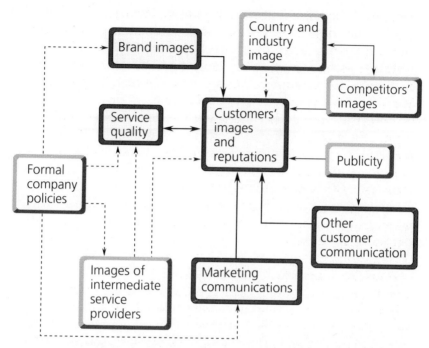

Figure 2.3   Factors Affecting Customers' Corporate Reputations

There is now a vast amount of research which shows that service quality leads to satisfied customers, and satisfied customers think more highly of the organisation which provided the quality service.[6] As the organisation's reputations improve, we also find that it is easier to create satisfied customers. That is, a positive feedback effect operates where people expect good service from an organisation with a good reputation, and if they can't judge whether it is good or bad (for example, a visit to a dentist, doctor, lawyer, accountant) they will tend to think that it is good, if for no other reason than to confirm their own expectations. For example, one US study found that firms which had developed a reputation for high perceived quality had fewer dissatisfied customers, and that these customers were more likely to provide positive word-of-mouth recommendations about the firm.[7]

The final factor to discuss in Figure 2.3 is that of the image of intermediate service providers. Many studies have shown that different types of distributors and retailers have distinct images in customers' minds. For example, the mention of a visit to a (new or used) car dealer to most people will elicit some unsavoury beliefs about what to expect. Similarly, many people expect that 'duty free' stores at international airports will have cheaper prices. Boutiques, supermarkets, department stores, warehouses, and 'markets' all have distinct images which shape customers' expectations about the range of merchandise offered and the overall price level. Research indicates that when a brand or corporate image is linked with a retailer image, then an averaging process occurs in consumers' minds. For example, if the *Apple* computer company sells its PCs through the *ComputerLand* chain of stores, then some of Apple's reputation will 'rub off' onto *ComputerLand's* image and vice versa. *ComputerLand* gains a little prestige and *Apple* loses a little prestige (assuming that *Apple* starts off with a better reputation than *ComputerLand*).

Sometimes a 'retailer' will try to shift its image from one category to another category by altering its name. For example, a furniture store which calls itself a 'furniture warehouse' is effectively trying to 'rent' the image of lower price which people associate with warehouses. Alternatively, when *McDonald's* (the fast food chain) calls their outlets (family) 'restaurants' they are trying to upgrade their image by associating them with restaurants (rather than say a café).

To round out the discussion of how people in the various stakeholder groups form their reputation of your organisation, the next section briefly examines one aspect of the social dynamics of these groups. We know from research in social psychology and marketing that in any group where the members communicate with each other, some people are more influential in shaping the opinions of other people. These influential people are often labelled 'opinion leaders' and their role in the reputation formation process is worth understanding.

Opinion Leaders

Within each stakeholder group the question arises as to 'who really matters with respect to shaping your organisation's reputations?' A related question is 'how do these people evaluate the different types of information they receive about your organisation?' These questions direct us to academic research on personal influence for their answer. Because theories abound, the following discussion focuses around the role of opinion leaders

The idea that some receivers of corporate communication may act as opinion leaders is a fascinating one. It suggests, for example, that corporate advertising and publicity can be most effective if it is targeted to these opinion leaders as well as to other members of the stakeholder group. The role of opinion leaders is to act as an extra channel of communication for the information. The $8 million *Nestlé* corporate advertising campaign discussed in Chapter 1 was targeted directly to opinion leaders in the grocery trade, in business, the family grocery decision maker, and key members of the community. The word-of-mouth (WOM) communication of these special people is likely to be more influential than the original mass media information. (Hopefully they will repeat the same message designed into the corporate advertising.)

Like many other simple ideas, this one turns out to be more complicated than a simple two-channel flow of communication. Namely, (a) mass media messages to opinion leaders and other stakeholders, plus (b) opinion leader communications to other people in their social network. There is value to be gained, however, by enriching our understanding of the way in which information is received by, and then disseminated by members of particular stakeholder groups.

The first insight is that opinion leaders are not 'leaders' as we would commonly know them. Leadership here is a much more subtle process. For many of your stakeholder groups, it will be almost invisible. Often it will occur simply as the result of a person's becoming aware of other people's attitudes and behaviour. This is particularly true for many consumer groups. For example, if your company designed and sold fashion clothing, then opinion leaders in your target market would 'lead' other customers' fashion opinions by talking about fashion and 'being seen' in various garments. In a professional field like advertising, the leading advertising agencies influence opinion through their clients' advertising as much as their formally stated opinions about good/bad advertising and the awards they receive.

There are some occasions, however, where the personal influence of opinion leaders may be much more transparent. The leaders of lobby groups, political parties, unions, professional societies, and regulatory authorities can at times be quite open and blatant in their opinion forming activities. In such cases, it is easier to monitor the position of these groups and their potential impact on the reputations of your organisation.

A second complicating factor to explore is sometimes referred to as 'the strength of weak ties'.[9] This is a colourful way of highlighting the fact that relationships in the social networks of which opinion leaders and other people are a part, vary in strength. The strength of relationships varies both within a particular network and between networks. Strong and weak interpersonal relationships can play a crucial role in the way information is diffused throughout a social system. For example, consider your organisation's employees as a social system. Co-workers in the same work unit would tend to have stronger relationships with each other (strong ties) and weaker ties with people in different units of the organisation. For WOM communication, weak ties facilitate the (informal) flow of information from one social network to another, while strong ties influence the flows of information within a particular group. Strong ties have been found to be more influential than weak ties, and they are more likely to be used as sources of information.[10]

From a corporate reputation perspective, an important question is the degree to which opinion leaders are likely to react differently to (mass media) information about your organisation. While there is little direct evidence to show that this occurs, there is less evidence to show that it doesn't. Also, there is some indirect empirical evidence to show that it probably does. This is a rather complicated way of saying that I think opinion leaders use mass media information differently to other people. My academic research on the adoption and diffusion of innovations suggests that a segment of customers called innovators often play the role of opinion leader. We have found that these innovators are more confident to evaluate a new product without seeking the social support of other people. They also tend to rely more on mass media sources of information to keep their product knowledge up to date than other groups of adopters.[11] In short, these 'innovative communicators' are likely to form a reputation about your organisation based on their own personal experience and your (and other sources of) media communications. This positive or negative reputation will then influence what they say about your organisation to other people.

The degree of influence of an opinion leader's WOM communications will depend on a number of factors. One such factor mentioned above is the strength of ties within and across social groups. That is, how many people opinion leaders contact and how frequently they talk with them. A second factor which can modify the impact of this source of influence is the credibility of the opinion leader versus the credibility of your organisation's media communications. Psychologists have demonstrated that in general, WOM communication is more influential than media communication.[12] Also, the personal characteristics and role of the opinion leader will influence the credibility of this person's opinions. For example, physically attractive people are generally more persuasive, as are people with more power and prestige.[13] These factors combine to provide the opinion leader with a certain amount of 'source credibility'.

One additional factor which can impact on the personal influence of an opinion leader is the strength of the reputation a person currently holds about your organisation. A person who has a well-formed reputation is less likely to have this changed than someone whose reputation is weak. This concept of a strong versus a weak reputation means that some people will base their reputation of your organisation on better information, and sometimes a wider variety of factors, than other people. For example, employees typically know more about the organisation they work for than customers. Because their base of information and experience is extensive, their overall reputation will be a composite of many factors. It is therefore more difficult to change this reputation (or web of information) than one based on a few less well connected pieces of information.

Finally, a recurring question about opinion leaders is 'how do you find them?' Researchers have tended to use one, or a combination of the following approaches:[14]

1   The *sociometric method* asks people to nominate who they turn to for information and advice about particular issues. By asking a set of people in a social network, it is possible to identify the people whose opinion is sought most often (that is, the strong ties). Also, by asking people if they seek advice from people in other networks, opinion leaders who have weak ties to other groups can be located. This method of identifying opinion leaders is quite good for small groups.[15]

2   The *key-informant method* asks a set of judges (or informed experts) to identify the opinion leaders in a group. The validity of this method rests on the knowledge of the judges about the social characteristics of the group in question.

of this method rests on the knowledge of the judges about the social characteristics of the group in question.

3 The *self-designating method* asks individuals in the group to assess whether they see themselves as an opinion leader. An alternative approach is to ask them about the quantity and types of information they share with other people. The validity of either of these approaches, however, can be questioned because of the tendency for people to misstate their influence.

4 The *observation method* measures opinion leadership by recording information exchanges and influence as it occurs. Such an approach, however, often requires that the observer be a part of the group. If the group is aware of the observer's role then this can bias the group's behaviour.

Given the crucial role that opinion leaders may play in shaping other stakeholders' reputations of your organisation, it is a good policy to identify who these people are, and to constantly monitor their reputations and opinion leadership behaviour. Reputation formation among stakeholder groups is similar to the 80 / 20 law of marketing which states that 'often, 80 per cent of your business comes from only 20 per cent of your customers'. In this case, 80 per cent of the reputation of your organisation will be formed by 20 per cent of the stakeholders (in a particular group).

Conclusion

This chapter describes the major groups of stakeholders which your organisation should monitor. It identifies these without using research to confirm that each group does hold a different reputation. Hence, it breaks one of my fundamental marketing rules, namely, 'that the most dangerous place to look at your stakeholders (customers) is from behind your desk'. At this stage of our discussion, however, using the taxonomy of stakeholder groups in Figure 2.1 is an acceptable compromise. Chapter 9 describes various research techniques which can be used to check the number of stakeholder groups to monitor.

While employees and customers are often the two most important groups, other stakeholders should not be ignored. Most people form their links with the organisation based on how it can help fulfil their needs. These needs are important to understand because they will influence the set of factors which activities (for example, journalists and regulators). The adversarial nature of many of these relationships requires special care and attention.

Managers need to understand the social dynamics of how people interact and communicate information about an organisation. Opinion leaders are crucial to identify, and it is important to monitor their strong and weak ties. It is also important to understand how to stimulate favourable word-of-mouth communication among stakeholders—especially the opinion leaders. Jerry Wilson has written a book on this topic.[16] While it focuses on customers, many of its ideas can be used to shape the communications of other types of stakeholders.

End Notes

1 In fact, in blind taste tests many, if not most, people will make errors of identification when nominating whether they have just sampled a Coke or a Pepsi. The same outcome is likely when people taste similar alcoholic beverages.

2 7-UP is a lemonade and the uncola positioning was later changed (in Australia) to 'it's cool to be clear'. This is another (vague) reference to the colour of cola.

3 This scheme is a modification of the one presented in: D. ten Berge, *The First 24 Hours*, Basil Blackwell, Oxford, 1988.

4 D. Schumann, J. Hathcote & S. West, 'Corporate advertising in America: a review of published studies on use, measurement, and effectiveness', *Journal of Advertising*, vol. 20, September, 1991, pp. 35–56.

5 P.M. Blau & M.W. Meyer, *Bureaucracy in Modern Society*, Random House, New York, 1987.

6 W.H. Davidow & B. Utal, *Total Customer Service*, Harper & Row, New York, 1989.

7 W.P. Rogerson, 'Reputation and product quality', *Bell Journal of Economics*, vol. 14, 1983, pp. 508–16.

8 T.S. Robertson, J. Zielinski & S. Ward, *Consumer Behavior*, Scott, Foresman and Company, Glenview, 1984, Ch. 16; H. Gatignon & T.S. Robertson, 'Innovative decision processes', in T.S. Robertson and H. Kassarjian (eds), *Handbook of Consumer Behavior*, Prentice-Hall, Englewood Cliffs, 1991, pp. 316–48; D.A. Aaker & J.G. Myers, *Advertising Management*, Prentice-Hall, Englewood Cliffs, 1987.

9 M.S. Granovetter, 'The strength of weak ties', *American Journal of Sociology*, no. 78, May, 1973, pp. 1360–80.

10 J.J. Brown & P.H. Reingen, 'Social ties and word-of-mouth referral behavior', *Journal of Consumer Research*, no. 14, December, 1987, pp. 350–62.

11 D.F. Midgley & G.R. Dowling, 'A longitudinal study of product form innovation using a contingent factor approach', *The Journal of Consumer Research*, vol. 19, no. 4, 1993, pp. 611–25.

12 W.J. McGuire, 'Attitudes and attitude change', in G. Lindzey & E. Aronson (eds), *The Handbook of Social Psychology, Vol II*, Random House, New York, 1985, pp. 233–346.

13 D. Aaker & J. Myers, *Advertising Management*, McGraw-Hill, New York, 1987, Ch. 11.

14 E. Rogers, *Diffusion of Innovations*, The Free Press, New York, 1983, Ch. 8.

15 P.H. Reingen & J.B. Kernan, 'Analysis of referral networks in marketing: methods and illustration', *Journal of Marketing Research*, vol. 23, no. 4, 1986, pp. 370–8.

16 J.R. Wilson, *Word-of-Mouth Marketing*, John Wiley & Sons, New York, 1991.

PART 2

Factors Which Affect Corporate Reputations

CHAPTER 3

Vision: The Guiding Hand

In some organisations, managers have a clear vision and a degree of enthusiasm that is noticeable even to an outsider. In others, the visitor may see a copy of a vision statement but struggle to find any evidence that employees believe in its sentiments or have even read it. Vision statements in and of themselves are unimportant. However, having a group of managers and employees with a clear sense of vision is a vital factor in creating a strong reputation for most organisations. Organisations which have a strong vision generally inspire a higher level of commitment among their employees than organisations which do not.

In the early 1980s, the management consulting firm *McKinsey & Company* argued that organisations needed to understand the interrelationship of seven key factors which were critical to their success. This scheme became known as the *McKinsey 7-S* framework.[1] Three factors were considered to be the 'hardware' of success—strategy, structure, and systems. (These are discussed in Chapter 4.) The remaining four were the 'software' of success—style, staff, skills, and shared values. (The first three of

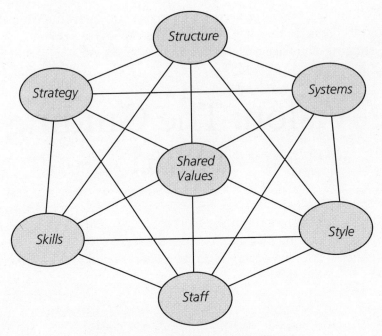

Figure 3.1   McKinsey 7-S Framework

Source: Peters, T. & Waterman R. 1982, *In Search of Excellence: Lessons from America's Best Run Companies*, Harper & Row, New York.

these are discussed in Chapter 5.) Their research showed that one way in which the operations of US and Japanese companies differed was the relative emphasis placed on the hardware versus the software elements of the organisation. In the USA most management concentrated on the hardware elements, while in Japan there was a better balance between the importance of hardware and software factors.[2] In order to communicate that firms often neglected to fully appreciate the role of the software factors, the McKinsey consultants would present their 7-S framework as a set of six factors hinged together by the shared values factor. This is shown in Figure 3.1.

Having shared values as the hub of the set of key success factors did not indicate that it was more important than the other factors. Rather, it suggested that the role of this factor was to act as a 'compass' to guide the activities of all employees. At *IBM*, these shared values once dictated that no employee should ever sacrifice customer service, while at the giant Japanese firm of *Matsushita* they meant that nobody would ever cheat a customer by knowingly producing or selling defective merchandise.[3] These shared values, or superordinate goals as they are sometimes known, can play a very pragmatic role by influencing the day-to-day activities of employees. They will also play a key role in shaping your organisation's culture—the topic of Chapter 5.

Vision

All organisations have a vision of one type or another. Some, however, have attempted to encapsulate their shared values in a formal document. This may be called a vision statement, credo, mission statement or charter. The choice of title does not matter. Typically, these documents are only a page or two in length and will contain a statement of 'what the organisation stands for' as this relates to the major stakeholders. Their value to an organisation derives from both the process used to create them, and the general guidance they provide to employees in the workplace. By creating a vision statement management must consciously contemplate, debate, and articulate the nature of the business, the reasons for the organisation's existence, and the customers and markets to be served. Creating a vision statement entails some risk because it can lead to disagreement and dissent among managers. Many managers, however, believe that the benefits far outweigh the risks. These benefits relate to the role that the formal vision statement can play in strategy formation and evaluation, performance evaluation, and setting the expectations of internal and external stakeholders.[4] Table 3.1 on the next page shows the famous *Johnson & Johnson* credo which the company has used on many occasions to guide its business decisions.[5]

Most vision statements are designed as an explicit statement of organisation philosophy. They also reflect many aspects of the organisation's ideal reputation (for example, being environmentally concerned, respected, responsive to customer needs). However, a severe criticism of these statements by many employees is that they are just platitudes. Considerable time and effort is devoted by senior management to developing the vision statement and then communicating it throughout the organisation. Many employees struggle to see the direct relevance of these general values to the organisation's overall strategy, and/or to their specific day-to-day activities.

To try to overcome this criticism some organisations print their vision statement on a card or plaque to be kept close to employees at all times. For example, Australia's international

Table 3.1

The Johnson & Johnson Credo

We believe our first responsibility is to the doctors, nurses and patients, to mothers and all others who use our products and services. In meeting their needs everything we do must be of high quality. We must constantly strive to reduce our costs in order to maintain reasonable prices. Customers' orders must be serviced promptly and accurately. Our suppliers and distributors must have an opportunity to make a fair profit.

We are responsible to our employees, the men and women who work with us throughout the world. Everyone must be considered as an individual. We must respect their dignity and recognize their merit. They must have a sense of security in their jobs. Compensation must be fair and adequate, and working conditions clean, orderly and safe. Employees must feel free to make suggestions and complaints. There must be equal opportunity for employment, development and advancement for those qualified. We must provide competent management, and their actions must be just and ethical.

We are responsible to the communities in which we live and work and to the world community as well. We must be good citizens—support good works and charities and bear our fair share of taxes. We must encourage civic improvements and better health and education. We must maintain in good order the property we are privileged to use, protecting the environment and natural resources.

Our final responsibility is to our stockholders. Business must make a sound profit. We must experiment with new ideas. Research must be carried on, innovative programs developed and mistakes paid for. New equipment must be purchased, new facilities provided and new products launched. Reserves must be created to provide for adverse times. When we operate according to these principles, the stockholders should realize a fair return.

Source: Gray, J. 1986, *Managing the Corporate Image*, Quorum Books, Westport, USA, pp. 25–66.

airline *Qantas* printed their vision statement on a plastic credit card so that each employee could carry it in his or her wallet. This strategy was probably created by an advertising enthusiast who believed that repetition was an effective way to get employees to rote learn the organisation's values. Few western organisations tend to translate the values in the vision statement into a company song like some Japanese companies. (Singing this at the start of each working day being another form of repetition.)

Other companies feel that to get the most benefit from their vision statements they need to make (parts of) them 'public'. When an organisation adopts this strategy it will print the vision statement in the annual report, and / or include its central values as a theme in corporate advertising. Making a vision statement public is one way to put employees and managers on notice that customers and other external stakeholders now fully understand what the organisation stands for. This strategy can also be used to help differentiate competing organisations from each other.

These concerns about the usefulness of vision statements are often well-founded. However, they relate more to coming to grips with how a vision statement can and should be used, rather than the value of spending the time and effort to create such a statement of purpose. The next section of this chapter describes some different types of vision statements and how to create them. The following section then shows how the essence of the vision statement can be used as a unifying theme for all the organisation's communications with its stakeholders. I then outline how to write a vision statement that has relevance for a wide range of employees. This section is based largely on the experience of a colleague who has developed vision statements for many Australian organisations.[6] The chapter concludes with a brief discussion of some research which indicates that companies which have a vision statement tend to be better performers than those that do not.

Types of Vision Statements

Vision statements are useful to an organisation to the extent that they can help achieve the following aims:

a to motivate and focus all employees on a common super-ordinate goal
b to define the boundaries of the business
c to provide an overall unifying theme for advertising and publicity
d to help differentiate the organisation from its competitors.

This is a difficult set of objectives for a one- to two-page document to fulfil. However, it is important to list objectives such as these before setting out to design a statement of philosophy. In fact, to achieve your objectives it may be necessary to design more than one type of vision statement.

Whether one or a set of coordinated vision statements is to be developed, they must all address the basic question of: 'What is our business, and what should it be in the future?' The answer to this question represents what marketers sometimes call the *Core Benefit Proposition* of the organisation. (In advertising parlance it is often called the *Unique Selling Proposition*.)

A useful first step in developing your vision statement is to identify the following factors and outline how they impact on your organisation's activities.

1 The broad *environment* within which operations are carried out, namely, economic conditions, social factors, legal restraints and competitive conditions.
2 The organisation's *role*, or unique contribution to its parent company, government, or community in which it operates.
3 The fit between the organisation's *objectives*, its *distinctive competences*, and the *key success factors* for operating in its chosen markets.
4 *Future trends* in the operating environment.
5 The basic *customer needs* served by the organisation.

These five factors define the broad constraints within which your organisation currently operates, and which will shape its future activities. They reflect the 'fit' between the organisation's overall objectives, its strengths, and the opportunities and constraints inherent in the marketplace. For example, it is not uncommon to see a business plan which has an objective to grow sales by 20 per cent next year. On closer inspection, one also finds that the market is mature, competition is fierce, and the company has no major strength which would provide it with obvious growth prospects. Understanding the fit among these important determinants of business success helps an organisation to define 'the business it is in'. As we will see in Chapter 4, business definition is not an easy task for many organisations.

Organisations can develop three types of vision statements. Two of these are for internal use and one is for external stakeholders. The contents of all three must be coordinated to ensure a unified purpose is communicated to your organisation's various target audiences. Two different internal vision statements may be necessary for organisations which have different strategic business units, branch networks, regional or international operations, or functional groups. Each operational unit typically needs a *Purpose Statement* to reflect its unique activities and its contribution to the parent organisation. For example, the activities carried out by scientists in a research and development department will be so different to those of the head office accounting and finance department, that a single vision statement for both groups may not be relevant to either group.

The potential problem caused by having a number of different Purpose Statements is that they may have no obvious relationship to one another. A good way to coordinate various purpose statements is to develop an *Umbrella Vision Statement* to link the individual purpose statements to the activities of the parent organisation. This umbrella statement can be a separate (one-page) document. Or it can be a short paragraph which expresses the overall role and goal(s) of the organisation. If this second approach is preferred, it can be written as the first part of each purpose statement. For example, an umbrella statement which can be used by the various schools and faculties of the *University of New South Wales* in Australia is:

> Together with other universities of the western tradition, The University of New South Wales shares a responsibility to support scholarly activity in the humanities and the natural and social sciences, and to express this activity in under-graduate teaching, postgraduate teaching, continuing education and research.[7]

Figure 3.2 outlines how to coordinate different types of purpose statements. When different parts of the organisation carry out essentially the same function like the retail branches of a bank, then one purpose statement can be used for all the branches. In fact, this will help ensure that the service customers receive from each branch will be of a consistent type and standard. This is something that many customers appreciate as fast food chains like *McDonald's* and *Pizza Hut* have discovered. However, when parts of the organisation are distinctly different, each should develop its own purpose statement. Trying to use one broad vision statement for different business units is one reason many employees feel that these statements are vague and meaningless.

Vision statements designed for external stakeholders are often referred to somewhat sarcastically as 'motherhood statements'. Their purpose is to communicate a sense of mission for the organisation as a whole, or for a particular strategic business unit. They are often reported in corporate advertising, sales

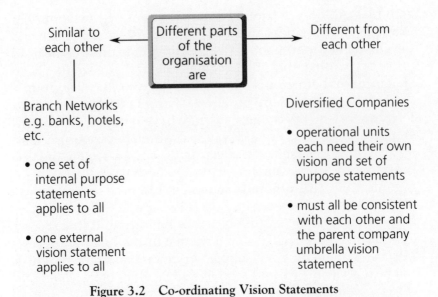

Figure 3.2   Co-ordinating Vision Statements

unit. They are often reported in corporate advertising, sales brochures, the annual report and press releases. These statements are designed to make employees, shareholders, journalists, politicians and investment advisers feel good about the organisation. In many cases, however, they are of little practical use for enhancing the successful operation of the organisation. Some examples of published vision statements are shown in Table 3.2.

When there is little competition among organisations (like public utilities), the umbrella statement may form the basis of the external vision statement. However, when an organisation has direct competitors, the external vision statement should seek to differentiate it from these competitors. In this case, the external vision statement helps to position the organisation in the marketplace. (Ideal reputations and competitive positioning are topics covered in Chapter 10.)

Compare the published vision statements in Table 3.2 to the internal mission statement used by the Japanese earth moving equipment company *Komatsu*: 'Beat *Caterpillar*'.

Every employee in *Komatsu* (and probably *Caterpillar*) knows why they come to work each day. In fact, the art of summarising a vision statement into something as clear and meaningful as *Komatsu*'s internal mission is a job which is often given to the organisation's advertising agency.

Table 3.2

Published Vision Statements

Mount Isa Mines (1991)

MIM's Corporate Vision has been crystallised
We strive to be the best mineral resource company in the world. We will achieve this through innovation, focus and a resolve to out-perform others.

Source: Mount Isa Mines, Annual Report 1991

American Marketing Association (1990)

Mission Statement

The American Marketing Association is an international professional society of individual members with an interest in the practice, study, and teaching of marketing. Our principal roles are:

First, to urge and assist the personal and professional development of our members, and second, to advance the science and ethical practice of the marketing discipline.

To further these roles we will:

Lead in the development, dissemination and implementation of marketing concepts, practice and information.

Be the focal point for marketing interests of business, education, government, and other institutions.

Probe and promote the use of marketing concepts by business, non-profit, and other institutions for the betterment of society.

Encourage the application of professional standards so that marketing knowledge and practice are used toward legitimate ends.

Offer services to our members and the marketing community both locally through professional and student chapters and internationally through the Association's divisions, other units and professional staff.

Source: American Marketing Association, Membership Information Brochure 1990.

Arthur Andersen & Co—UK (1990)

Arthur Andersen & Co. is one of the largest professional services organisations anywhere. More than 40 000 staff work from over 200 offices across the world, ten of them in Britain. The firm provides financial and business consultancy, audit and accountancy services, tax consultancy and advice and business solutions based on information technology.

We have grown rapidly because we deliver services of the highest quality. We work closely with our clients to gain a thorough understanding of their business and provide constructive advice to help them realise their full potential. Many of our largest clients came to us as start-ups; we have helped them grow and our practice has grown with them.

Our commitment to quality means that we seek to recruit the ablest people and give them the best possible training. That training is based on industry expertise, a strong business perspective and on methodologies that apply worldwide. Using these resources, we work with our clients to add value to their businesses.

Source: Arthur Andersen, Practice Publicity Brochure, UK Office, 1990.

Advertising the Vision

One way to communicate your vision statement to various stakeholder groups is to distil its essence into a 'corporate promise'. A good advertising agency can write the core benefit proposition of the vision statement as a 'tag-line' or slogan to be used with your organisation's advertising. These tag-lines are generally three to eight words in length, and together with the organisation's name they are used to 'sign off' many advertisements. For example, at the time of writing this book *Sony* uses the tag-line 'the one and only', while the oil company *BP* signs off its product and corporate advertising in Australia with the tag-lines 'on the move' and 'for all our tomorrows'. The automobile manufacturer *Toyota* uses the phrase 'Oh what a feeling' in its advertising. This signature has become well known because it is set to music, and is generally accompanied by a picture of target customers jumping high into the air.

Tag-lines which summarise an organisation's vision can be used for a variety of communication objectives. For example, to:

- Position a company against a competitor, for example, *Qantas* airlines 'the spirit of Australia' versus *Lufthansa* 'German airlines'.
- Explain what the company does, for example, *Schott* 'nobody knows more about glass'.
- Target a segment of customers, for example, *SAS* 'the business airline of Europe'.

- Communicate industry leadership, for example, *British Airways* 'the world's favourite airline'.
- Help mould customer expectations by making a promise, for example, *Cathay Pacific* 'arrive in better shape'.
- Link products together, for example, the various models of *Mercedes-Benz* cars are 'engineered like no other car'.
- Ask the consumer to take some type of action, for example, *Mitsubishi Motors* 'please consider' (their cars); *Philips* 'take a closer look' (at their products).
- Issue a challenge, for example, the *US Army* 'be all you can be'.
- Explain the company's name, for example, *CIG* 'Commonwealth Industrial Gases'.
- Establish trust in the company, for example, *Westinghouse* 'You can be sure ... if it's Westinghouse'.
- Help customers justify (past) purchase behaviour, for example, *AT&T* 'the right choice'.
- Communicate a vision, for example, *ICI* 'we're making the future'.

Many tag-lines used in advertising, however, do not convey any real meaning to the target audience. They (and the accompanying advertising) fail to pass what a colleague of mine calls the IDU test.[8] This test says that advertising should seek to link the benefits of the company's products or services to customer needs. These benefits should be *Important* to customers, and the company must be able to *Deliver* these *Uniquely* via its products or services. To help avoid creating a visionary tag-line which lacks impact, it is useful to know which parts of the vision statement are more likely to contain information relevant for communication to outside stakeholders.

The next section outlines the contents of a good vision statement. Arguably the best place from which to abstract a tag-line is the section dealing with the organisation's distinctive competence as this relates to an attribute which is highly valued by customers. One of the worst sections to use as the basis for a tag-line is the section dealing with the future directions of the organisation. Your employees may be interested in the future direction of the organisation; however, most external stakeholders (especially customers) would prefer something now, rather than a vague promise about the future. To illustrate this point, I think that *AT&T*'s 'the right choice' is better than *ICI*'s 'we're making the future'. (How is *ICI* making the future? My future or some other person's future?)

Contents of a Vision Statement

The contents of vision statements are as varied as the companies that have developed one. However, one survey could be found which analysed the components of vision statements of USA companies.[9] These researchers identified eight types of information in a 'typical' vision statement. These are organised into seven paragraphs below. This framework is suitable for drafting either a vision statement or a purpose statement.

Strategy Sections
1 Context
2 Business Definition
3 Distinctive Competence
4 Future Directions

Stakeholder Sections
5 Employee Value Systems
6 Employee Development and Work Practices
7 Stakeholder Commitment

1 *Context* This paragraph sets the context for the other six paragraphs and 'introduces' your organisation to the reader. It should outline the organisation's broad area of operations in a way which does not inhibit the future directions of the organisation (which are outlined in paragraph 4). For example, a person unfamiliar with *Johnson & Johnson* who read their credo in Table 3.1 for the first time would not get a clear picture of what the company actually does. Reference to doctors, nurses, and patients indicates that the company has interests in the health care industry. However, exactly what *J&J*'s field of operations is, or its relative expertise in this industry is somewhat unclear. By contrast, the first sentence of the *American Marketing Association*'s mission statement (in Table 3.2) provides a clear indication of the *AMA*'s field of activities. In a purpose statement, this first paragraph should also state what the relationship of the business unit is to the parent organisation.

2 *Business Definition* This paragraph describes the organisation's business and what it might be in the future. It is important to define the scope or boundary of the business in terms of the customer needs, and the technology and people used. In his classic *Harvard Business Review* article titled 'Marketing

Myopia', Professor Ted Levitt vividly illustrated the consequences of a poor business definition.[10] The railroads thought they were in the railroad business rather than the transportation business and as the demand for passenger and freight transportation grew their share of this market steadily declined. Companies operating fleets of cars, trucks and aeroplanes realised that customer needs varied, and that they could be better served by companies not in the railroad business. The list of organisations which have lost touch with their customers is long—very long indeed! The movie industry took years to adapt their products for television; the postal monopolies failed to update their products and services and provided the opportunity for courier companies to enter the market; telephone companies were fixated with their phone networks and allowed the electronics companies to develop telecommunications equipment such as fax machines. The list goes on and on. In Chapter 4 more time is spent outlining how to define your business.

3 *Distinctive Competence* These are the essential skills, capabilities and resources which underpin your organisation's success. They are the things which are not easy for your competitors to emulate in the short term (otherwise they are really just a differential advantage). For example, while a bigger advertising budget than a competitor offers a potential advantage, it can be quickly emulated. On the other hand, a strong brand image (created from past advertising) is difficult to develop and something that other organisations may pay a lot of money to acquire.

Appreciating the fundamental things that your organisation does better than its competitors, and the fit these have with the needs of a particular market can be a difficult task. In fact, it is often one of the reasons why once successful organisations lose their way. For example, the *Apple* computer company entered the market with a product that allowed users easier access to the power and applications which computers could offer. Many customers were prepared to trade off speed, power, disk storage, and more dollars to acquire these benefits. However, *Apple* lost the plot. Not only did R&D stop delivering in this area (they were one of the last major manufacturers to introduce a portable PC), for a time the company stopped communicating this value proposition to customers. Its famous George Orwell 'Big Brother' TV commercial shown during the

1984 US superbowl football game symbolised *Apple*'s fight with *IBM*, rather than its value proposition for consumers.

4 *Future Directions* This paragraph provides the dynamics of the vision statement. It signals the future direction(s) likely to be pursued. These, however, will be restrained by the organisation's past activities (a point not fully appreciated by many CEOs), and should be contingent on the business definition and distinctive competence(s) built up by the organisation. Hence, this paragraph should be a logical extension of the first three paragraphs. It should rarely signal that the firm is about to embark on a program of discontinuous change.

In the 1970s many CEOs decided that growth was the central theme of their corporate plan. They decided to grow by adopting a strategy of (unrelated) diversification. That is, by acquiring other companies rather than by attempting to grow new enterprises. Many corporate raiders soon discovered, however, that the skills which led to their past success were not suited to managing a set of unrelated enterprises. Not all firms fully understood that distinctive competencies are only partially transferable across industry sectors. So the 1980s saw a slightly different growth strategy—'focused' mergers and acquisitions. Many of these were also unsuccessful. For example, in 1970 Maurice and Charles Saatchi started their own UK advertising agency called *Saatchi & Saatchi*. Through a series of takeovers of independent advertising agencies, *Saatchi & Saatchi* became the UK's biggest agency by 1979. In pursuit of still further growth the Saatchi brothers kept buying agencies, many of which were in the USA. Soon their empire was the world's biggest advertising conglomerate. The Saatchi brothers' next move, however, signalled the beginnings of their demise. They diversified into management consulting, market research, and public relations so that they could provide a full range of management services to their clients. By the late 1980s the Saatchi empire was on the verge of collapse.[11]

5 *Employee Value Systems* For many employees this and the next paragraph are regarded as the essence of the organisation's vision statement. They tune into radio station *WII–FM* or 'What's In It For Me'. Hence, this paragraph must clearly reflect the value system of management and employees, or as discussed in the next chapter, the 'organisation's internal culture'. It has to communicate how the basic values and

attitudes an employee brings to the workplace can help the organisation achieve its goals and further develop its distinctive competencies.

For organisations which employ many professionally trained staff, the way the organisation's culture is expressed in this paragraph can have a big impact on the behaviour and priorities of these employees. For example, accountants, engineers, and lawyers often need direction to balance the values developed during their professional training with the values needed to make their organisation competitive and successful in the marketplace. This tension between profess-ional and corporate values can be addressed in the vision statement. For example, in many professional service firms partners only want to do work associated with their vocation. The important tasks of new business development and account service may get second priority or relegated to specialists like a marketing manager. My experience suggests that a firm staffed by market-oriented professionals is more likely to succeed in the long run, than one staffed by a group of professionals and a marketing manager.

6 *Employee Development and Work Practices* This part of the vision statement makes a commitment to ongoing staff development, the renewal of the organisation's value system, and desired work practices. To be taken seriously by employees, these activities must be linked to the organisation's formal policies. This link is extremely important because it creates a 'contract' between the organisation and its employees concerning acceptable behaviour and rewards. There is an old saying in the discipline of human resource management that 'people do what is inspected, rather than what is expected'. Because much of the vision statement focuses on what is expected, an explicit statement of how these expectations will be formally rewarded is important for gaining commitment to the organisation's vision. This is a part of many vision statements which is underemphasised. A good example of this is shown in the *Arthur Andersen & Co* vision reproduced in Table 3.2. Here, the second and third paragraphs cover much of the material recommended in this section; however, there is no indication that *Arthur Andersen*'s formal policies will explicitly reward staff who commit to achieving excellence by adding value to clients' businesses.

7 *Stakeholder Commitment* Chapter 2 outlined how your organ-

isation might go about identifying various key groups of stakeholders. The last paragraph of the vision statement should make explicit mention of any groups which have not been identified in the previous six paragraphs and how the organisation relates to them. For example, manufacturing companies may want to state their preferred type of relationship when dealing with suppliers and distributors (such as a strategic partnership versus an 'arm's length' relationship). In the case of companies listed on a stock exchange, this is the place where a commitment is made to a balance between shareholder wealth creation, the payment of taxes, protection of the environment, and service to the community. Also, for organisations which aspire to something more inspirational than shareholder value, this is the section in which to state these inspirations. In effect, this paragraph is a statement of the organisation's ethical position. The *Johnson & Johnson* credo in Table 3.1 focuses almost exclusively on these issues.

Creating a Vision Statement

While the process of creating a vision statement has been alluded to throughout this chapter, it is now appropriate to briefly outline how your organisation can commit its vision to writing. Generally, the first task is to gain the commitment of the CEO and key senior managers. As noted earlier, there is often scepticism to the idea of a formal vision statement. Familiar criticisms are: 'we know what we are doing and where we want to go, so there is no point in wasting time writing this down' or 'we have already got one somewhere in the annual report' or 'they are just motherhood statements and the staff will not take any notice of them' or 'is this the latest gimmick from the management consultants?'. Without commitment at the top of the organisation then you should not proceed.

The second task is to agree on a set of objectives for the vision statement. For *Johnson & Johnson*, their credo is used as an internal guide to direct the company's everyday business activities and its social responsibilities. For *Hewlett-Packard* it explains the 'H-P Way' that ties the behaviour standards of employees together. Whatever the objectives, they should be agreed to prior to writing the first word because they will guide the type(s) of vision statement to be developed, and the appropriate channels to communicate the vision. For example, a 'motherhood statement' for inclusion in the annual report may contain only the information normally found in paragraphs 3, 4 and 7.

Having gained commitment to create a formal vision statement and a set of objectives to be achieved, a senior manager should write a one-page outline of the framework for the vision statement. This can be circulated to the top team who will write the first draft. Half a day can be set aside to produce a first draft of the various paragraphs. Often this meeting is stretched for time because some fundamental differences of opinion about the organisation's activities emerge. If a first draft can't be produced at this meeting then individuals can be assigned to write various paragraphs which summarise the group's position. These summaries can be used to start discussion at the next meeting. This process should continue until an overall first draft is crafted. Now comes the hard part of the process.

With a first draft clearly labelled as such, the vision writing team must start to internally market the document to (represent-atives of) all groups who will be affected by the vision statement. To many people, the contents of this first draft will come as a surprise. This should not be too disconcerting because the perceptions of the top management team will seldom be exactly the same as those of people in other parts of the organisation. In fact, the revelation of these different perceptions (or realities) can be one of the benefits of the process of creating a vision statement.

Comment and discussion about the draft vision should be collected and tabled at the next drafting meeting at which a second version is produced. This can be shown to key opinion leaders within the organisation for their feedback and hopefully their acceptance. When a final set of words is agreed upon, the vision statement can be printed and circulated throughout the organisation. At this stage, the CEO needs to personally sell the vision statement to target stakeholders. He or she needs to explain the statement's objectives, how it was created and how individuals within the organisation should use it. A key part of this sales pitch is to demonstrate (not just communicate) that the CEO and top managers are committed to the philosophy contained in the document.

Contrast this procedure with the way the chief of the *London Metropolitan Police* created a sense of mission for his men and women.[12] After the Brixton race riots in 1982, he decided that the force had lost sight of the old 'bobby on the beat' values that made the British police so special. In an 80-page book titled *The Principles of Policing*, he set down the behaviour standards and values that his police were to follow in their work. The book was circulated to every police officer on the force, and discussion groups were organised to 'sell' the message about changing some of the current policing practices. Individual police had two options: either change their behaviour, or ridicule the book as an example of how their leaders had lost touch with the problems of policing. Not surprisingly, they chose the latter option. Visions 'from above' are seldom enthusiastically endorsed by employees.

Conclusion

The case is advanced in this chapter that the time and effort required to develop a formal vision statement is a worthwhile investment. In many cases the evolution of vision statements over time will also serve as a partial record of the history of the organisation. The 'downside' of creating a vision statement, however, is that the CEO may use it as a substitute for leadership (as was the case with the London police example). As a supplement to the CEO's leadership, however, the vision statement can play a valuable role in helping to shape your organisation's strategy and day-to-day operations—but it can never replace personal leadership.

To conclude this chapter, I briefly note some findings from three survey research studies which support the development of a vision statement. (I could not find any published surveys which argued that vision statements are a serious 'health hazard' for an organisation.) Given the widespread use of vision statements, research into the effects of (the process of creating) vision statements on an organisation's behaviour is quite scarce. (In Australia, I estimate that about 50 per cent of medium and large firms have some type of vision statement. This estimate is based on discussions with businesspeople from approximately 300 companies who have attended short courses I have been involved in at the Australian Graduate School of Management.)

Two US researchers, John Pearce and Fred David, set out to examine the proposition that a comprehensive mission statement is linked to making better strategic decisions, which in turn should contribute to improved organisational performance.[13] They found that a sample of better financially performing (in terms of profit margin) *Fortune 500* companies had more extensively developed mission statements than low performers. In effect, these mission statements were used as a surrogate measure of the comprehensiveness of the firm's strategic plans. (Other research has also shown that firms that engage in strategic planning outperform firms that do not.[14])

Two surveys of managers in US firms have focused on what I call purpose statements. One study showed that managers of firms that had a written customer service mission statement were more likely to believe that customer service was a strategic weapon for their firm.[15] The other survey found that firms with a customer service mission statement were more likely to use quantitative measures of customer service performance. Also, these firms monitored more customer service related activities. These findings were true for the three types of firms surveyed: manufacturers, industrial service firms, and consumer service firms.[16] As we are all coming to appreciate, satisfying customers is a key success factor for most organisations.

In conclusion, the best way to create a vision statement is to do it *slowly*, and with the participation of as many people as practical. Over-eagerness on the part of the CEO and/or the executive management team can depreciate the value inherent in both the process of writing a vision statement, and its effect on employees. If it is done poorly, the process sends signals to employees that top management does not fully understand and appreciate its employees.

Knowing what parts of the internal vision/purpose statements to communicate to external stakeholders will depend on how much confidential information they contain, and whether or not they add to the store of information which people use to form their reputation of your organisation. For many organisations, the vision statement provides the only concise public statement of the organisation's ethical position. Given the definition of reputation outlined in Chapter 1 (Figure 1.1) your vision statement can play an important role in the reputation formation process.

End Notes

1 T.J. Peters & R.H. Waterman Jr, *In Search of Excellence: Lessons from America's Best Run Companies*, Harper & Row, New York, 1982.

2 R.T. Pascale & A.G. Athos, *The Art of Japanese Management*, Simon and Schuster, New York, 1981.

3 ibid.

4 R. Germain & M. Bixby Cooper, 'How a customer mission statement affects company performance', *Industrial Marketing Management*, vol. 19, 1990, pp. 47–54.

5 J. Gray, *Managing the Corporate Image*, Quorum Books, Westport, USA, 1986.

6 Dr John Gattorna of the consulting firm *Gattorna Chorn Strategy* (located in North Sydney, Australia) was the first person to introduce me to the seven paragraph framework for writing a vision statement.

7 Mission Statement, University of New South Wales, Kensington, NSW, 1988.

8 J. Rossiter & L. Percy, *Advertising & Promotion Management*, McGraw-Hill, New York, 1987.

9 J.A. Pearce & F. David, 'Corporate mission statements: the bottom line', *Academy of Management EXECUTIVE*, vol. 1, no. 2, 1987, pp. 109–16.

10 T. Levitt, 'Marketing myopia', *Harvard Business Review*, July–August, 1960, pp. 45–56.

11 P. Kleinman, *The Saatchi & Saatchi Story*, Pan Books, London, 1987.

12 A. Campbell, 'The power of mission: aligning strategy and culture', *Planning Review*, September–October, 1992, pp. 10–12, 63.

13 Pearce & David, 1987.

14 ibid.

15 M.J. Kyj, 'Customer service as a competitive tool', *Industrial Marketing Management*, vol. 16, 1987, pp. 225–30.

16 Germain & Bixby Cooper, loc. cit.

CHAPTER 4

Formal Company Policies: Strategy and Structure Do Matter

This chapter reviews some research dealing with the strategic management of organisations. It is an interesting area of inquiry which is of vital importance to the management of your organisation's reputations. In essence, the development of a strong reputation, which is consistent across various stakeholder groups, is driven by the organisation's business strategy and tactics. Much of what has recently been written in this area, however, is faddish. Concepts such as benchmarking, outsourcing, relationship marketing, strategic partnerships and total quality management are often new names for what has always been a sound business practice. Those basic ideas which have stood the test of time form the basis of the following discussion.

A key element influencing the way your organisation develops its reputations with various stakeholder groups is the formal policies which guide the strategy, structure, and control systems of the organisation. The business an organisation chooses to participate in, and the way it seeks to create a competitive advantage will have a profound impact on what people think about your company. Figure 1.2 on p. 12 shows that these formal policies influence the organisation's culture, employee images and reputations, product and service offerings to customers, and all forms of communication with stakeholders. Over the past two decades, managers have been pressured to rethink some of the most fundamental aspects of their business strategy. Most of the sources of this pressure have come from the environment in which the organisation operates.

The response of managers to these pressures, and the study of how they have coped with them has helped researchers and management consultants isolate a set of factors which differentiate successful and unsuccessful organisations. This field of inquiry, often referred to as 'strategic management' has focused on three major factors: strategy, structure, and environment. The basic idea is that the environment in which an organisation operates dictates a limited number of generic strategies which can be used to gain a competitive advantage in the marketplace. These strategies, in turn, will have a higher chance of being successfully implemented if they are supported by certain generic types of organisational structures.

While this is a somewhat oversimplified view of reality, research is showing that it is more difficult for an organisation which does not fit one of the general strategy–structure configurations to remain successful for an extended period of time. In effect, there are some basic building blocks which largely determine the long term success potential of organisations operating in a competitive market. These are best understood as they relate to the operations of a Strategic Business Unit (SBU) rather than the organisation as a whole, which may control a number of such SBUs. (An SBU is a business unit that can be planned for separately, has its own competitors, and its own management team that has responsibility for its operations.)

Chapter 1 argued that successful organisations are the ones which get a double payoff from success, namely, higher financial rewards and a better reputation. The first crucial decision that your organisation must make which will impact on its potential success is 'what business to compete in'. This decision defines the environment for the firm's operations, and the set of pressures which it must monitor and respond to over time.

Business Definition

One of the most fundamental and difficult questions that managers must ask about their organisation is 'what business are we in?'. How can such a simple question be so difficult to answer well? One reason is that senior managers tend to spend most of their time managing the operational aspects of their organisation. They develop an operational mindset which is characterised by short-time horizons, and a 'maintaining–stabilising–reactive' orientation. Also, many managers find it difficult to say 'no' to a potential new business opportunity that may enhance their career, and/or their revenue stream. Another difficulty is that many organisations try to serve every customer who walks through the door.

These factors can create a problem of having a business definition that is too broad. Resources get dissipated and the organisation struggles to provide excellent products or service to any single customer group. As people in the advertising industry say: 'you don't stand for anything which is important and unique in customers' minds'. When this happens, the organisation is unlikely to have a strongly focused image. At best, it may be known by its association with the industry in which it operates. As a contrast, think of the *Disney* organisation. *Disneyland* and *Disneyworld* are a unique product in which everything is focused around entertainment. The *Disney* organisation's other products complement these theme parks. The result is a strong and distinct image of both the company and its products. In fact, the *Disney* organisation tends to set the standards for the whole theme park industry. That is, it is a market-driving organisation which helps to create the industry image.

A more important problem for many organisations in a competitive market situation is that the business is defined in terms of what the organisation does rather than what its customers want from it. That is, the concern of managers is for 'means' (products, production processes, R&D) rather than 'ends' (what customers need or want). In his classic marketing article, Professor Ted Levitt of the Harvard Business School advanced the proposition that market definitions of a business are superior to product-based definitions.[1] He argued that products are transient, but that basic needs and types of customers endure. For example, new products which are often based on new technologies cannibalise the sales of the existing products. Portable electronic calculators have replaced slide-rules, and audio tapes and CDs have replaced music records. The basic customer needs these original products served have endured, but they are now serviced by completely different products.

Levitt has encouraged companies to define their businesses from a market, not a company perspective. In this way, you can avoid the trap of being caught in the 'sliderule' or the 'music record' business. Instead, managers should focus on the under-lying need for (portable) numerical calculation, or high quality music reproduction. To further illustrate the application of Levitt's approach, Table 4.1 provides a number of examples of product and market definitions for the same business enterprises.

The notable business writer, Derek Abell, has suggested using three criteria to create a market-oriented business definition.[2] These are:

- the customer groups to be served
- the customer needs to be met
- the technology used to satisfy these needs.

For example, the lighting division (SBU) of the *Philips* com-pany serves a variety of customer groups (such as homes, factories, offices, outdoor stadiums), with incandescent and fluorescent lights (technologies), to satisfy the needs of illumina-tion, safety and security. That is, the business definition of the Philips Lighting Division is defined by the intersection of these three factors.

Organisations which define their business according to these three criteria are in a good position to answer the question 'how will we compete?' For example, based on the business definition of the Philips Lighting Division above, it is a relatively straight-forward task for *Philips*' managers to survey the needs of differ-ent customer groups, identify competitors (and their strategies), and monitor the relevant technologies which will impact on the production process for different types of lights.

Fit or Failure

A guiding principle in the process of strategic management is to ensure that an organisation's strategy, structure, and manage-

Table 4.1

Product-oriented Versus Market-oriented Business Definitions

Company	Product Orientation	Market Orientation
Apple	We sell computers and programs	We provide the opportunity for people to enhance their skills ('The Power to be Your Best')
BP	We explore for oil and retail petrol	We provide convenient sources of energy for people
Carrier	We make air conditioners and heaters	We provide (home) climate control
Columbia Pictures	We make movies	We provide escapism and entertainment
National Geographic	We sell magazines and support research projects	We record history and society
Polaroid	We make cameras that produce instant pictures	We sell entertainment and having fun (for young people). We help minimise the risk of poor photos (for the professional photographer)
Revlon	We make cosmetics	We sell beauty and hope
Westpac Bank	We design and sell financial products and services	We help manage money and create wealth
Xerox	We make copying equipment	We help improve office productivity

ment processes complement each other. In a landmark strategic management paper, Raymond Miles and Charles Snow illustrated that successful organisations are the ones that achieve a strategic 'fit' with their market environment, and support their strategies with appropriately designed structures and management control processes.[3] They identified two types of fit:

1 *external fit* between the market environment and the organisation's resources and competencies
2 *internal fit* between the organisation's strategy, design, and functioning.

A minimal level of internal fit is essential for all organisations to operate effectively. Organisations with a fragile external fit tend to be vulnerable to changing market conditions unless they are in a 'protected' environment such as that provided by government regulation. Organisations with tight internal and external fits are usually associated with excellence—both financial and reputational.

The dividing line between an acceptable level of fit, and misfit, is generally difficult to detect. Misfit tends to creep up on organisations and can come from internal sources, and/or environmental change. Miles and Snow offer the *Chrysler Corporation* as a classic example of internally generated misfit. From a strong position in the 1930s as the second largest US automotive manufacturer, *Chrysler* began its decline after the Second World War when it changed its strategy without significantly altering its organisation structure or management processes. *Chrysler* decided to broaden its product line and compete with both *Ford* and *General Motors* worldwide. However, it did not support this new diversified product–market strategy with a modified organisation structure. In fact, *Chrysler* tried (unsuccessfully) to use its functionally departmentalised and centralised structure to support its new strategy. The rest is history, so to speak. Lee Iacocca was appointed CEO to rescue the company and *Chrysler* needed Federal Government assistance to avoid bankruptcy.[4]

A good example of externally generated misfit is the demise of the UK motorcycle industry.[5] From the early 1900s until the 1960s, the UK was a major force in the manufacture and sale of motorbikes. By the 1980s, however, the famous names of *BSA*, *Norton*, and *Triumph* were out of the market. The early 1960s saw the entry of the Japanese into the UK market—*Honda, Kawasaki,*

Yamaha, and *Suzuki.* The entry strategy of *Honda* was to avoid head-on competition with the established manufacturers. Instead, it targeted 'first time buyers' with lightweight, easy-to-handle 125cc bikes, and a dealer network that provided good customer support to this 'beginner' market segment. From this base, the Japanese moved up to the next engine size category (250cc), again with innovative design and strong marketing support. Many customers were their original first-time buyers who were trading up from smaller machines. This group was also a potential purchaser of British bikes. When the Japanese dominated this segment, they moved up to the segment of the market which wanted big bikes.

The response of British manufacturers was very slow. They seemed to believe that they could rely on their established reputation to keep (attracting) customers. In fact, it was probably their reputation that helped to speed up their demise! At the time of the Japanese entry to the market, customers thought that the British manufacturers had a weak dealer network and poor product availability. Also, in contrast to the Japanese manufacturers, the British bike makers did not seem to have any type of long-term strategy. It took just ten years for a group of companies with good strategic insight, and the organisation structure and management systems to back it up, to destroy the established market participants who had no sustainable competitive advantage.

Miles and Snow argue that 'finding the right strategy' is not as important to success as achieving a tight fit. The primary reason for this is that many competitors will have a similar understanding of the forces driving the evolution of their market, and will be considering similar market development or market penetration strategies. They argue that what differentiates the winners from the not so successful companies is the organisation's ability to articulate a good strategy, and the ability to develop a structure to support this before competitors. In essence, successful companies achieve tight internal and external fit *before* their competitors. The main factors which drive tight fit are shown in Figure 4.1. This is a contingency framework where strategy and positioning (relative to competitors) are determinants, while information technology, human resources, structure, and culture enable and constrain what the organisation can do.

The next section reviews some market-based strategic options. Then a brief outline of the major types of organisational

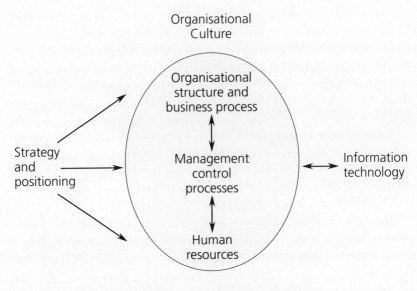

Figure 4.1   A Model of Strategic Fit

Source: Adapted from Craig, J. & Yetton, P. 1993, 'Business process redesign', *Australian Journal of Management*, vol. 17, no. 2, pp. 285–306.

structures is presented. Finally, some examples of successful strategy–structure fits are presented. The theme developed here is that given a particular strategy (which is a direct outcome of business definition), there are only a limited number of suitable structures.

Strategic Planning

That famous author, Anonymous, once identified three types of people: those who make things happen, those who watch what happened, and those who wonder what happened. In the context of strategic planning we can identify three similar types of companies: those which are *market driving*, those which are *market driven*, and those which are *market tolerant*. Companies which drive (that is shape) their market have the ability to understand customer needs. They also have the technology and management systems to design and market products which fulfil these needs. A good example is the *Sony* Corporation. In the field of consumer electronics, *Sony* has specialised in making small, high quality, user-friendly products. Its Walkman portable music systems are regarded as a design classic.

Market-driven companies can only 'read' customer needs. They spend their market research budgets on customer satisfaction surveys, usage and attitude studies, and advertising tracking studies. They also tend to segment their markets using demographic factors which describe customers (age, gender, socioeconomic status, media used), or psychographic factors which describe the psychological profile of customers (activities, interests, opinions). In contrast, market-driving companies will use demographic and psychographic factors as descriptions of market segments which have been formed to directly reflect customer needs.

The big four Australian banks (*ANZ, Commonwealth, NAB, Westpac*) are good examples of market-driven companies. Since deregulation of the banking industry they have been some of the biggest spenders on advertising and market research in Australia, yet they have a generally poor reputation among customers, journalists, and public policy makers. In fact, the Australian banks ruined their reputations to such an extent that the Federal Government set up a banking inquiry to review their operations and customer service practices. Also, a bank ombudsman was appointed to help mediate customer complaints. During the late 1980s and early 1990s, customer needs and expectations changed faster than the banks' internal structures could cope with. Also, the banks' bad debt and property write-offs rose to alarming levels. These four banks have both a fragile internal and external fit.

Market-tolerant organisations know that they must serve customers, but customers tend not to be assigned priority. In public service (government) organisations, procedures, career enhancement, and a host of other factors often seem more important than understanding and serving customer needs. Many 'old' capital intensive industries like automobiles, chemicals, electricity generation, mining, and steel making really only tolerate their customers. An emphasis on achieving production efficiency often makes it difficult to respond to changing customer needs. For example, the demand for a clean environment can only be catered to by the old industries within the constraints of their current resources and technology. In these cases, the internal fit can be so tight that this inhibits achieving some aspects of a tight external fit.

A market-oriented strategic plan for an SBU involves five core elements: business definition, environmental analysis, product-

1 Business Definition
  a What business are we in?
  b What business should we be in?

2 Environmental Analysis
  a External
    • opportunities
    • threats
  b Internal
    • strengths
    • weaknesses

3 Product-Marketing Strategy
  a Market penetration
  b Market development
  c Product development
  d Diversification

4 Competitive Strategy
  a Differentiation
  b Cost leadership
  c Focus
  d Asset management

5 Market Positioning
  a Segmentation
  b Targeting
  c Positioning

Figure 4.2   Strategic Planning

market strategy, competitive strategy, and market positioning. See Figure 4.2. Business definition has been referred to above, and competitive strategy will be discussed in the following section. Market positioning will be covered in Chapter 6. The remainder of this section discusses environmental analysis and marketing strategy.

Environmental Analysis

Most books on planning, and many business plans, include a section on what is known as a SWOT analysis. SWOT is an acronym which stands for internal Strengths and Weaknesses and external Opportunities and Threats. An organisation's internal strengths and weaknesses should be assessed for a particular market (as per the business definition), and in relation to a benchmark. In many cases, this benchmark is best industry practice, or a particular competitor. Likewise, opportunities and threats are described as they relate to a particular market.

Market research, secondary data sources, and the organisation's internal information systems provide raw information about the market: its current and projected size, competitive activity, technological trends, the preferences and buying habits of customers, legal regulations and distribution channels. Collecting and analysing this information can highlight potential market opportunities. These can be prioritised in terms of their attractiveness and success probability. Environmental scanning should also reveal potential threats to the organisation's current business activities. Threats are often prioritised in terms of their seriousness and probability of occurrence. Without some type of purposeful action, these threats may lead to an erosion of the organisation's market position and/or reputation as we will see in Chapter 11.

Because the factors which combine to run a business are not equally important to its success, each factor needs to be given an importance weight to reflect its relative contribution. A process often used by marketing planners is to rate the importance of each factor and its current performance level relative to the competition. (The performance rating is similar to classifying it as a strength or a weakness.) This type of importance–performance analysis can be used to search for factors where the organisation has a *distinctive competence*, and/or a *competitive advantage*. When a business has a major strength in a particular factor—a distinctive competence—this will only provide it with a competitive advantage if it is important to customers. Also, a weakness may not necessarily lead to a competitive disadvantage if it is unimportant to customers. These competitive advantages often help shape an organisation's reputation, especially for financial analysts and business people.

Marketing Strategy

There are many ways to think about marketing strategy. One of the founding fathers of strategic management, Igor Ansoff, proposed a useful framework for identifying four basic marketing strategies.[6] He summarised the environment in which a business operates into two dimensions—what is sold (current or new products/services for the firm), and to whom it is sold (the firm's current market or a new market). Ansoff's product–market matrix is illustrated in Figure 4.3. For the sake of simplicity, the range of technological and market newness has been classified into only two levels. This provides four basic marketing strategies: market penetration, product development, market development, and diversification (which is either related or unrelated to the organisation's core competencies).

A business not seeking to grow its market is located in Cell 1 of the Ansoff matrix. It will adopt a defensive marketing strategy to maintain market share, and profit improvement will result largely from cost reductions. A firm embarking on growth, however, may select any of the four growth options in Figure 4.3. The least risky growth option is generally considered to be a market penetration strategy. Here the company is familiar with both the products it is selling, and the market(s) in which they are sold. This strategy is implemented by either 'push' and/or 'pull' marketing. Push marketing involves a stronger selling effort to existing distributors to encourage them to stock more

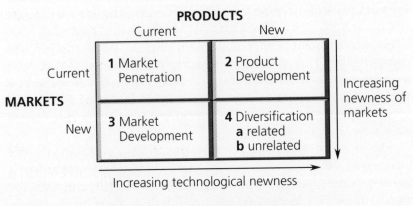

Figure 4.3   Product–Market Matrix

Source: Adapted from Ansoff, I., 'Strategies for diversification', *Harvard Business Review*, September–October 1957, p. 114.

product. Pull marketing involves trying to increase the amount of the product demanded by users. Advertising and promotion are typically used for this purpose, and customer demand forces distributors (and retailers) to stock (more of) the product.

Because many markets have reached saturation, there is a natural tendency for firms to try to sell their current products to a new market. A market development strategy (Cell 3) can be implemented by getting a different type of distributor to sell the product (for example, selling personal computers direct to big clients, and through speciality retail chains to smaller clients), by entering a new geographic market (for example, the Japanese exporting their motorbikes to the UK), or by finding a new use for the product in a different market (for example, 3M's yellow *Post-it* note pads were originally targeted to the business market and later sold to the home market).

An often used growth strategy is to launch a new product into an existing market (Cell 2). This product development strategy seeks to build on the existing internal strengths (distinctive competencies) of the business. In the frequently purchased packaged goods area, one of these strengths is often the name (or image) of a brand. *Line extensions* (such as a new flavour, variety, or pack size) are a very common form of new product introduction. Sometimes a *brand extension* will be used to implement this strategy. For example, in the early 1980s *Levi Strauss* (the blue jeans makers) introduced a line of upmarket, wool-content men's suits through their existing retailers under the *Levi* name. This brand extension, however, was a spectacular failure costing the company a lot of money and damaging the brand image. (Customer surveys showed that the Levi name meant denim, durable, working men, and good value. This image was incompatible with a fashionable, top quality suit.) Many new product introductions like Levi's men's suits may not reflect a realistic market opportunity. Also, there is a vast amount of research attesting to the fact that many (some say most) new products are failures.

The last growth strategy is diversification (Cell 4). During the early 1980s this was a popular option for many companies. It turned out, however, to be a high risk strategy. Here, both the product and the market are new to the firm. To reduce some of this risk, the firm could develop new products which have a technological and/or marketing synergy with the firm's current operations. If, however, diversification is unrelated to the firm's current technology, products, or marketing expertise, then the SBU is exposing itself to multiple sources of risk, and the potential for failure increases dramatically. Many successful organisations are unwilling to take more than one major risk at a time. Hence, it may be advisable to create a separate SBU for such a venture (to limit any potential adverse spillover effects on the company), or take over an existing business.

Each strategy identified in Figure 4.3 makes different demands on a company's reputations. They are numbered from least risky (1 market penetration) to most risky (4b unrelated diversification). Risk here is defined as the potential for business and hence, reputational loss. Also, the greater the variety of activities a stakeholder knows an organisation is involved in, the less focused will be the organisation's image and/or reputation.

Competitive Strategies

The last fifteen years have seen some significant advances in the field of competitive strategy. The conceptual work of Michael Porter and the empirical research using the PIMS (Profit Impact of Market Strategies) database have largely transformed the way in which we answer the questions 'how to compete?' and 'how to gain a competitive advantage?'.[7] As noted above, these quest-ions can only be comprehensively answered by considering all the elements in Figure 4.1 on p. 68. Here, however, the focus will be on strategy, then structure, and then the link between strategy and structure.

Generic Strategies

The strategic management literature suggests that there are four generic strategies: differentiation, overall cost leadership, focus, and asset management. These are summarised in Table 4.2, and briefly described below.[8] Each strategy drives the organisation's operations which in turn have a significant effect on employees' and external stakeholders' perceptions of the firm.

Differentiation strategies rely on delivering a product and/or service that is uniquely attractive to customers. The primary methods of differentiation are either product, service, technology, or marketing based. Two companies which have established technology-based differentiation are *Boeing* and *Hewlett-Packard*. One organisation which strives to be a new product leader is the *Sony* corporation. It introduces up to 1000 new products and variations of existing products each year. Alternatively, companies may try to deliver superior perform-ance on quality, style, reliability, or some other attribute valued by consumers. Marketing differentiators usually create a strong brand image and/or corporate reputation as the signal of uniqueness. The classic example of a brand–image based differentiation strategy is *Coca-Cola*. Another good example was *IBM*, whose computers were seldom state of the art, but the company's reputation for marketing service and support was legendary.

Table 4.2

Generic Strategy Alternatives

Differentiation
a Product
  • new products
  • superior performance on an important customer benefit
b Marketing
  • unique brand or corporate image

Overall Cost Leadership
  • production, and/or
  • distribution

Focus
  • on a particular type of product
  • market segment
  • geographic region

Asset Management
a Parsimony
  • use of few, or other organisations' resources
b Access
  • high capital requirements, patents, copyright
c Flexibility
  • resources used for multiple purposes
d distribution
  • large, well-established distribution system

Overall cost leadership is a strategy which seeks to achieve the lowest cost of production and distribution so that products can be sold at the lowest price in the market. The management consultants *BCG* (Boston Consulting Group) made this strategy fashionable in the late 1960s and early 1970s. The overall aim of this strategy is to achieve a large enough market share (usually over 15 per cent) to capture the rewards of production experience (the experience curve effect). Production cost savings allow low prices which are attractive to price sensitive consumers. Alternatively, cost leaders may price their products similarly to competitors, but operate at a higher profit margin. Cost leaders are high volume producers with R&D focused on productivity improvements more than product improvements.

Henry Ford's *Model T Ford* is probably the classic example of an overall cost leadership strategy. (Customers could have these cars in any colour as long as it was black!) Later in the 1960s the Ford motor company's cars the *Falcon* and the *Mustang* were also based on a cost leadership strategy. A different example of this strategy is the Australia–Japan coal trade which is the single biggest commodity trade flow in the world. The Australian coal producers traditionally concentrated on mining large volumes of high quality, cheap coal, while the Japanese users (cement, power generation, steel) took prime responsibility for blending different types of coal to suit their needs.[9]

The old strategic orthodoxy suggested that a differentiation and cost leadership strategy would not blend well together. The joint pursuit of both strategies typically led to a 'stuck in the middle' position where the organisation did not achieve the advantages of either strategy. Many of these 'stuck in the middle' companies also had a 'fuzzy' reputation because it was difficult for customers to identify any element of superiority for the products or for the company.

While being stuck in the middle may have been the fate of some US companies, many Japanese companies have been able to avoid this problem. For example, the success of Japanese automotive and consumer electronics makers is built on elements of both product differentiation and cost leadership. Continuous technology development and manufacturing process flexibility allow the frequent introduction of a wide range of high quality new products, produced with lower costs and faster cycle times. In the stagnant breakfast cereal market, *Kellogg* has also prospered by simultaneously

- introducing large numbers of new products
- heavy spending on advertising to build brand equity
- plant and equipment modernisation to gain manufacturing cost efficiencies.

Hence, it is time to rethink the conditions under which the (old) stuck in the middle 'rule' applies.

Corporate strategists suggest that a focus strategy is more likely to be employed by small companies or new entrants to a market. It may also be used to complement either a differentiation or a cost leadership strategy. As Table 4.2 illustrates, a focus strategy is all about concentrating the organisation's resources on a particular type of product, customer, or geographic market. The basic idea is that resource concentration allows the organisation to differentiate its products, or to reduce costs in order to serve a particular market segment(s). Focus or niche strategies are probably the most feasible strategy for most companies.

Many large firms organise their activities to practise a multiple focus strategy. Divisions of companies like *General Motors, Nestlé, Procter & Gamble* and *Unilever* use a strategy of product variety and mass marketing. They produce a range of (similar) products to offer variety to buyers, and/or to appeal simultaneously to many segments of the market.

Asset management is the fourth generic strategy. Table 4.2 identifies four types:

a   parsimony—where an organisation uses few assets per unit of output in comparison to its competitors
b   access—where there are high capital requirements (such as steel making), or where access to resources is limited (such as diamond mining), or where patents and copyrights constrain other companies from producing identical products (such as pharmaceutical, biotechnology, and computer software companies)
c   flexibility—where resources can be used for multiple purposes (such as management consulting)
d   distribution—where a company has a strong distribution system in place (such as retail banking), or a big personal sales force.

In industries like professional business services, asset management is a key strategic consideration. For example, merchant banks differentiate themselves from traditional banks by their focus on particular types of financial transaction, and access to resources (both investors' money and skilled staff). Their profits come via success fees and asset flexibility (for example, using the same staff on multiple (types of) 'deals').

Like a focus strategy, asset management is often used as a complement to one of the other strategies. For example, the availability of skilled staff often determines the types of practice areas developed by a law firm. In turn, the range of practice areas differentiates one law firm from another. The business definition and strategic mix of the firm sets the foundation for developing its reputations.

Organisation Structure

In 1979 Henry Mintzberg drew together a lot of the work on the structure of organisations. His ideas are widely used and are still appropriate for understanding the basic structural configurations of many SBUs.[10] He called the most basic type of organisation *The Simple Structure*. This organisation is one with little or no formal structure. It typically consists of a boss (owner or manager) and the workers. Coordination of tasks is achieved by direct supervision, and strategy is formulated by the manager. Such organisations are flexible, but very limited in their capacity to cope with complexity. They tend to operate simple technologies in simple environments.

Most organisations quickly become more formalised as they start to grow. Work is divided to facilitate specialisation, and the organisation strives to achieve reliability, predictability, and efficiency. The primary coordination mechanism is the standardisation of operations. A key part of the organisation is the group of people who design work practices, and the formal and informal monitoring and control mechanisms. Information systems are often developed to monitor costs, throughput, and sales rather than market needs. They tend to resemble the rest of the organisation—being centralised, efficient, long-term, but not very flexible. Strategy, power, and decision-making are also centralised with the senior executives. Mintzberg described the extreme form of this type of organisation as a *machine bureaucracy*. Such mechanistic organisations are suited to operating in a stable or predictable environment.

Organisations which carry out complex tasks, and operate in a stable or predictable environment, are not restricted to being organised as a machine bureaucracy. Coordination of operations can be achieved by standardising the skills and knowledge of workers, rather than their work practices. These organisations are decentralised, in both the vertical and horizontal dimensions. The key people are trained and indoctrinated professionals who are given considerable control over their work. Much of the early training and indoctrination is controlled by the profession to which the person belongs, and these professionals may identify more with their profession than the organisation in which they work. Structural configurations like this were called *professional bureaucracies* by Mintzberg, and are common in universities, research institutes, hospitals, schools, and public accounting firms. Strategy within a professional bureaucracy is often a blend of personal agenda, acceptable practice, and the desires of the organisation.

Like a professional bureaucracy, a *functional* organisation is a set of quasi-autonomous entities (such as manufacturing, logistics, marketing) linked together by an administrative structure. Unlike the professional bureaucracy, however, the departments are more tightly coupled to achieve an integrated output. Often they are self-contained cost (or profit) centres run by a senior manager. This structural form is used primarily by organisations which can benefit from the accumulation of a set of focused operations. Because each functional unit has a specialised purpose, these organisations tend not to be highly flexible. Hence, they too are only an appropriate structural choice when the organisation's environment is stable or predictable.

When an organisation's environment tends to be turbulent (complex and/or dynamic), and when people must perform unusual or complex tasks which change each time they are performed, then the various types of bureaucracy described above are generally unsuitable. Here, the organisation must be designed for change. To compete under these conditions firms decentralise decision-making, broadly define jobs, use as few rules and procedures as they can, and subjectively evaluate individual performance. Information technology systems are often distributed throughout the organisation to provide specialised information processing capabilities to support the innovativeness of individuals.

Professional business consultants (management consultants, corporate lawyers, advertising agencies) are good examples of such organisations. People with different skills, goals, and time horizons must coordinate their work to satisfy the expectations

of customers. Frequent meetings, often 'on the run', and pro-
posals, briefing papers, and reports are used as coordinating
mechanisms. Power and authority tend to be situational and
expertise based. Within work teams communication is open, and
environmental (customer) monitoring is extensive. Mintzberg
called this type of organisation an *organic structure* or an
adhocracy.

Strategy–Structure Configurations

The choice of an appropriate strategy and structure configuration is determined by the opportunities and threats posed by the
SBU's market(s). The internal strengths and weaknesses of the
organisation then determine how it tries to adapt its products
and services to fit (new) market requirements. Hence, the quality
of environmental monitoring (using such frameworks as SWOT
and market research) is the key to developing an appropriate
strategy–structure configuration. It is also the key to the success
potential of the organisation. The value of being visibly successful is that employees and external stakeholders enhance their
reputations of the organisation. (Most people like and respect
'winners' more than 'losers'.)

To illustrate strategy–structure fit, take the case of a small
management consulting firm. These firms generally start business with a few highly trained people and a handful of support
staff—flexible, simple structure organisations. A key success
factor is their ability to convince potential clients that the
consultants can provide a new insight into the problems that
keep the CEO awake at night. Consultants typically spend as
much time as possible in the market (rather than their offices)
gathering information about client needs, and developing
'models' to solve particular types of problems. They are classic
new product differentiators, driven by the ever changing needs
of their clients. In these firms, organisational culture is more
important than structure as a mechanism for coordinating activities and focusing effort. As consulting firms grow in size, an
organic structure typically develops to ensure that they remain
flexible and responsive to client needs.

Recognition and reward systems are a critical element in the
performance management of new product differentiator–organic
organisations. Rewards need to be linked directly to the key

success factors of teamwork, information sharing, and performance output. In these organisations, the human resource manager can help the organisation develop its innovation capabilities through personnel selection, training, and reward management.

Performance-based reward systems are not appropriate for all types of organisation structure. An alternative is the hierarchy-based reward system, which is used more in bureaucratic organisations. Here, sometimes elaborate performance appraisal mechanisms are used to both develop and evaluate managers. Bonuses are a smaller part of the total remuneration package than in a typical performance-based system. Also, managers in a bureaucratic organisation are more likely to be transferred across departments on a regular basis to develop their general management capabilities.

In the early part of the 1990s, the crucial role that information technology plays in aligning an organisation's strategy and structure became appreciated. To gain a competitive advantage in their markets, some companies developed information systems to help achieve the joint benefits of production efficiency and product/service customisation. The strategy was known by names such as mass customisation, and maximarketing.[11] In essence, this strategy relies on a network organisational structure where a number of generic, modular production units share material and information to design, advertise, and deliver new products to customers. Computerised databases containing information about the purchase history, media habits, and interests of an individual is one type of such modular production unit. For example, the US company *Equifax* boasts that it has a database of nearly 100 million consumers with as many as 340 items of information on each one.[12]

The diversity of ways that an organisation can strive to gain a competitive advantage means that there are no simple rules about what are, or what are not appropriate strategy–structure configurations. Instead, managers must choose a generic strategy mix and then support this strategy with a suitable structure and complementary control activities. Major changes in business strategy are often triggered by some form of crisis (such as the threat of a takeover, entry of a new competitor, change in technology). Minor changes in business strategy often involve marketing the organisation and/or its products and services differently to customers. However, the consistent presentation of

an organisation to its stakeholders, based on a shared understanding of its business strategy, is essential to the formation of
a distinctive reputation.

Conclusion

The argument presented in this chapter is simply that successful
organisations learn how to read their environment, and couple
their strategy, business systems, and structure to deliver value to
their customers. They create a tight (but not too tight) internal
and external fit. In the future, information systems will play a
key role in facilitating this process. Integrated formal policies are
a necessary but not sufficient condition for developing a strong
set of reputations among various stakeholder groups. The
organisation's formal policies get translated through the reward
systems used to evaluate employees, such that staff will often 'do
what is inspected, rather than what is expected of them'.

An organisation's formal policies define how it wants to
compete, and an integral component of its competitive strategy
is the organisation's positioning relative to its competitors. That
is, how will your organisation favourably distinguish itself from
the other organisations which also seek to serve your customers.
Good competitive positioning is usually based on the functional
and/or psychological benefits your organisation, and its
portfolio of products and services, offer to stakeholders. Strategy
and positioning get implemented by developing a supportive
organisational structure, and a set of appropriate business
systems. The sequence of planning is business strategy mix, then
positioning, then structure and business systems. Chapter 10
elaborates the positioning element of competitive strategy, for
this is the key attribute of your organisation's desired reputation.

End Notes

1 T. Levitt, 'Marketing myopia', *Harvard Business Review*, July-August, 1960,
   pp. 45–56.
2 D. Abell, *Defining the Business: The Starting Point of Strategic Planning*,
   Prentice-Hall, Englewood Cliffs, 1980, Ch. 3.
3 R. Miles & C. Snow, 'Fit, failure and the hall of fame', *California Management
   Review*, vol. 26, no. 3, Spring, 1984, pp. 10–28.
4 L. Iacocca with W. Novak, *IACOCCA: An Autobiography*, Bantam Books,
   Toronto, 1984.

5 M. Christopher, S. Majaro & M. McDonald, *Strategy Search*, Gower, Aldershot, 1987, pp. 14–16.

6 I. Ansoff 'Strategies for diversification', *Harvard Business Review*, September–October, 1957, pp. 113–24. It seems that Ansoff was not the first person to publish this product–market matrix. See for example, S. Johnson & C. Jones, 'How to organize for new products', *Harvard Business Review*, May–June, 1957, pp. 49–62.

7 M. Porter, *Competitive Strategy*, Free Press, New York, 1980; M. Porter, *Competitive Advantage*, Free Press, New York, 1985; R. Buzzel & B. Gale, *The PIMS Principles*, Free Press, New York, 1987.

8 Most of these strategies are outlined in: D. Miller, 'Configurations of strategy and structure: towards a synthesis', *Strategic Management Journal*, vol. 27, 1986, pp. 233–49.

9 G.R. Dowling, 'Buying is marketing too—Japan's influence in the Australian coal business', *Long Range Planning*, vol. 20, no. 1, February, 1987, pp. 35–43.

10 H. Mintzberg, *The Structure of Organisations*, Prentice-Hall, Englewood Cliffs, 1979.

11 A.C. Boynton, B. Victor & B.J. Pine, 'New competitive strategies: challenges to organisation and information technology', *IBM Systems Journal*, 1993; S. Rapp & T. Collins, *The Great Marketing Turnaround*, Prentice-Hall, Englewood Cliffs, 1990.

12 ibid.

CHAPTER 5

Organisational Culture: The Invisible Web

People are aware of differences in national cultures. This awareness results from travel, personal contacts and international news stories. Cultural differences are rooted in very basic beliefs about the origins of life, the role of time and nature in shaping people's lives, and how people should interact. These belief systems are a powerful force which shape our behaviour as a society, and our business dealings. With trade and commerce becoming more international, an appreciation of such differences is an important prerequisite to competing globally. This is despite the fact that the language used for much of the world's international business is English.

To the anthropologist, a culture is revealed by its language, ritual, kinship structure, architecture, and symbols. The history of culture has often demonstrated how important a name (or other identity symbols such as a flag) is to helping people identify with a culture. An interesting example of this occurred with the recent renaming of the city of St Petersburg. In 1703 the young Russian tsar, Peter I, began to build a city to project his self-image, and to be the new Russian capital. The name Peter gave to his new city was not Russian, but rather Germanic in honour of his patron saint. St Petersburg was designed to be different from other Russian cities (especially Moscow), and in time it developed its own distinct cultural identity. To appease anti-German feelings arising during the First World War, the city was renamed Petrograd in 1914. A decade later to commemorate Lenin's death, the city was given the new name of Leningrad. In 1991 the city's residents held a referendum and returned the city's original name—St Petersburg. The power of the cultural identity symbolised by the city's original name somehow survived a generation of inhabitants, and powerful new identity forming events such as 'the siege of Leningrad' during the Second World War.

It is not a big step from thinking about national cultures to thinking about organisational cultures. However, it was only in the decade of the 1980s that researchers and consultants began to realise that an organisation's culture was a powerful force within the organisation which shaped many aspects of its behaviour. (See Table 5.1 for an interesting example.) As more studies of the creation and functioning of organisations were conducted, it became obvious that some intangible force was operating inside organisations which interacted with the easily observable characteristics such as size, structure, reward systems and technology utilisation to explain how organisations worked.[1]

In the context of the overall reputation formation process outlined in Chapter 1 (and Figure 1.2), the organisation's culture plays a pivotal role in translating the values in the vision statement into employee behaviour. It also impacts on how many aspects of an organisation's strategy, structure, and control systems get implemented (Chapter 4). These interrelationships are graphically shown in the *McKinsey 7-S* framework outlined in Figure 3.1 on p. 42, where the Shared Values and Style factors represent an organisation's culture. In fact, it is a lack of understanding of organisation culture issues that causes many reputation rejuvenation programs to fail to achieve their expected outcomes. Also the advocates of takeovers and mergers are discovering that it is often these 'soft' cultural issues which lead to the underperformance of many joint ventures.[2]

The following sections in this chapter outline what is meant by the concept of organisational culture. This understanding will help you to begin the task of assessing the culture of your organisation. The focus then shifts to how this powerful force

Table 5.1

R.J. Reynolds

In 1874 Richard Joshua Reynolds established his tobacco company in the North Carolina, USA town of Winston-Salem. The area was populated by the descendants of Czechoslovakian immigrants—a group called Moravians. This community's Moravian values of work, thrift and ingenuity became strongly imbued in the R.J. Reynolds corporate culture, and played a strong part in the company's early success. Winston-Salem, or W-S as it was sometimes known to the locals, jokingly stood for Work & Sleep.

In 1929 the company moved into its new 22-storey stone building that was considered such an architectural gem that it was rebuilt on a much larger scale in New York city as the Empire State Building. The magnificence of this icon was in stark contrast to the conditions enjoyed by its managers. No limousines or fat expense accounts were permitted in the early years.

By the mid 1950s Winston-Salem was an R.J. Reynolds company town. The company's senior managers seldom (for a company of its size and standing) travelled outside the company's sphere of influence in the Winston-Salem area. They were frugal, suspicious of outsiders, protective of the status quo, profoundly antiunion, good to their town and workforce, and hugely profitable.

(R.J. Reynolds introduced the first packaged cigarette—Camel, the first major filtered cigarette—Winston, and the first mass-marketed menthol cigarette—Salem.)

In 1985 R.J. Reynolds took over the Nabisco food company headed by the flamboyant CEO Ross Johnson. The new company was called RJR Nabisco and the two companies' senior management cultures were an uneasy mix—the staid RJR managers and the 'continuous change' Nabisco management cadre. Even the two companies' product lines clashed: the wholesome foods from Nabisco and the life threatening tobacco products of RJR. It was unlikely that two such strong organisational cultures could be blended, and they couldn't. Within a couple of years Ross Johnson had complete control of RJR Nabisco and led the company to the largest leveraged buyout (LBO) ever attempted.

Source: Burrough, B. & Helyar, J. 1990, *Barbarians at the Gate*, Arrow Books, London.

can enhance or hinder the development and use of the organisation's reputation among stakeholder groups. A word of warning, however, before we proceed. While most executives have a natural desire for quick and decisive action, corporate culture is a slow, evolutionary factor in the reputation formation process. You must avoid the attitude expressed in the following quote from a fictitious chief executive who just discovered the importance of corporate culture: 'That sounds great! I want one by Friday afternoon.'

What is Organisational Culture?

While there are nearly as many definitions of organisational culture as there are academic researchers in the area, the task of understanding this phenomenon is not hopeless. Over the past decade, enough has been written about the topic to provide good guidance to the practising manager. The perspective adopted in this chapter is to assume that culture is something that all organisations have to a greater or lesser extent. It is a variable, and so it makes sense to see if different types or amounts of culture are related to other aspects of organisations. For example, do organisations with a strong culture perform better in the marketplace than organisations with a weaker culture. Also, do different types of cultures enhance or inhibit internal communication in the organisation. These are the types of questions occupying the minds of management researchers and consultants. There aren't many definitive answers yet, but the questions are interesting ones, and we know that by assessing your organisation's culture you can begin to appreciate its potential effects on how the organisation functions as a whole.

Two good working definitions of organisation culture are:

The system of shared values (what is important) and beliefs (how things work) that interact with a company's people, organisational structures, and control systems to produce behavioural norms (the way we do things around here).[3]

A somewhat more 'academic' definition is:

The pattern of basic assumptions which a group has invented, discovered or developed, in learning to cope with problems in its environment, which have worked well enough to be considered valid and therefore to be taught to new members as the correct way to perceive, think, and feel in relation to those problems.[4]

A number of aspects of these definitions are worth elaborat-

Table 5.2

A Comparison of Cultural Stereotypes

Asia–Pacific Company	East–Coast USA Company
a Truth comes ultimately from older, wiser, better educated and higher status members.	a Ideas come ultimately from individuals.
b People are capable of loyalty and discipline in carrying out directives.	b People are motivated, responsible and capable of governing themselves.
c Relationships in the organisation are basically linear and vertical.	c All people should state their views.
d Harmony and consensus decision making are important.	d Group discussion and active debate is the best way to test ideas.
e The organisation is a 'solitary unit' that will take care of its members.	e The best people survive and prosper in the organisation.
f The organisation is more vision or mission-driven.	f Formal planning, budgets and organisation charts direct activity.
g The organisation places more emphasis on lifetime learning inside the organisation.	g The organisation relies for its training more on formal qualifications from external sources.

ing. First, cultures are developed by people (a group), and comprise people's beliefs and feelings (corporate values or assumptions). These beliefs and values will vary depending on the nature of the work group to which a person belongs, and the types of problems they face in the work environment. Broad national cultural factors will also impact on an organisation's culture. An example of how these various factors can shape an organisation's culture is shown in Table 5.2. Here a contrast is drawn between a 'typical' Asia–Pacific company and a 'typical' East-Coast USA company.[5]

Subcultures

The variety of factors which can affect an organisation's culture mean that within any medium to large organisation, we should group is likely to view the organisation differently from how it is viewed by the workers on the production line. In the field of retail banking, the culture in the branches is often quite different from the culture in head office. One of the principal reasons for this is the lack of face-to-face dealings with customers by head office managers. Regional diversity can also encourage the formation of subcultures. For example, in the early years of the *American Express Company*, the company's Eastern (New York) and Western (Chicago) Departments had two very different subcultures. In the East, J.C. Fargo's autocratic leadership was followed to the letter, while in the West, the 'Chicago Rule' prevailed. It said: 'J.C. Fargo could be persuaded, and if he could not be persuaded, he could be deceived'.[6]

For your organisation's subcultures to unite and drive the overall desired reputation, they must share a dominant core set of values. One way to achieve such integration is to use the vision statement and other forms of internal communication as vehicles to promote these core values. For example, in some of the giant Japanese companies employees regularly sing their company song as a way of reinforcing the company's core values.

When a core set of values are in place, the CEO and other senior managers need to monitor and control the unique beliefs and feelings which characterise the various subcultures. In other words, there can be some cultural diversity within an organisation—but not too much, otherwise it becomes dysfunctional. Research has uncovered three types of 'pure' subculture which will play a different role in shaping your organisation's desired reputation.

The first case is where one subculture drives the overall culture of the company. For example, in the early days of the *Apple* computer company, the technical development people created a distinct subculture based on their unusual work habits and dress code. This subculture was often used as a way of demonstrating to visitors that *Apple* and its products were innovative—look at the people who created them! Another example is the research and development unit of the German car maker *Mercedes-Benz*. The values of engineering excellence and technological leadership which this group hold, are used in much of the company's advertising. The phrase (or tag-line to use the advertising term): 'engineered like no other car' is used as the *Mercedes* signature on many print advertisements.

A subculture which drives the overall culture of the organisation has been labelled an 'enhancing subculture'.[7] The problem with managing enhancing subcultures, is to ensure that they do not come to completely dominate the way the organisation views its competitive environment. If either *Mercedes-Benz* or *Apple* believe that their products are their key success factor, then they run the real risk of trying to fit their customers to their products (a product-oriented business philosophy), rather than being responsive to customer needs (a market-oriented business outlook).

A second type of subculture is one that tries to have little or nothing in common with the overall organisational culture, or other subcultures. These groups create their own unique set of values which coexist, but don't compete with the organisation's core values. An example of such a subculture is sometimes found in organisations which have their own internal legal department (for example, in television stations and newspapers), or advertising agency (for example, in a large retailer). Here, the professional values associated with the specialist activities of the group dominate its culture. The management task here is to assess whether or not such a coexisting subculture enhances or detracts from the functioning of the group and the parent organisation.

The third type of 'pure' subculture is one that is in conflict or incompatible with the dominant organisational culture. In the 1970s and early 1980s in Australia, many craft-based unions had a set of social values and assumptions about work practices which were directly opposed to the efficient and effective functioning of the organisations which employed their members. The result was very high levels of workplace disputation, and the use of government industrial tribunals to arbitrate these disputes. The extent of this workplace disruption ultimately led to Australia gaining an international reputation as a country with an uncooperative workforce.

Subcultures which diverge from the dominant culture can, in some cases, serve useful purposes for an organisation. For example, they can create 'safe' havens for groups or taskforces to create new products in companies which do not have a formal new product development process. They may also provide management with a breeding ground for initiating change. If a particular group is perceived by others in the organisation as being more innovative, then their 'internal reputation' may help management to use this group to start a new project or initiate change throughout the organisation. The *Australian Graduate School of Management* has sometimes filled this role within its parent university. As a business school it was one of the first units of the university to introduce a scheme of performance-based salary supplementation. It was also an early adopter (in the Australian public university system) of the practice of charging student fees for an MBA degree. Both these initiatives were compatible with the image of a small innovative business school.

Cultural Strength

The discussion of subcultures leads naturally to the question of the strength or intensity of an organisation's culture. Organisations with a strong culture tend to have a high level of consensus among members about what basic assumptions and values guide the organisation. While there may be various subcultures, they will hold a common set of core values. In a strong culture, there is also likely to be an obvious link between the organisation's reward and control systems and 'acceptable' behaviour. For example, Chapter 4 mentioned hierarchical versus performance-based reward systems. These reward systems can influence the development of what is known as a 'clan culture' or a 'market culture'. Clan culture organisations exhibit more homogeneous values about the organisation than market culture organisations.

A third dimension of a strong culture is the degree of commitment to consensus. Is there really a core set of beliefs and values? Are these widely held? Are people committed to them? Even if people in the organisation share a common set of values about work, for a strong culture to exist, these will need to be ascribed to the organisation rather than to the individual or his/her profession. Researchers search to see if stories and myths, rituals and ceremonies, and heros and villains in work-life are linked to the organisation. Other manifestations of a strong organisational culture are the use of particular vocabulary and jargon, and whether employees use the company logo and colours to identify themselves with the organisation.

It is important to recognise that cultural strength may not be related to organisational effectiveness. This will be a function of the overall fit between the organisation's strategy, structure, and culture (internal fit), and between these factors and the threats and opportunities posed by the organisation's operating environment (external fit).[8] Cultural strength, however, will be related to the reputation employees hold of their organisation. As Figure 1.2 in Chapter 1 illustrates, these reputations can be a prime determinant of the images and reputations external groups hold of the organisation.

Monitoring the gap between what employees think, and the ideal image and reputation of your organisation can signal potential problems. For example, employees of big Australian organisations have become much less loyal in the past six years. This is a key finding from extensive surveying of workers coordinated through the Australian Employees Survey Group.[9] The group of thirty member organisations includes *Ford*, *IBM*, *Qantas*, *Kodak*, and *Hewlett-Packard*. Their pooled results enable them to compare performance on key issues such as morale, training, and pay. Results during 1986–1992 involved almost 70 000 worker responses. The main findings were:

a Satisfaction with work has not changed—77 per cent of workers continue to enjoy their jobs.
b Workers' satisfaction with their organisations has steadily declined—from 79 per cent to 55 per cent.
c The image of the organisation has also declined. The proportion of employees who rated their organisation as superior to other workplaces has fallen from 91 per cent to 58 per cent.

If similar symptoms are applicable to your organisation, then culture change may be necessary to help rectify this situation.

Changing Organisational Cultures

The previous description of organisational culture suggests how to change or manage culture. A good way to illustrate the dynamic aspects of culture is to consider its role in a new, founder-dominated organisation. Here, the main issue is how to form a number of individuals into a work-group, and to establish a growth path for the organisation. The work-group, which is the organisation now, needs to establish an identity, and to develop work procedures to accomplish its tasks. The emerging culture will act as a focal point to assimilate different perceptions of the goals of the organisation, and how it should interact with its key stakeholders. Culture changes that occur during this early formative stage of development are concerned with clarifying the dominant beliefs and values of the group. They also shape the communication devices used to signal important aspects of the organisation's culture to other people.

As new organisations grow, an effective culture emerges, otherwise the organisations would not have survived. To change the culture of these organisations requires an appreciation of how the culture originally developed. This is especially important when some of the original members of the organisation still hold positions of power and influence. The classic example of this situation occurs when the original founder of a company is about to abdicate his/her position, and the new management team (which often includes one or more family members) charts a course to 'modernise' the company. There may be a feeling at this crucial transition stage, that some major changes are necessary. The new team feels that the founders held too tightly to a set of values which were applicable to a past era. Culture change in this situation can be traumatic, and may result in replacing large numbers of people who want to hold on to the old culture.

In mature organisations which have a history spanning two or more generations of managers, the early history of the organisation may provide only limited insight into the key factors which have shaped, and which reinforce the existing culture. In these organisations research to describe culture strength, the existence of subcultures, the signalling devices used to communicate culture, and the degree of internal fit between strategy, structure and culture is necessary. It is also necessary to assess the external fit between the demands of the organisation's markets and the internal factors which shape its response to these markets. Culture change is typically extremely difficult for large, mature organisations and often requires a major external shock to stimulate action. A well-documented example of an organisation which experienced such a shock, and which spent years trying to change its culture (strategy and structure) to survive in a changing market is the story of Lee Iacocca's reign at the *Chrysler Corporation*.[10]

Forces Driving Culture Change

When Lee Iacocca took control of *Chrysler* in 1979, there was a huge 'gap' between the way the US car market was evolving and the company's strategy for serving this market. (This was the era when small Japanese cars were making significant inroads into the market.) There was an equally serious gap between *Chrysler*'s flawed strategy and the organisation's capability to implement it. In short, *Chrysler* was in deep trouble—it faced a crisis of survival. The pressure for change was enormous, and employees understood the consequences of failing to change. Iacocca's appointment as the new chief operating executive gave him the mandate to make vast changes in the *Chrysler* empire.

When thinking about how to change *Chrysler*'s, or any organisation's culture, a good metaphor is that of an iceberg. The part we can see above the waterline is only a small part of the total iceberg. Likewise with organisation culture. Changing the bits that are easy to see such as rituals and vision statements, will have only limited effect on the overall culture. To significantly change an organisation's culture requires that first we 'unfreeze' the total iceberg, and then we 'refreeze' it into a different shape. Now, whether your organisation's culture is a strong or a weak force in determining success, will determine whether you set out to unfreeze/refreeze an iceberg (as in the case of the *Chrysler Corporation*) or an iceblock!

Consultants who help organisations to change their cultures often approach the problem using a simple model of change.[11] The first element to consider is whether or not there is significant pressure for change. This pressure may result from a crisis such as the death of the founder, or an accident like the grounding of the Exxon Valdez oil tanker. It may also emanate from an environmental threat such as the entry of a powerful competitor into the marketplace. *IBM*'s entry into the personal computer market is a good example. When this occurred, all the PC suppliers realised that customer service would become a key marketing factor because this was an important attribute of *IBM*'s reputation among customers. Culture change was necessary for many PC suppliers because their emphasis prior to *IBM*'s entry was very product (as opposed to customer) focused. Both management and employees must agree that the consequences of failing to respond to such threats will cause serious problems for their organisation and themselves. Otherwise, the organisation is likely to defer change in the hope that things will return to normal.

When the need for change becomes accepted by employees, a clear shared vision for the direction of change must be established. Top management plays an important role in articulating this vision and demonstrating its commitment to the implementation of this vision. The leadership role of the CEO is a critical success factor here because unless employees understand the nature of the company's changed circumstances, management's new direction may appear illogical and/or unreasonable. Lee Iacocca at *Chrysler*, John Scully at *Apple*, Jan Carlson at *SAS Airlines*, James Strong at *Australian Airlines*, and Lord King of *British Airways* have all been credited with having a big impact on gaining commitment for their company's new direction, and for mobilising the human resources necessary to implement such change. Chapter 10 reviews the different approaches these people used within their organisations.

The next factor which determines the potential effectiveness of change is whether the organisation has the capability to change. These capabilities are of two types: people and business systems. Management consultants see many instances where a person responsible for a particular job is ill equiped to handle the task. Sometimes the problem can be rectified by training, while in other cases the information on which decisions are based is inadequate. Another source of systems failure can result from poor design. In the area of customer service, this is a common problem. For example, many large retail banks (in Australia at least) have customer service systems which have been designed to facilitate the bank's data storage and handling requirements rather than to provide a money management service to customers. The large scale of the investment in these systems makes it almost impossible for the banks to make a rapid response to changing customer needs, and/or to tailor their services to different segments of the market. In effect, the bank's systems and infrastructure constrain its capacity to make anything other than incremental change.

A crucial step in the change process is to get started. The actionable first steps should be simply stated, clearly demonstrated, and they should lead to some successful outcomes. In other words, get some early successes so that you can publicise your achievements. Then publicly reward those people who have been instrumental in helping to achieve these successes. Because people tend to do what is inspected rather than what is expected, compliance with the desired changes should be tied directly to the organisation's reward system. The reward system—who gets rewarded and why—is an unequivo-

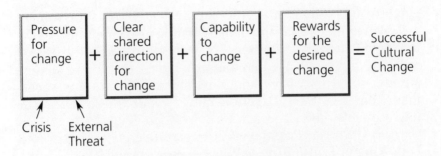

Figure 5.1   Forces Driving Cultural Change

successes. Because people tend to do what is inspected rather than what is expected, compliance with the desired changes should be tied directly to the organisation's reward system. The reward system—who gets rewarded and why—is an unequivocal statement of the organisation's beliefs and values. It is a key to understanding and influencing the organisation's culture.

Successful cultural change is a function of the four factors outlined in Figure 5.1. Each factor is necessary but not sufficient to change an organisation's culture. The timeframe over which such cultural change is likely to occur is typically slower than anticipated by many managers. The main reasons for this are that it is often necessary to raise the 'cultural awareness' in an organisation before embarking on a program of change. Also, it takes time to get a widespread commitment that change is necessary, and to develop a clear shared direction for change.

Evolution versus Revolution

Cultural change can be of two types—evolutionary or revolutionary. Which type you set out to achieve will depend on the degree of internal and/or external misfit currently being experienced by your organisation. Evolutionary change does not destroy the basic underlying beliefs and values of the culture—it merely modifies them. This type of cultural change typically leads to incremental changes in the organisation's behaviour. Revolutionary cultural change, however, sets out to replace one system of beliefs and values with another system (hopefully) more appropriate for the organisation's survival. Many managers believe that this type of change is too dangerous, and if they are forced into a situation where it becomes necessary, they will often use external consultants to facilitate the process.

and sewerage, and power generation organisations caused these classic bureaucracies to adopt a more market (customer) orientation.

Measuring Your Organisation's Culture

Much of the discussion in the two previous sections has assumed that you know, or can measure your organisation's culture. For example, it would be difficult to evaluate the success of a culture change program if it were not possible to describe the old and the new culture. Also, it would be foolhardy to try to change various beliefs and values if you did not know how strongly and widely they were held. The aim of measuring organisational culture is to transform it from an 'invisible web' to a visible web. When it becomes visible, it can be used as a mechanism to monitor and shape employee behaviour, which in turn will have a big impact on the signals employees send to customers and other stakeholders.

An outsider (consultant, investor, potential employee) seeking to measure the culture of an organisation is generally forced to rely on its visible indicators and identity symbols. A site visit may show a new building, quality furnishings, expensive cars in the carpark, open-plan offices or well-dressed people. Also, the organisation's advertising—the media in which it appears, its tone of voice, and frequency—may provide clues about certain aspects of its culture. (For example, companies selling high quality products tend to have high quality advertising, and employees tend to believe that technology, production, and product quality are the key success factors.) Other sources of cultural information are publicity, the annual report, and internal company newsletters. Information from such external indicators, however, is generally unrepresentative of the true culture.

To measure the true culture you need to get 'inside' the organisation. Once inside, there are a variety of ways to map the various subcultures. At one extreme is the type of research done by cultural anthropologists. They live in, and become part of the organisation for an extended period of time, studying the internal workings, decision-making processes, and rituals of the organisation.[12] Another version of this approach is the (investigative) journalist who writes a history of the organisation.[13] From both approaches you would typically wait a year or more, and receive a long-winded description of your organisation's culture based on the perceptions of an 'expert witness'.

There has to be a quicker way—and there is. It involves doing a survey among a representative sample of employees at all levels, and in all locations of the organisation. The three main survey techniques are

- in-depth personal interviews
- focus groups
- self-completion questionnaires.

In-depth personal interviews on a one-to-one basis can be time consuming, and if they are unstructured, the information they provide can be difficult to interpret. A focus group is composed of six to eight people and a professional moderator to guide the discussion. The interaction among the individuals will usually stimulate thoughts and insight not easily obtained from individual interviews. Personal interviews and focus groups are valuable for building up an understanding of the way people think about the organisation, and for discovering the language they use to describe their relationship with it.

A widely used method of data collection is to start by interviewing some of the longer-serving members of the organisation and some people who have recently joined the organisation. If possible, try to find these people in various parts of the organisation, and at various levels in the hierarchy. Stage two involves using the information gained from these in-depth personal interviews to select people to participate in two or three focus group sessions. (The number of focus groups is typically determined by the number of subcultures that seem to exist in the organisation.) The information from the personal interviews and focus groups is then used to construct a questionnaire to be completed by a representative sample of employees. The individual and group interviews ensure that the questionnaire reflects the beliefs, values, language and customs of the organisation.

The major alternatives to this approach are to

- modify one of the various questionnaires available in the published academic literature,[14] or
- employ a human resources consultant who specialises in measuring organisational culture.

The use of the second approach can add an extra dimension to culture mapping, as these consultants can often compare the profile of your organisation to other similar organisations.

The first time a culture survey is conducted, it is difficult to predict how employees will react to the survey. Hence, it is a good idea to use the services of someone whom employees regard as 'independent' to send out the questionnaires, and to conduct the data tabulation, statistical analysis, and feedback of the results. When analysing data from a questionnaire, look for a pattern of results. For example, is there a heavy emphasis on internal rituals and ceremonies but little emphasis on outwardly visible signals? What types of rituals and ceremonies do various parts of the organisation use? Is fun at work something that only parts of the organisation seem to indulge in? Do various levels in the organisational hierarchy think that the reward system is fair and equitable? How do different parts of the organisation regard customers? A good organisation culture profile is one that has a balance among such factors, and that stresses those aspects which contribute to internal and external fit.

In summary, the aim of measuring an organisation's culture is to answer these questions.

1 What is the level of 'cultural awareness' among the top management team?
2 Is your organisation characterised by many subcultures? Do these enhance, coexist, or compete with the dominant organisation culture?
3 How strong is the organisation's culture?
4 How is culture used to enhance the implementation of strategy? How is it used to influence the reputations that internal groups project to external groups of the organisation?

Conclusion

Culture in large organisations is like national culture: it is reinforced and modified over many years. It is rooted in the countless details of organisational life—how rewards are administered, how plans are made, how conflict is resolved, how the CEO interacts with staff. We have come to realise that significant strategic and structural change cannot take place unless it is supported by the organisation's culture(s). Many organisations have also discovered that a key success factor in the management of their external reputations is the management of the internal culture. If the various subcultures can be moulded into a force which projects a consistent set of signals to outside stakeholders, then there is potential to use the organisation's culture as a powerful force to help shape its desired reputation. An organisation with a 'healthy' inside is one that is more likely to project a good image to outside stakeholders.

Two good examples of communicating a company's internal culture to both employees and external stakeholders were the corporate TV advertising campaigns of BP (British Petroleum) and BHP (Australia's largest steel, minerals and oil producer) in Australia during the 1980s. BP's 'Quiet Achiever' campaign projected the company as one which quietly went about developing petroleum products and upgrading its service stations. (Understatement and quiet achievement are two highly respected qualities of Australians.) This campaign was replaced by one with the theme 'For All Our Tomorrows' which is discussed in the next chapter. BHP's corporate campaign showed the variety of jobs done by the 'ordinary' people who worked for the company. These advertisements showed the human face of Australia's biggest company. Both campaigns won awards from the advertising industry, and both were favourably received by internal and external stakeholders.

End Notes

1 The interested reader could consult these two references for more information on organisation culture. A. Pettigrew, 'On studying organizational cultures', *Administrative Science Quarterly*, vol. 24, no. 4, 1979, pp. 570–81; B. Arogyaswamy & C. Bayles, 'Organizational culture: internal and external fits', *Journal of Management*, vol. 13, no. 4, 1987, pp. 647–59.

2 M. Lefkoe, 'Why so many mergers fail: the main reason is a clash of corporate cultures', *Fortune*, 20 July 1987, p. 113.

3 B. Uttal, 'The corporate culture vultures', *Fortune*, vol. 17, 1983, pp. 66–72.

4 E. Schein, 'Coming to a new awareness of organizational culture', *Sloan Management Review*, vol. 25, Winter, 1984, pp. 3–16.

5 R.T. Pascale & A.G. Athos, *The Art of Japanese Management*, Simon and Schuster, New York, 1981.

6 P. Grossman, *AMERICAN EXPRESS: The Unofficial History of the People Who Built the Great Financial Empire*, Crown Publishers, New York, 1987.

7 J. Martin & C. Siehl, 'Organizational culture and counterculture: an uneasy symbiosis', *Organizational Dynamics*, vol. 12, no. 2, 1983, pp. 52–64.

8 R. Miles & C. Snow, 'Fit, failure and the hall of fame', *California Management Review*, vol. 26, no. 3, Spring, 1984, pp. 10–28.

9 T. Thomas, 'For industrial efficiency, try asking the workers', *Business Review Weekly*, 11 June, 1993, pp. 70–3.

10 L. Iacocca with W. Novak, *IACOCCA: An Autobiography*, Bantam Books, Toronto, 1984.

11 I was first introduced to this framework by Dr Norman Chorn of Gattorna Chorn Strategy Consultants in Sydney, Australia.

12 A. Coombs, *AdLand*, William Heinemann, Melbourne, 1990. This is a good example of the inside workings of an advertising agency.

13 Grossman, 1987. This is a good example of the investigative journalist's approach.

14 Pettigrew, loc. cit.; Arogyaswamy & Bayles, loc. cit.; Schein, loc. cit.

CHAPTER 6

Communication: What You Do and What You Say

Like corporate identity which is discussed in the next chapter, corporate advertising is often oversold as a mechanism for creating a desired image. Ralph Nader once made the comment that: 'I don't care how many lobbyists (here read advertising) you have. If you're weak in the streets, you're weak.'[1] Nader's advice reflects an age-old marketing 'law' which says that stakeholders, and especially customers, are more interested in what companies do rather than what they say about themselves.

Advertising and other forms of communication, such as direct mail, identity symbols, publicity, the salesforce, and sponsorships are all important devices for organisations to help project a desired image. Advertising is the high-profile member of this team. It can be segregated into two basic types: product-based and corporate. Corporate advertising, as its name implies, tends to focus on broad issues relating to the organisation. A recent review of this type of advertising in the USA found that it has experienced a number of shifts of emphasis. In the 1970s the primary emphasis was on goodwill (for example, public relations and public service). In the 1980s two themes were prominent, namely, advertisements which combined the promotion of products and services with general messages about the company, and advocacy and issue advertisements which promoted political, social and economic ideas.[2]

The authors of this historical analysis of corporate advertising went on to suggest that the next fashion could be corporate advertisements which keep customers and the public better informed of the customer-oriented nature of business activities. For example, in the early 1990s three prominent US companies started to use corporate advertisements to describe the parts of their internal management processes that demonstrated their capability to deliver the promises made to customers: *3M* talked about its innovation process, *Ford* about its quality techniques, and *Motorola* about participatory management.

An issue which troubles many communication managers is what proportion of each type of communication will give an organisation the most effectiveness per dollar spent? This is a question which often raises strong opinions within organisations and their advertising agencies. While there is no simple answer to this question, the contents of this chapter illustrate the factors which need to be taken into account in order to use corporate advertising effectively.

Before outlining a brief communications planning framework, it is valuable to reflect on the amount of money spent on corporate, as opposed to product-based, advertising. It has been reported that companies in the USA spent approximately $1.2 billion in 1988, up from $158 million in 1971.[3] Television and magazines were the two most preferred media. Also, the giant companies *AT&T*, *General Electric*, *DuPont*, and *US Steel* have been using corporate advertising for more than fifty years. While $1.2 billion represents less than 5 per cent of the USA's total advertising expenditure, it is still a sizeable amount of money. It also indicates that most advertising messages sent to consumers focus on specific products and services. Hence, this type of advertising is the prime type of communication which is used to set stakeholder expectations about a company, and which its behaviour tries to match.

The next section focuses on the marketing mix organisations use to serve their customers. It explains that consumers judge product (or service) quality to be the most important factor used in their choice process. In Figure 1.2 of Chapter 1, marketing communications and product/service offerings are grouped together to reflect the fact that the emotional properties of the advertising often enhance the perceived quality of a product or service. It is established that management should use the various forms of communication at their disposal to build on, rather than replace product quality, and the remaining sections of this chapter outline a well-tried framework for planning a communications campaign.

The Marketing Mix

In 1960 a US academic, E. Jerome McCarthy, popularised a four-factor classification of the marketing decision variables which managers can use to implement their marketing strategy.[4] This classification is generally referred to as 'The 4 Ps': *product*—brand name, features, options, packaging, quality, services, warranty; *price*—list price, discounts, credit terms; *place* (of distribution)—channels, locations; and *promotion*—advertising, personal selling, sales promotion, publicity. Consultants and marketing managers will often expand this framework by adding a fifth P—*people*, who are especially important in service organisations. Figure 6.1 illustrates how an organisation will arrange the marketing mix to offer products to customers, and to communicate this offer to them.

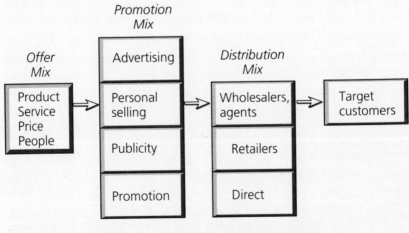

Figure 6.1   Using the Marketing Mix

Source: Adapted from Kotler, P. 1991, *Marketing Management*, Prentice-Hall, Englewood Cliffs, p. 69.

Figure 6.1 illustrates that each element of the marketing mix is necessary but not sufficient to serve customers. In fact, all four (or five) elements are combined to offer a product or service to customers. This combination can also facilitate or hinder the projection of a unified image to customers and other stakeholders. For example, when customers have trouble judging the quality of a product (such as perfume, video cassette recorders, legal services) they may use price, and/or their image of the retail outlet as signals of quality. In product categories where customers think that all products offer essentially the same set of functional benefits (for example, petrol, washing powder), the advertising and identity symbols can often become more important determinants of choice than the functional benefit itself. The essential point to remember is that the various elements of the marketing mix interact to create value for customers.

Research from the USA conducted during the 1980s indicated that, in the long run, the most important single factor affecting a business unit's marketing and financial performance is the relative perceived quality or value of its products and service. Relative, that is, to that offered by competitors.[5] The key word from our perspective here, is 'perceived'. Quality is defined by customers (and other stakeholders) relative to

- an intended purpose, and
- a set of alternatives.

It is similar to, but different from the three types of quality usually associated with Total Quality Management awards, namely

- actual or objective quality, which is often measured in terms of superior delivered performance
- product-based quality, which incorporates superior ingredients and/or features
- manufacturing quality, which implies the fewest defects.

All these factors are important, but they are no substitute for 'customer perceived quality'. Unless customers actually think that your product or service is of valuable quality, then to them it is inferior.

Perceived quality generates value for consumers by giving them a reason to buy the product. Everybody likes to buy 'quality' products. Quality, however, comes at a price. When the benefits derived from quality (and other elements of the marketing mix) are compared to the price of the product, this comparison presents a 'value proposition' to customers. The better the value, the better the chance of (a) sales, (b) a good brand and company image, and (c) a good corporate reputation. Perceived quality also differentiates a product from competitive products. For example, *Rolls Royce* cars have come to be associated with 'the best' quality, even though the top of the line *BMWs* and *Mercedes* have better actual, product-based, and manufacturing quality. Old images can endure for long periods of time, and competitors like *BMW* and *Mercedes* don't try to compete head on with such an image. Rather, the advertising tag-lines of these manufacturers position *BMWs* as 'The Ultimate Driving Machine' and *Mercedes* cars are 'Engineered Like No Other Car'.

Perceived quality can support a price premium. The 'get what you pay for belief' is widespread among many segments of consumers. It is especially prevalent where consumers lack the ability, or the information to judge actual, product-based, or manufacturing quality. For example, companies like *Caterpillar* (heavy construction equipment), *Hewlett-Packard* (electronics), and *Michelin* (automotive tires) have pursued profitable market share growth using an actual and perceived quality strategy. Alternatively, perceived quality can be used to achieve high levels of market penetration as many Japanese automotive and consumer electronics companies demonstrate. Also, Philip Crosby, in his book *Quality is Free*, argues that building more quality into products does not necessarily inflate costs.[6] The manufacturing process usually causes less scrappage, and after-sales servicing is reduced.

Perceived quality is often used as a basis for a brand extension. Here, the brand name is used on different types of products, and the quality reputation built up by the original product is 'rented' by the new product. For example, *Rolls Royce* cars and aircraft engines both share a quality position in the marketplace. Also, *BMW*'s motor bikes use the tag-line 'The Ultimate Riding Machine' to trade off the quality image of the better known cars. When a company's products and services are known for their quality position in the marketplace, a naming strategy which links all the brands or models to the company name is often used. In effect, each quality product adds to the perceived quality of the other products in the portfolio. For example, both *BMW* and *Mercedes* label their models using the company name and a particular model identification—*BMW 318, 320, 325,* etc; *Mercedes Benz 180, 190, 230,* etc.

Marketing quality, and using its positive associations to enhance your organisation's desired images, is a three-step process. First, establish quality in your products and services. For products this can be achieved by offering superior performance, more features, better reliability, better ingredients, more durability, easier serviceability, a better fit and finish. For services, quality can be achieved by making the service more tangible than its competitors, more reliable, or more responsive to customer needs. These attributes can be delivered by having staff who are more competent, and/or who have more empathy with customers. A key aspect of delivering service quality, is to manage (or set) the expectations of your customers about the level of service they will receive. These service levels are of two broad types: functional performance (such as getting access to money in the customer's bank account), and expressive performance (such as the way staff in the bank deliver the service). There are many good books which provide frameworks for delivering service quality.[7]

The second step in marketing quality is to discover the signals customers use to infer quality. These can be many and varied, and customer research is the most reliable way to discover what they may be. For example, dark coloured beer is thought to be 'stronger' than light coloured beers; a solid-sound when closing a car door is thought to indicate quality; lots of suds and/or a lemon scent have been found to signal cleaning power for household detergents; an expensive office location and fitout for a professional service provider signals quality (and usually high overheads and a high fee). It doesn't really matter whether or not the signals people use to judge quality are based directly on product or manufacturing quality; what is important is that these attributes help consumers to perceive quality. The signals of quality can't, however, be used as a substitute for actual quality because customers will soon learn and communicate that the product or service doesn't fulfil its (functional) expectations.

The final step in the marketing process is to communicate quality. There are a number of quality positions available in any market; the job is to pick one and to manage the signals of quality to tell customers what your organisation's quality position is. When quality is combined with price, it is the concept of 'value' which becomes relevant. Be it simply quality or value, a good communication strategy is to explain why quality is to be expected, how much it will cost, and how it will be delivered. Different segments of customers will generally want different quality levels, and these can be priced to offer value to each segment.

This discussion about quality does not imply that the other elements in the marketing mix (Figure 6.1) cannot be used to help establish a desired corporate reputation. They can, and are often used for this purpose. The point being made in this section is that because most customers will sooner or later consider the value (quality and price) of your products and services, then perceptions of value should be actively managed. In this way, the impact of value and quality on your organisation's desired reputation can be explicitly designed in.

Product Versus Corporate Advertising

When product advertising is tied directly into corporate advertising, each type of advertising helps the other. Corporate advertising helps create an overall environment of familiarity and confidence, while brand advertising signals credibility and the functional benefits offered by the company. Many advertisers believe that customers and other stakeholders don't distinguish between the different types of message in corporate and brand advertisements. In effect, they often think that the company is the product in corporate advertisements. This is a good result, especially when there is a long time between purchases of the company's products and services (such as automobile tires, personal computers, electrical appliances).

Corporate advertising is often thought to be a waste of money by many advertising agencies and many managers (although not the ones who do it). Such scepticism is healthy. If brand advertising can sell products and help project the company's desired image, well and good. However, as Chapter 2 pointed out, every organisation has a number of different types of stakeholders. In many cases, non-customer stakeholders want to know what the company stands for—as well as what they make and sell. Customers are often interested in this too. Hence, it makes sense to support brand advertising with corporate advertisements to ensure these different messages don't get blurred. In any case, it is rare that a corporate campaign will reduce sales. It is far more common for some brand advertisements to degrade the reputations which customers and other stakeholders hold of the company!

One reason many executives think that corporate advertising is self-indulgent is that so many of the advertisements are awful! They are either long-winded, flat and dull, or short and vague with a large abstract photo (print advertisements) unrelated to the company's vision or operations. Look at the major business magazines such as *Business Week*, *The Economist*, *Forbes*, and *Fortune*. Most corporate advertisements are simply uninspiring. If they are lucky, they generate a 'ho-hum' reaction. If they are worse, they may be ignored completely, or they may generate a counter-arguing response such as 'Rubbish' or 'Says who?'

A good example of a 'ho-hum' corporate campaign was the British oil company *BP*'s 'For All Our Tomorrows' global advertisements. This campaign was designed to focus on three themes—environmental concern, community help, and research-based product development. The corporate advertisements showed *BP* conducting mineral exploration, providing solar energy systems to help developing countries, and so on. These advertising themes, however, could apply to any oil company—or to nearly any manufacturing company for that matter. There is nothing unique to *BP* about wanting to be a good corporate citizen. With such a broad, vague set of claims, *BP*'s advertising agency (*Saatchi & Saatchi*) had to work extremely hard to make the (TV) advertisements interesting enough to reward viewers for their time and attention.[8]

In contrast, the US-based *Chevron* oil company combined the two themes of environmental concern and community responsibility into a successful corporate campaign. With a number of different advertisements showing how *Chevron* people helped various species of wildlife to survive, this corporate advertising campaign helped minimise the potential adverse effects of *Chevron*'s takeover of *Gulf Oil*. The advertisements illustrated that *Chevron* was a company with values similar to those of *Gulf*'s customers. It led to a significant increase in the overall favourability rating of the company among petrol buyers.[9]

Dick Wasserman, a noted US adman, says that many dull corporate advertisements go to air because corporate executives think that when they are spending a large amount of money, they should talk about something 'weighty'. Naturally, the tendency is to do this in a 'weighty' or 'sombre' tone. Unfortunately, this often leads to advertisements depicting what the company wants to say with abstract images and intangible symbols. He says that since the reader or viewer of corporate advertising will not be rewarded with information about a tangible benefit, the reward for paying attention to the advertisement must be in the reading or viewing itself. Most successful corporate advertising must contain some sort of built-in tension producer, like an unusual twist or a surprise which makes the advertisements seem novel to the audience. The closer the advertisements are to straightforward, literal speeches, well-reasoned arguments, or declarations of solemn corporate credos, the less successful they are likely to be.[10]

Whether the decision is taken to use a combination of corporate and brand advertising, or just brand advertising, the manager responsible for the advertising campaign and the agency producing the advertisements must agree on a set of communication objectives. Most advertising people agree that the first such objective should be to gain awareness for the company. In the next section, the pivotal role of awareness is outlined. Then a more comprehensive communication planning framework is presented. Together these two sections provide much of the information necessary to answer the question about what is the desirable balance between corporate and brand advertising for your organisation.

Gaining Awareness

One of the best print advertisements ever written shows a picture of a tough, sceptical, professional buyer sitting in a chair looking at the reader of the advertisement. Next to this picture are the following words which represent the thoughts going through the buyer's mind as he meets a salesperson (see p. vi).

I don't know who you are.
I don't know your company.
I don't know your company's product.
I don't know what your company stands for.
I don't know your company's customers.
I don't know your company's record.
I don't know your company's reputation.

Now—what was it you wanted to sell me?[11]

As the *McGraw-Hill* company, the sponsor of this world-famous advertisement says at the bottom of the advertisement— '**Moral**: Sales start before your salesman calls—with business publication advertising.'

This *McGraw-Hill* advertisement, which is reproduced in the Preface of this book, has been used since the mid-1950s, and is an excellent summary of the role of corporate advertising. In a simple, clever and informative way, it gets across the message that people like to deal with companies they know. This finding has been supported by research. For example, at the 11th Public Relations World Congress in 1989, the *Roy Morgan Research* company (the Australian member of *Gallup International*) presented the results of a survey of almost 10 000 people from nine countries (Australia, Canada, Finland, UK, Japan, Netherlands, New Zealand, Norway, USA). The aggregate results showed that the more people said that they knew about a company, the more they believed that the company had good products and services.[12] An earlier study (reported in 1986) done for the advertising agency *J. Walter Thompson*, found that if respondents (1000 financial analysts, corporate executives, and affluent consumers in the USA) knew a company well, they were more likely to rate the company as a winner. Good corporate communications were found to play an integral part in projecting a winning corporate image.[13]

Company awareness occurs when a stakeholder recognises or recalls that the company is involved in a certain industry, and/or sells certain products (brands). There has to be a link, however, between the company and the industry, and/or the product class. There is not much point in people knowing your company's name but not knowing anything about it. This type of meaningless awareness may occur as the result of corporate or brand advertising seen in an irrelevant context for the viewer. For example, the French Open tennis tournament is sponsored by *BNP*. These three letters are telecast around the world to millions of viewers. What do they stand for? *Banque Nationale de Paris* is the answer. How many people outside France or Europe could make the link between *BNP* and the bank? Probably a good deal fewer than could recognise the three letters or where they saw them. As a contrasting example, *Rado,* the Swiss watchmaker, is a co-sponsor of the Australian Open. Like *BNP*, its advertisements appear at the end of the tennis court and receive thousands of exposures to each viewer. Unlike *BNP*, however, the advertisement appears as 'RADO—Swiss Watches'. Most viewers who pay attention to this advertisement know what *Rado* sells.

Company (and brand) awareness is often measured by calculating the percentage of people who say they are aware of, or have heard of the company. A better way of estimating the level of awareness for your organisation, is to supplement this measure with the percentage of various stakeholder groups which recognise, recall, and give prominence to the company within its relevant industry. This set of measures can be arranged as a pyramid—where we would expect more people to be able to recognise your company's name than to be able to recall it. Similarly, we would expect more people to recall that your company is in a specific industry, than to say that it is the only company they can recall. Figure 6.2 illustrates these various types of awareness.

At the base of the awareness pyramid is recognition. This is typically measured by giving respondents a list of companies in a specific industry, and asking them to nominate which ones they have heard of. Recognition is the most basic of all communication objectives. Without the ability to recognise the company name, there is little point in trying to communicate a set of attributes which describe the desired image of the company. The industry represents an 'address' in the stakeholder's mind; the company is the resident at this address in which facts and

Figure 6.2   The Awareness Pyramid

feelings about the company are stored for later use. No address equals no storage, and a waste of advertising.

The next level in the awareness pyramid is recall. It is measured by asking a person to name all the companies they can think of in a particular industry. This is done in an unaided fashion. That is, unlike a recognition measure, which shows the respondent a list of names and asks them to nominate various companies, recall would simply ask the person to name 'all the computer companies you could think of'. The first company mentioned is classified as 'Top of mind'. If only one company is mentioned it is the 'Dominant company' in our awareness pyramid. Dominant is better than top of mind, and recall is better than recognition. Achieving recall is important because it will generally place a company in what marketers call the buyer's 'evoked set'. It is this set of companies that a person will select from when the need for the companies' products or services arises. If your company isn't considered, then it won't be on the short list, and you won't be chosen.

Below the awareness pyramid, are those people who say they have never heard of a company, or who say they have heard of the name, but who can't relate this to the correct context. This second group exhibits name confusion. This may benefit an organisation if it is confused with a more prestigious company in the same industry. Alternatively, it may handicap an organisation confused with a poorly regarded company in its own industry, or one in another industry. This type of problem is more likely to happen to companies with those three letter names—ABC, BBC, NBC.

As I wrote this section I recalled an interesting computer advertisement I saw in 1978. It was a three-page corporate advertisement in the Australian business magazine *Rydges*. The first page of the advertisement was a right-hand page showing two signwriters who had written a big letter 'I' on the wall of a building. The headline said 'The world's first, large-scale, solid state business computer was marketed by a large international company with a three letter name'. Most people mentally filled in the other two letters, and concluded it was *IBM*. On turning the page the reader was confronted with a picture of the two signwriters' completed work—it read *NCR*. The final page of the advertisement went on to explain that it was *NCR* who, in 1957, announced the first commercially viable large-scale, solid state business computer, and it rewarded the reader with a brief

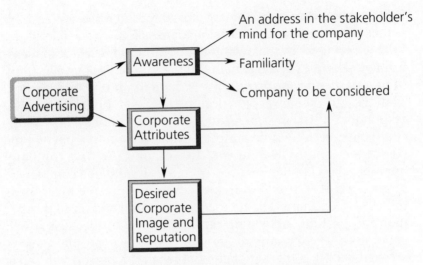

Figure 6.3   The Role of Corporate Advertising

historical account of *NCR*'s first machine. The idea behind the advertisement was to get buyers to consider *NCR* along with *IBM*, which at that time was on nearly every short list.

Figure 6.3 summarises the discussion so far. It outlines the dual role of corporate advertising in gaining awareness, and how this can contribute to communicating desired attributes of your company and its operations to stakeholders. A good corporate reputation is of strategic value to your company, and it can facilitate the decision-making process of individual stakeholders. These outcomes were discussed in Chapter 1. The next section outlines an overall communication planning framework which can be used to guide the use of corporate advertising.

Planning Corporate Advertising

The framework outlined below was originally developed by John Rossiter and Larry Percy. John is an advertising academic (and a colleague), and Larry is an advertising practitioner. Their book, which describes the full framework, is one of the leading texts in its field.[14] Here, only four parts of this framework are used to plan corporate advertising.

1 *Target Audience Selection*
   The first stage in this process is to identify the target audiences (or stakeholders) for your corporate advertising. Figure 2.1 (Chapter 2) classified these into four groups—normative (e.g.

government), functional (e.g. employees), diffused (e.g. the press), and customers. People within each customer group can be subdivided into a number of subgroups. For example, customers can be profiled as:

a potential new company users, that is, people who have not yet dealt with the company (or its products/services)

b our-company loyals, that is, people who are loyal to our company

c other-company loyals, that is, people loyal to another company

d multiple-company acceptors, that is, people who deal with a group of companies, which may or may not include our company

e multiple other-company acceptors, that is, people who deal with a group of companies, none of which is ours

f company switchers, that is, people who switch from one company to another over time, without loyalty or continued acceptance.

The planning process proceeds by outlining an action objective for each target audience. (I assume here that you know the approximate size and importance of each group, and whether or not any advertising is warranted.)

2 *Action Objectives*
Action objectives are merely statements of 'What do we want people to do?' For example, here are some typical action objectives:

a potential new company users: learn about the company using our information (rather than publicity, and/or word-of-mouth communication); trial of the company's products or services

b our-company loyals: repeat use; increase use; say favourable things about our company

c other-company loyals: enquire / gather information about our company, and its products or services; consider using our company

d multiple-company acceptors: higher share of use of our company

e multiple other-company acceptors: consider our company; (re)try our company's products

f company switchers: consider our company; retry our products or services; switch to our products.

Action objectives for the other groups of stakeholders are developed in a similar manner. For example, for key government employees the action objectives may be to develop a favourable attitude towards the company; for financial analysts—accurate evaluation of the company's past performance and future prospects; for journalists—a fair reporting of events; employees—a positive attitude; for investors—a higher stock price. Each of these action objectives can then be linked to a communication objective.

3 *Communication Objectives*
The question here is 'What factual or "image" information do we communicate to achieve our action objective?' Advertising, direct marketing, and promotion can help to achieve four communication effects:

  a *Category Need* This occurs when the stakeholder (target audience member) seeks some benefit, or wants to solve a particular problem using a company or its products and services. Stimulating the category need is synonymous with stimulating primary demand. That is, it applies to all companies which offer these services.

     If the category need is not present, or it is weak, then the company must 'sell' this basic need prior to selling the company. If the category need is latent, then this need only has to be mentioned to remind the buyer of the previously established need. Companies selling infrequently purchased products, or new products for the first time (fax, mobile phones, insurance, consulting services), will often need to 'sell the category *and* sell the brand'.

  b *Company Awareness* This links the company to the category need. The Awareness Pyramid in Figure 6.2 illustrates that this linkage can be of various strengths: dominant, top of mind, recall or recognition. The aim is to achieve dominant or top of mind status.

  c *Company Reputation* This refers to the stakeholder's overall evaluation of the qualities associated with the company (image), and the emotional reaction those qualities produce (reputation). This evaluation, like awareness, must be linked to the company's perceived ability to meet the stakeholder's current need. Often the primary motivations for forming an overall evaluation of a company are risk avoidance (making a 'wise' choice), and social approval (being associated with a respected company).

Depending on what research indicates, management may pursue one or more of five options with respect to this communication effect:

i   create a favourable reputation (for people previously unaware of the company)

ii increase an already favourable reputation (for people who hold a moderately favourable reputation)

iii maintain or reinforce the established very favourable reputation

iv change an unfavourable reputation people hold of the company

v   modify, or reposition people's reputations when they are at odds with the company's activities, or when competitors are seen to be very similar. (For example, one *American Express* advertising campaign attempted to reposition the company's card services from a problem avoidance motive—as communicated by their famous advertising tag-line 'don't leave home without it', to a social approval motive, by using a series of famous people in their advertisements and the tag-line 'cardmember since 19XX'.)

d   *Delayed (Soft Sell) Company Consideration and Support* All corporate advertising should aim to achieve the effects outlined in Figure 6.3. Hence, when the need arises, the stakeholder should use the company's products and services, and support its community participation, and dealings with government. Much corporate advertising is also aimed to get potential employees to consider a career with the company.

The first three communication effects are always communication objectives, while the fourth will occur as a natural outcome of good corporate (and product) advertising. The fundamental issue facing management is to develop a coordinated approach to corporate and product advertising, so that there is a positive carryover from each type of advertising to the other. The key point is that stakeholders are unlikely to be bothered to figure out these associations for themselves—often you will have to make the linkages explicit.

When the company equals the brand such as *Boeing, Coca-Cola, IBM, Levis, McDonald's*, this carryover effect is automatic. Also, for many professional service providers (advertising agencies, consultants, law firms, market research firms) corporate advertising is really brand advertising. Government agencies like health services, police, and schools also fall into this category, that is, all their communications promote the body corporate. It is for those companies which have multiple brands, divisions, or strategic business units that corporate advertising can act as an umbrella. Companies like *Westinghouse* in the USA often run corporate advertisements which describe the broad range of its activities. One such advertisement had the headline, 'The Best-Known Unknown Company in America'. It went on to state that *Westinghouse* was involved in electrical energy, broadcasting, office systems, financial systems, and so on. It ended with the tag-line 'You can be sure ... if it's Westinghouse'.

4 *Creative Strategy*
All advertising works only when it is 'processed' by the target audience member. Processing is defined as the person's immediate responses to elements of the advertisement while it is being looked at, listened to, or thought about. There are four main processing responses that may occur: attention, learning, acceptance and emotion. Many advertisements automatically gain attention, just by being in the medium in which the person is involved with. The advertiser, however, must creatively use stimuli in the advertisement to maintain continued attention. Learning in this context is of the simple or 'rote' type. It requires little mental activity, and can result in two communication effects: company awareness and the formation of a low involvement image and/or reputation about the organisation. Acceptance, on the other hand, refers to the viewer's personal (dis)agreement with the elements in the advertisement about the organisation. It will lead to the formation of a high involvement reputation about the organisation. Emotions elicited by advertisements 'feed' learning and acceptance. Emotional responses are critical to the effectiveness of advertising. As noted earlier by Dick Wasserman, it is a lack of emotion which makes much corporate advertising *dull*.

What often differentiates one advertisement from another is the advertising agency's ability to illustrate an organisation's benefits, or how it provides a solution to a problem to stakeholders in an emotionally more compelling or engaging way.

Rossiter and Percy suggest that for advertisements used to present organisations to their stakeholders, the types of creative tactics outlined in Table 6.1 are appropriate. They combine the emotional portrayal of a motivation for using or being associated with the organisation, and information about the benefits of this association. In times of a crisis, a more 'informational' approach may be appropriate—a topic covered in Chapter 11. Managers who must commission corporate advertisements can use this framework to help evaluate their agency's creative approach.

Corporate advertising, in contrast to product advertising, is much like political advertising. It will be more effective in changing attitudes about an organisation with people who have less interest in the organisation. The reason for this is that more interested people will already have more information about the organisation and its products and services. Hence, the amount of 'new' information in the 'typical' vague corporate advertisement will be less than that for less interested people. As Table 6.1 indicates, viewers or readers of corporate advertising must like the advertisement *and* identify personally with the organisation's message. This is less likely to happen when people hold a lot of information about a company. The more likely outcome is a 'ho hum' reaction.

Table 6.1

Corporate Reputation Advertising Tactics

High Involvement—Turning on a Positive Motive

A *Involvement*
  1 Benefit claims for the company are usually explicit.
  2 'Long copy' is OK if it is well presented.
  3 Tend towards overclaiming rather than underclaiming.
  4 Repetition serves to build up interest, image, and to reinforce claims.

B *Motivation*
  5 The target audience must identify personally with the company in the advertisement, and not merely like the advertisement.
  6 Lifestyle and emotions used to portray any relationship with the company must be authentic.

Source: Adapted from Rossiter, J. & Percy, L. 1987, *Advertising and Promotion Management*, McGraw-Hill, New York.

Conclusion

Some companies are in the risk management business, that is, they sell products and services which many people think are risky to make or to use, such as airlines, chemicals, nuclear power, pharmaceuticals. These companies rely on public trust to carry out their basic operations. Banks, car makers, insurance firms, public transport operators, and schools also fall into this category. The reputations held by various stakeholder groups of the firms in these industries are crucial to the success of their operations. This becomes painfully obvious when a disaster such as the grounding of the Exxon Valdez oil tanker occurs. As Chapter 11 later shows, the investment put into creating a good reputation can make the difference between an adverse media and public reaction, or receiving help from the media, government, and the public to recover from the crisis situation. In this situation, informational corporate advertising can help present the company's 'case' and intended response to the crisis. For companies without a good reputation, corporate advertising during or after a crisis is generally of little or no value. (The possible exception is when it is used as part of a takeover defence strategy.) In fact, it is likely to spur the media into a frenzy of company bashing if it is conducted at this time.

Corporate advertising by the major companies in an industry is one way to build awareness, familiarity, and respect for industry participants. It is a long-term investment and can also be undertaken by the industry association on behalf of all its members. Accountants, bankers, container manufacturers, farmers, foresters, lawyers, miners and other industry groups often use advertising and public relations activities to help establish a desired reputation in the minds of their stakeholders. Sometimes these associations even take a leaf out of the packaged goods marketers handbook, and create a brand name for their members. For example, the letters *CPA*, which stand for Certified Practising Accountant in Australia, and Certified Public Accountant in the USA, effectively signal a certain minimum product standard in accounting professions.

If corporate advertising is the vehicle used to promote a desired reputation, then as we have seen in this chapter, it can be effective for such things as creating awareness and familiarity, projecting a desired image, thanking customers and employees for good service to the company, and taking a stand on public issues. What managers, and their advertising agencies need to avoid, is vague and meaningless messages about the company. Stakeholders tune into only one radio station in the world of advertising—Radio Station WII-FM, or *What's In It For Me!*

End Notes

1 R. Nader, *The Consumer and Corporate Accountability*, Harcourt Brace Jovanovich, New York, 1973.

2 D. Schumann, J. Hathcote & S. West, 'Corporate advertising in America: a review of published studies on use, measurement, and effectiveness', *Journal of Advertising*, vol. 20, September, 1991, pp. 35–56.

3 ibid.

4 E. Jerome McCarthy, *Basic Marketing: A Managerial Approach*, Richard D. Irwin, Homewood, Ill, 1960.

5 R.D. Buzzell & B.T. Gale, *The PIMS Principles: Linking Strategy to Performance*, The Free Press, New York, 1987.

6 P.B. Crosby, *Quality is Free*, McGraw-Hill, New York, 1979.

7 W.H. Davidow and B. Uttal, *Total Customer Service: The Ultimate Weapon*, Harper & Row, New York, 1989.

8 G.R. Dowling, 'BP catches the global brand fad', *Australian Institute of Management Magazine*, February, 1991, NSW Edition, pp. 7–8.

9 L.C. Winters, 'The Role of Corporate Advertising in Building a Brand— Chevron's "Pre-Conversion" Campaign in Texas', paper presented at The Tenth Annual Advertising and Consumer Psychology Conference, San Francisco, California, 16–17 May 1991. See also L.C. Winters, 'Does it pay to advertise to hostile audiences with corporate advertising?' *Journal of Advertising Research*, June–July, 1988, pp. 11–18.

10 D. Wasserman, *That's Our New Campaign*, Lexington Books, Lexington, 1988.

11 D.A. Aaker & J.G. Myers, *Advertising Management*, Prentice-Hall, Englewood Cliffs, 1987, p. 100.

12 Staff Reporter, 'Is your global public image good?', *Marketing*, February, 1989, p. 31.

13 Staff Reporter, 'To the winners belong the spoils', *Marketing News*, vol. 20, no. 1, 10 October 1986 pp. 1, 13.

14 J. Rossiter & L. Percy, *Advertising & Promotion Management*, McGraw-Hill, New York, 1987.

CHAPTER 7

Corporate Identity: What You See Is All You Get

The subtitle of this chapter is meant to be mildly provocative—especially to many corporate identity consultants. As noted in Chapter 1, corporate image and corporate reputation are not the same as corporate identity—they embody much more. Many CEOs and their senior management teams, however, have been conned by consultants into believing that a change of their company's visual presentation—its identity—will change the company's desired image, and then hopefully the reputation people have of the organisation. Only rarely will such a simple change of identity cause this to happen. The con works so often because when an organisation tries to change its image, it can change either its advertising, identity symbols, and/or its behaviour. What is easier to change—advertising, identity or corporate behaviour? You guessed it, employ an advertising agency or a design consultant to help change the advertising and identity, and be seen to have made an explicit attempt to improve the company's reputation.

Hence, beware of wolves in sheep's clothing or, in the terminology of this book, beware of advertising agencies and design consultants masquerading as corporate image consultants. Sometimes these wolves may come dressed as corporate name consultants who say your company needs a name change. Beware of this variety of wolf too, because they often do not understand the equity that your company has built up in its name. A full program of corporate identity change can be expensive, and may take a year or two to complete—for very limited results if it is the *only* thing that is changed.

This chapter has three aims. First, to draw your attention—yet again—to the fact that corporate identity is not the same as corporate image. It may be one of the more visible elements of your organisation's communication with its stakeholders, but it is only a minor part of the overall corporate image formation process. The second, and most important aim is to outline how identity symbols can influence the desired image of your organisation. This aim motivated the subtitle of this chapter—'what you see is all you get'. The third aim of this chapter is to warn managers about corporate design consultants who oversell the power of their work, namely, corporate logos and signage.

The Evidence

There are two types of evidence which justify the claim that corporate identity has only a relatively limited impact on the images which people hold of various organisations. The first, and what many people claim is the most persuasive type, is common sense. For example, who really believes that updating the corporate signage of, say, a bank by something as simple as tilting the letters of the bank's name slightly to the right, and drawing four faint white lines through them, will cause staff and customers to change their images of the organisation. For a start, most customers will not notice any difference, and why should they? They are bombarded with visual symbols in an over-communicated society. Also, they are more interested in customer service, not window dressing.

The second type of evidence is more subtle, and is based on surveys of various stakeholder groups. Occasionally, these are done by academic researchers, but mostly by firms such as *Landor Associates*—a highly respected firm of strategic design consultants headquartered in San Francisco. *Landor Associates* regularly surveys people to measure their recognition (awareness) of various companies, and the 'esteem' (reputation) in which these companies are held. These two variables are combined to produce an index of 'Image Power' (their trade-marked concept). Landor's surveys often show that when a company changes its name to something which has no intrinsic or recognisable meaning, that the company's awareness (and hence image power) falls. A good example is when *United Airlines* changed its name to *Allegis*. Its image power dropped from 85 per cent to 4 per cent.[1] Whoops! (It quickly changed its name back to *United Airlines*.)

This type of image power research is then used to advance the claim that corporate identity is a powerful image-forming device. It is, but only if you define corporate image as awareness *combined with* esteem. Awareness, as we saw in Chapter 6, has little to do with corporate image. It is simply the communication goal of every organisation. People have to be aware of your company before they can develop an image and/or reputation of it. When companies change their names people may become confused and/or the level of name awareness falls. This is especially so for names such as *Allegis*, *Navistar* (which replaced the name *International Harvester*), and *Unisys* (coined when the two computer companies *Burroughs* and *Sperry* combined). Shareholders may even become angry, as they did when they forced *Allegis* to change back to *United Airlines*. But where is the evidence to suggest that a simple name change causes people to suddenly increase or decrease their reputation (esteem) of the company. Did shareholders (suddenly) sell their stock in United, or did consumers stop flying with United? These effects have yet to be documented.

We need to understand a lot more about the role of corporate identity in the corporate image formation process before we can evaluate the potential impact of a change in identity on the images people hold of organisations. The next section starts this process by defining what is meant by the term corporate identity, and then outlining a model of how corporate identity can impact on awareness, image, and reputation. Following this, each of the major elements of corporate visual identity is reviewed. This chapter concludes by illustrating how to integrate visual identity into the culture of the organisation so that it can achieve its maximum potential to impact on the images people hold of an organisation.

Visual Identity

There are four basic components of an organisation's identity: its name, logo/symbol, typeface, and colour scheme. In addition to these, the company's buildings, office decor, signage, stationery, uniforms, cars and trucks can all play a part in helping stakeholders and others to identify the organisation. All these elements are visual. Companies often combine them to create a visual style which can help to make a statement to people about what the company stands for. For example, many professional service firms combine various identity symbols (office decor, staff dress, letterhead) to project an image of high quality. (This being only one attribute of the firm's overall desired image.)

Hence, a second part to the definition of corporate identity stated in Chapter 1 (Figure 1.1) is that the organisation's various identity symbols represent: 'the visual manifestation of the organisation's desired image'.

This definition also describes two of the primary roles of the various visual identity symbols, namely, (a) to create awareness, and/or to trigger recognition of the organisation, and (b) to activate an already stored image of the organisation in people's minds. In this way, identity is more tactical than strategic. Whether the organisation's tactics (the way it coordinates its identity symbols) support its strategy (its desired image and reputation) is a question best answered by research.

The tactic versus strategy distinction is a crucial point, and it is where this book differs from the views of many corporate identity consultants. Visual identity is a device for helping people to recognise an organisation and to recall their image and reputation of it. In some circumstances, like the example of professional service firms noted above, it may help to define some of the attributes of the company's desired image. Never, however, does it become *the* corporate image. Used cleverly, visual identity can also help a company to differentiate itself from its competitors. However, this is a far cry from the identity being the same thing as an image of an organisation. As Chapter 1 demonstrated, the images and reputations which people hold of an organisation will be made up from a wide variety of experiences, only one of which is related to the visual symbols used to identify, or 'badge', the organisation.

Figure 7.1 elaborates the role of an organisation's visual identity. It suggests that the name and other visual identity

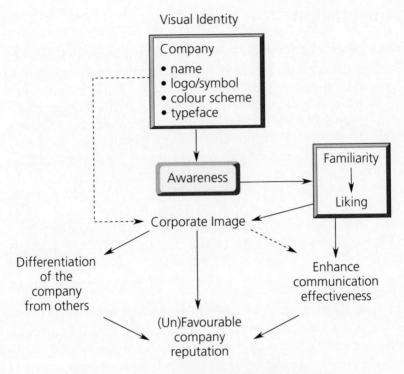

Figure 7.1   The Role of Corporate Visual Identity

symbols act primarily to trigger awareness (recognition, recall). The dashed arrow on the left indicates that *sometimes* the name of an organisation may directly help the image formation process. (This point is elaborated in the next section.) High levels of awareness often lead to increased familiarity and liking (as discussed in the previous chapter), which in turn activates a person's mental image. It is this image which helps differentiate one organisation from another, and which may enhance communication effectiveness—people tend to believe messages more from sources they know and like.

The reader may question what we gain by interposing the formation of a mental image between awareness, and the two outcomes—company differentiation, and communication effectiveness. The main insight is that it suggests that to understand the effects of an organisation's images on the overall evaluation of the company, we need to measure the company's images directly, as well as measuring the constructs: awareness, familiarity, and liking. In short, the Landor approach is too simplistic to give a comprehensive picture of either a company's various images, or their potential effects on the overall (un)favourable reputation of the company. Chapter 9, which deals with the measurement of corporate reputations, returns to this point.

The Elements of a Company's Visual Identity

The basic building blocks of an organisation's visual identity are its: name, logo or symbol, colour scheme, and type font, (the style of lettering it uses to write its name). Sometimes, the company's building architecture, its location (for example, in the central business district), the internal decor of offices and the uniforms of employees will also help people recognise the company. By far the most important of these devices, however, is the corporate name.

Company Names

In the early days of commercial enterprise, many companies were named after their founders as a way of assuring customers and investors that a (noteworthy) person stood behind the company. This naming practice is still common among professional service firms, where the names of the founders often crowd the firm's letterhead. Another early practice was to name a company after its generic product, such as *Bank of New South Wales, National Cash Register, US Steel*. Here, the name communicated the company's core products or services, and probably helped to sell the product category as well as the company. For example, if you are an early entrant into the cash register market, then you may as well be known as the National Cash Register company.

Advertising gurus Al Ries and Jack Trout revived interest in names.[2] They argued that a company's name is usually the first point of contact for a stakeholder. Because names denote and connote meaning, a good name can enhance communication with stakeholders. In their terminology, the name helps to position the company in the prospect's mind. To illustrate, consider how the following names tell customers about the product's core benefit:

- *Compaq* personal computers
- *Weight Watchers* (frozen) foods

- *Head & Shoulders* shampoo
- *Intensive Care* skin lotion
- *Close-Up* toothpaste
- *DieHard* batteries
- *U-haul* trailers.

Ries and Trout argue that many special interest groups recognise the power of a good name, for example, *Right to Life*, *Freedom from Hunger*, *Greenpeace*, fair trade laws, consumer protection and child safety campaigns. Sometimes even a national government will understand the communication value of a clear naming strategy. For example, during the Pierre Trudeau administration in Canada, a two-word naming system was adopted for identifying government departments—The Canadian Ministry of Air Transport became *Air Canada*; the Ministry of Health and Human Services became *Health Canada*.[3]

Many companies struggle to derive the full value from their names. Sometimes this is the result of industry convention, but often it results from failing to appreciate the marketing power of a good name. For example, many (most) accounting, engineering, management consulting, and law firms are named after the founding partners. One problem with founder names is that they signal who are, and who are not, the most important people in the firm. If certain clients are not served by one of these 'owners', then they may think that the service has been second-class. Also, when the founders are no longer with the firm, it is debatable what role the original names contribute over their awareness value. A second problem is that unless the founder names are associated with an already established reputation, they do nothing to help new clients choose a firm which may offer the type of service they require. In the world of advertising, many old and new advertising agencies also use the names of the founders. I suppose that one should never underestimate the feeling of seeing one's own name in print (or in lights).

One way to calibrate the communication value of your organisation's name is to compare it with the names of your competitors. This can be done formally using various consumer research techniques, or it can be done by comparing it with the various alternative types of company names in common use. Table 7.1 lists ten commonly used types of company names, and examples of each. Scanning this list usually raises the two following questions.

1 What is an appropriate type of name for our company?
2 Should we change our company name?

Wally Olins, one of the most prominent corporate identity consultants, says that the naming process usually 'works' when the company is committed to it, and fails when it isn't.[4] I think this is good advice. However, we have learnt that brute-force commitment (often in the form of a large advertising budget) can be expensive if it breaks some of the 'rules' discovered by advertisers and by communication researchers. Here are some of these rules which seem to make sense:

1 Names (and advertising copy) often communicate better in print if they are designed for radio first. That is, if the name sounds good to the ear then it is likely to communicate well in any medium. Mostly, however, names are created the other way round!
2 Only when a company pioneers a new product or service that customers really want is it safe to use a mean-nothing name like

	Table 7.1	
	Types of Company Names	
1	Founder Names	Ford, Philips, Rolls Royce, Marks & Spencer, Nestlé
2	Location	Lloyd's of London, Saks Fifth Avenue
3	Animal/Object	Caterpillar, Shell, Apple, Jaguar, Eagle Star (Insurance)
4	Descriptive	Tubemakers, Bond Brewing, The Free Press
5	Abbreviated	Pan Am, Nabisco (The National Biscuit Co). US Air
6	Initials	BP, IBM, ICI, KLM, DEC, NEC
7	Abstract	Exxon, Kodak, Unisys, Xerox
8	Analogy	Burger King, Cadillac (Canadian chief), Royal Viking Line
9	Dynamic	Whirlpool, Travellers Insurance Co., Surf, Dive & Ski
10	Combination	British Airways, Boston Consulting Group, Australian Graduate School of Management

Kodak, Coca-Cola or *Xerox*. When the new product is good, customers are willing to learn that *Xerox* means photocopiers, *Coke* means cola, and *Kodak* means film.

3 Avoid alphabet soup names like *ABC, ADI, AGC, AMP, ANZ, BHP, BRW, CCH, CIG, CRA*. (These are all substantial Australian enterprises.) Only when you dominate a category (hence most customers know who you are anyway), is it 'safe' to use the company's initials. Until research shows that customers and other stakeholders are starting to shorten the company name, use the words. Also, if initials create another word some people will start making fun of the company name. (For example, if a company with a name like Titan Information Technology shortened its name to TIT, it could soon be the butt of many jokes.)

4 Have a name that is easy to pronounce, spell, and remember in the country in which it is used. In Australia, the pharmaceutical company *Hoechst* found that customers could not pronounce its name. (Some people thought hoechst was a drug rather than a drug company.) The company ran a television advertising campaign to demonstrate the correct pronunciation, and to help customers recognise the name! The German company *Siemens* has had a similar problem, namely that people outside Germany often have trouble spelling its name. There is only negative equity in a meaningless name. (In the *Hoechst* case, it was the cost of the advertising campaign and customer confusion.)

5 Try to avoid new names beginning with the country name, or the words such as General, Global, International, National. These words are now overused, and mostly they reflect the company's aspirations rather than commercial reality.

6 Don't play semantic games with your company name. A good name is the first phase of seduction, but it should not be a mystery. For example, a small Australian design consultancy calls itself the *Leda Consulting Group*. Most people might expect that Mr or Ms Leda was the founder. Not so; the first page of their corporate brochure links the origins of the Leda name to the father of the Gods, Zeus. Clever—but do potential clients really care? Also, if you don't ask the company for a brochure you don't get the message!

7 Be careful when considering a name change. Many long-established names have built up customer equity. See Table 7.2 for an interesting example. While they may no longer accur-

Table 7.2

The Datsun-Becomes-Nissan Story

When Datsun returned to making cars after World War II, they chose to market them in Japan under the name Nissan. However, in 1961 the U.S. car market was entered under the old Datsun name. By 1981 the name Datsun was used not only in the U.S. but in many other countries, even though the firm was marketing its cars, trucks, and other products under the Nissan name in Japan. In fact, the awareness level of Nissan in the U.S. was only 2% compared to 85% for the Datsun name.

The decision to change the name from Datsun to Nissan in the U.S. was announced in the fall of 1981. The rationale was that the name change would help the pursuit of a global strategy. Industry observers however, speculated that the name change was designed to help Nissan market stocks and bonds in the U.S. They also presumed substantial ego involvement, since the absence of the Nissan name in the U.S. surely rankled Nissan executives who had seen Toyota and Honda become household words.

During the years 1982–1984 the change was implemented gradually. Advertising was the cornerstone of the name-change effort. The successful 'Datsun: We Are Driven' campaign which was initiated in 1977 and had a $60 million budget in 1981, was dropped. Around $240 million was spent on advertising the new 'The Name Is Nissan' campaign. The enlarged advertising budget was due to the added mission: to register the new name. It seems very likely that 'The Name is Nissan' campaign with its name registration mission was considerably less effective than the successful Datsun campaign it replaced.

The most incredible aspect of this story is the resilience of the Datsun name. In the spring of 1988, a national survey found that the recognition and esteem of the Datsun name was essentially the same as that of the Nissan name, despite the virtual absence of the Datsun name from the commercial scene for five years.

The greatest potential cost of the name change was the bottom-line effect upon sales. Nissan saw its share drop from 5.9% in 1982 to 4.5% in 1984, compared to the 0.9 share points that Toyota lost during the same period. However, during that time period there also were import restrictions, some quality problems with the Nissan line, and growth in the Honda line. Thus it is impossible to determine precisely to what extent the share drop was caused by the confusion of the name change—yet that surely was a contributory factor of some notable degree.

The cost to change the name could easily have exceeded half a billion dollars, and probably was much more. First, it is known that the operational costs, including changing signs at the 1,100 dealerships, cost about $30 million. Second, one may assume that $200 million was spent on advertising between 1982 and 1984 because of the name change, and that another $50 million was wasted because the 'Datsun, We Are Driven' campaign was prematurely stopped. Finally, assume even that .3% market share was lost for a three-year period because of buyer confusion. That loss alone would represent many hundreds of millions of dollars in marginal profit.

Source: Aaker, D. 1991, *Managing Brand Equity*, Free Press, New York, pp. 56–8.

ately reflect what the company does, they may stand for a set of corporate values (like quality or service) which are important to customers. Sometimes these names need to be revitalised, rather than changed. A good example is *American Express*. This company stopped doing what its name suggested in 1918 (it lost its US express delivery business). Its travellers' cheque business, and then its credit cards have created such strong equity for the corporate name that it would be unfortunate if the company stopped using the name *American Express*. Also, some of the big Japanese conglomerates have built up such strong corporate equity that their names can appear on a wide variety of products and services, such as *Mitsubishi* automobiles, bank, electrical products and heavy industry.[5]

Logos and Symbols

What flags are to countries, and heraldic shields and banners are to families, logos are to the founders of companies. They are a badge of identification and membership. For example, the giant US food company *RJR Nabisco*'s logo is based on a medieval Italian printer's symbol. It is a cross with two bars, on top of an oval (which contains the word NABISCO). Originally, the symbol represented the triumph of the moral and spiritual over the evil and the material.[6] (The irony of this is that the RJR part of the company is the *R J Reynolds Tobacco Company*.) The giant Swiss food company *Nestlé* also has a name and logo with symbolic meaning. *Nestlé* means 'little nest' in the Swiss German dialect, and the logo depicts a bird feeding its young in a nest (which seems very appropriate for a food company). To a suggestion that the Nestlé nest logo be replaced by the cross which appears on the Swiss flag, Henri Nestlé is reported to have said that 'The nest is not merely my trademark, it is also my coat of arms'.[7]

Logos are also used to signal consistency of product or service. The logo is often the most distinctive point of eye contact that employees and customers have with an organisation's visual identity symbols. Most logos, however, are remarkable for their anonymity. Wally Olins suggests that one reason for this is that at least boring, anonymous logos are 'safe'.[8] They are unlikely to cause too much impact inside or outside the organisation.

A few logos have gained widespread recognition. In Australia, the *Qantas* logo of a flying white kangaroo set in a scarlet triangle is probably the most recognisable. The big red W which forms part of the *Westpac* (bank) name is another. (*Westpac* changed its name from the *Bank of New South Wales* to help signal its expansion into the *Western Pacific* region.) A recent 'classic' example of a logo change which generated high awareness, but at the expense of high ridicule, was the *Commonwealth Bank*'s change from a yellow and black map of Australia surrounded by three concentric circles, to a yellow and black square, rotated onto one of its corners. (According to the design consultant it is supposed to represent a stylised version of the Southern Cross star constellation which appears on the Australian flag.) The design of this logo (yes, a square in two colours!) and the redesign of the bank's stationery took two-and-a-half years to complete, at an estimated cost of more than $1 000 000. (An

---

Table 7.3

The Shell Logo

Marcus Samuel Junior formed The 'Shell' Transport and Trading Company to carry on the business of transporting and trading oil products, initially to the Far East. The name 'Shell' was chosen for the sentimental reason that Marcus Samuel Senior had started the family's Far East trade fifty or more years earlier by importing decorative oriental sea shells.

The first 'shell' was a mussel, drawn in a charming rather than a distinctive way. But after only four years, the superior graphic possibilities of the scallop shell led to the introduction of the symbol that with only slight changes has remained ever since.

Since 1900 changes to the Shell logo have only been slight, to keep the symbol in line with current ideas of style. People should be taken with the message, not taken aback by the way it is communicated. Part of the success of the 'shell' as a symbol has been its ability to change with the times without customers being conscious of the changes.

The 'shell' of course is only one component, although the most important, in the Group's Visual Identity—which has to be extremely versatile. Its task is to identify and brand literally dozens of companies, hundreds of locations and service stations, thousands of widely different products, fleets of road tankers and sea tankers, not to mention countless advertisements, leaflets, booklets and letterheads—and do it in a babel of tongues and against a kaleidoscope of cultures.

Source: 'Shell's own Shell', *Shell Education Service*, UK.

Table 7.3 (cont'd)

The Apple Logo

To understand the creation of the Apple Logo is to understand how the name Apple Computer came about. When Steven Jobs and Stephen Wozniak started the company in 1976, they wanted a name that would reflect a new venture and a fresh, exciting company—a non traditional name that didn't conjure up a picture of a typical electronics firm.

The Company was founded during a time when the popularity of natural foods was growing. Steve Jobs, in particular, was an advocate. During a brainstorming session just prior to the deadline for filing a Company name, someone came up with the name Apple—a fruit the health-food conscious Jobs was fond of. And an Apple, after all represents something healthy, fresh and natural. It was an image that appealed to Jobs and the others. And since they couldn't come up with a name they liked better, Apple Computer was born.

A graphic image was needed to reflect the fresh ideas of the company, and Apple Computer chose the Regis McKenna Advertising Agency to develop a Logo. An Apple was the obvious choice, and the colours of the rainbow were chosen to enhance it and make it stand out among corporate Logos. Rainbow colours also generate positive feelings. The bite out of the Apple was a creative way to use the Logo as more than a corporate signature. It's a sales tool that artistically suggests to individuals that they purchase an Apple Computer. The word bite also can be tied to the world of electronics. Bytes (pronounced bites) are units that measure the memory capacity contained on the microcomputer chips that are the foundation for all personal computers.

Source: Internal Apple document

Postscript: A major trademark battle between Apple Computer and the Beatles' holding company Apple Corps over their company logos resulted in an out-of-court settlement in favour of Apple Corp estimated to be US $29m.

amount of $500 000 was also spent on the launch advertising campaign, plus the cost of new signs on 2000 branches.)[9]

Internationally, the two most recognised logos are the Red Cross and the Swastika. Table 7.3 provides a brief account of the origins of the *Apple* and *Shell* logos. The *Apple* computer company's rainbow-coloured apple with the bite missing from it is claimed (by *Apple*) to be one of the world's best known corporate/brand logos. Another well-known logo is the *Shell* petroleum company's shell. *Shell* says that this trademark, which is registered in more than 170 countries, is its most important marketing asset. (Shell is confusing identity with image.) Part of the value of the shell logo has been its ability to change with the times without customers being conscious of the change. The 'rules' for managing this logo and the other elements of *Shell's* visual identity are recorded in a manual several inches thick.

Colour

Colour is often an afterthought. Left to the designer's or corporate management's whim, a potentially important part of an organisation's visual identity can be chosen without regard to the psychology of the effects of colour on people's emotions. People are thought to notice colour more readily than form or shape, and it is thought to hold their attention longer. The red and white of *Coca-Cola*, the blue of *Ford*, the yellow arches of *McDonald's*, and the yellow of *Kodak* are now important parts of the corporate landscape. Most company colour schemes, however, do not elicit strong recall from stakeholders. Some companies will even use multiple colours to sign their name. For example, I wrote this book on an *IBM* personal computer where the *IBM* letters were printed in silver on the computer, brown on the keyboard, white on the monitor, and black on the printer. (And to think that *IBM* was once known as 'Big Blue'!)

Research has shown that certain colours can cause predictable emotional and psysiological effects. We also learn to respond to them in certain ways, for example, in all the world's traffic signals, red means stop and danger, while green means go. The cultural context within which a colour is used, however, can be an important factor to consider. For example, white often signals purity and cleanliness, but in some cultures it is the colour of mourning. Colour researchers have documented many generalisations regarding the effects of colour on people.[10] For example,

- red will stimulate appetite
- blue creates a condition of mental calmness, it decreases the appetite
- green is a cool colour, it is refreshing and tranquil
- grey creates a mood of dignity and safety
- yellow is friendly and cheerful, it is the happiest of colours.

The intrinsic physiological and emotional impact of colour contrasts to how people respond to a logo. Here a person always has to learn what a particular form or shape stands for—some-

Table 7.4

The Effect of a Corporate Colour Scheme

An interesting example of the effect of a company's corporate colours is found in the Japanese colour film industry. By the early 1980s the amateur colour film market was dominated by three companies: Kodak, Fuji and Sakura. Fuji had been gaining market share, while Sakura—the market leader in the early 1950s with over half the Japanese market—had been losing share to both its competitors. Blind tests showed that Sakura's problem was not product quality. Rather, it was handicapped by its choice of the colour of its packaging (red) and an unfortunate word association. Its name in Japanese means 'cherry blossom' which suggests a soft, blurry, pinkish image. The red colour and the cherry blossom associations somehow led amateur photographers to believe that Sakura's prints were perceptibly reddish. The name Fuji however, was associated with green trees, brilliant blue skies, and the white snows of Japan's sacred mountain. Fuji uses green for the colour of its film packaging and deliberately stresses its 'green image'. Sakura tried advertising as a way to overcome the negative associations which its name produced. This was not successful.

What could Sakura do to overcome its identity problem?

a   Change the brand name and the colour, and/or
b   Shift the competitive battleground from image and identity to either
    i   new technology, or
    ii   unmet customer needs.

It chose strategy b (ii) and introduced a 24-exposure film at the same price as competitors' 20-exposure film. This strategy was aimed at exploiting the growing cost consciousness of users at the time, and it drew attention to the economic issue (where it had an advantage) and away from its identity problem (which it could not win against Fuji).

Source: Ohmae, Kenichi 1982, *The Mind of the Strategist*, Penguin, New York, Chapters 4 and 11.

times through a large amount of advertising, and sometimes through experience. In contrast, many colours are liked or disliked intuitively, as we see (to our cost) each fashion season. Table 7.4 provides an example of this effect on the perception of product quality in the Japanese film industry.

Another example in the Australian context relates to the colours green and gold (or bright yellow) which are typically used by Australia's representative sporting teams. (The colours on the national flag are red, white and blue.) The oil company *BP* also uses these colours as an integral part of its corporate signature. (Do petrol sales increase during a period like the Olympic games when the country follows the exploits of its national sporting team?) By colour-coordinating their service stations, *BP* uses the hard colour yellow on a strong green background to project a distinct visual montage to the passing motorist. The company's research findings indicate that this visual montage can be a determinate choice factor for the casual petrol (and food) buyer when confronted with two or three service stations in a row with the same price levels.

Typeface

A look through any business magazine shows the variety of typefaces used by organisations to sign their names. In fact, there are hundreds of different typefaces from which a typographer can choose. In addition to selecting a typeface, the typographer needs to select the size of type, and the form (upper and/or lower case, light, bold, italic) in which it will appear. With so many possible variations, one would expect that no two companies would use similar typefaces. Not so. Advertisers have found that only a few are suitable for easy communication and recognition. For example, one favourite option for corporate names is UPPER CASE.

Apart from the distinctive way that *Coca-Cola* writes its name, I struggle to recall the typefaces used by the ten most recognised companies. For example, in 1990 the *Landor Associates'* global top ten Image Power companies were: *Coca-Cola, Sony, Mercedes-Benz, Kodak, Disney, Nestlé, Toyota, McDonald's, IBM,* and *Pepsi*. How many typefaces can you recall? (*Sony, Toyota, IBM,* and *Pepsi* all commonly write their names in upper case.) Better still, how many of your company's customers would know how your organisation writes its name?

A question which is often asked is, who cares how our company writes its name, (or what corporate colours we use) as long as it is clear and legible, and easy to reproduce? The answer is that some (a few) people may transfer meanings and sensations generated by visual elements of a company's identity to the company itself. It is best to find out if this occurs prior to deciding on a particular typeface. A fascinating way to test your company's typeface is to write it in several different styles, some of which are used by your competitors. Ask (different sets of) customers to rate each typeface on the attributes which describe your company's desired image (such as product quality, customer service). The results might surprise you. For example, a study of audiotape buyers showed that most customers preferred the *Memorex* name written in the typeface used by *Maxell*, a key competitor.[11]

The Meaning is the Message

All organisations have a visual identity even though they may never have employed a design consultant to integrate the various elements into a coherent whole. Every physical element of the organisation which a stakeholder sees helps to form this identity. The difference between the visual identity of *McDonald's* and most other companies is that of consistency and uniformity of presentation. *McDonald's* family restaurants (fast food outlets) have a similar appearance all over the world. This makes them easy to recognise for people of all ages, and it enhances the familiarity–liking linkage outlined in Figure 7.1. Few other multi-outlet organisations (with the notable exception of some petrol service stations) manage their visual identities so well.

The previous discussion in this chapter suggests that each element of an organisation's visual identity may elicit various meanings in the minds of stakeholders. These can vary across different cultures, and different types of stakeholders. This can make it difficult for a company to coordinate the signals sent from the various parts of the identity. One way to overcome these potential problems is to hire a corporate identity consultant, and trust the consultant's judgement. Consultants of the calibre of *Landor Associates* and Wally Olins will seldom make mistakes integrating the various elements of a corporate identity. Consultants with less experience, however, may be a bit of a gamble. (A key question to help you choose a design consultant is: does (s)he recommend research to examine image, and pretest design options?)

The minimum any organisation should seek to achieve is to coordinate all aspects of its advertising and visual identity. This will help the organisation present a consistent style to its internal and external stakeholders. What will have even more impact, however, is if the organisation can fuse its strategy and organ-isational culture with its visual style. The aim here is to link a single value proposition to the company name and logo, and to communicate this to every stakeholder. In this way, the company tries to avoid the problems associated with different people coining a range of different impressions from the visual identity symbols.

One approach which companies can use to create a single value proposition which will be linked to its visual identity is to create a 'tag-line' to be used with the company name and logo in all advertising. This tag-line should reflect the essence of the company's vision and strategy. At the product level, Coke's 'It's the Real Thing' was probably one of the most strongly effective summaries of the 'raison d'être' a brand ever used. Also, *Apple Computer*'s 'The Power to be Your Best' is a tag-line which nicely captures the essence of the company and its product promise. (As I write this chapter, however, *Apple* have just introduced a new tag-line in Australia—'There are no limits'. To me, this is not nearly as 'personal' as their previous tag-line.)

The discussion of vision statements in Chapter 3 is a good place to start designing a tag-line. Section 2—business definition, Section 3—distinctive competence, and Section 4—future dir-ections are the relevant parts of the vision statement. The task is to use this material to coin a four to six word tag-line that stakeholders can relate to every time they see the company's visual identity (and its advertising). In the 1980s the oil company *BP* used two tag-lines which research indicated that people in the UK and Australia responded to very well. Both relied for their appeal on a parochial theme, namely, 'Britain at its Best', and 'The Quiet Achiever' (which was a popular Australian trait). *BP* subsequently discovered 'global branding' and replaced both these popular tag-lines with 'For All Our Tomorrows'. Unlike the two previous tag-lines, the global one could apply equally well to any oil company.

Some tag-lines are better than others. Table 7.5 lists the tag-lines of some of the world's major airlines and asks you to see how many you can correctly match with the appropriate carrier. If you are an airline executive, consumer responses to such a quiz are important because they indicate whether or not consumers are aware of one of the core attributes of the airline's desired image/reputation.

Table 7.5

Slogan Test

How many of these slogans (tag-lines) can you match with their correct international airline?

Air France	Find out how good we really are
American Airlines	A great way to fly
ANA	The business airline of Europe
British Airways	The Spirit of Australia
Cathay Pacific	We're flying better than ever
Continental Airlines	Enchantment wherever you are
Delta Airlines	German airlines
Espana	The reliable airline
Iberia	A world of difference
JAL	Warm to the experience
KLM	Passion for life
Lufthansa	We love to fly and it shows
Malaysia Airlines	You don't get big by being second best
Pan Am	Arrive in better shape
Qantas	The world's favourite airline
SAS	Japan's best to the world
Singapore Airlines	Something special in the air
TWA	Ask the world of us

Answer: Tag-lines are in reverse order.

Conclusion

The major conclusion to be drawn from this chapter is that corporate identity does matter—but it is not nearly as important as what your organisation does, the products and services it offers, or what and how it communicates with stakeholders. For example, a logo can help a company like *Nestlé* communicate the core benefit of some of its products—as the birds in the *Nestlé* little nest logo do for the company's infant products. However, it is the quality and value of the products that are the key to their success.

The company name is arguably the single most important part of the identity mix. It can help communicate what the company does (for example, *Tubemakers*), link the company to an industry (such as *Virgin Airlines*) and associate the company with a particular country or region (such as *British Airways*). It can also be used as an umbrella for a variety of similar products (for example, *Sony*), or across a range of unrelated divisional activities (such as *Mitsubishi*). Colour and style can help customers recognise your retail outlets (such as *McDonald's*) or signal attributes of a company's service (such as *BP*'s clean motor service stations). Apart from creating and focusing awareness however, for most companies identity is mainly icing on the cake.

For companies which sell functionally identical products (such as beer, milk powder, mineral water, petrol), identity and advertising can be used to differentiate competitive offerings. For these types of products it is crucial to integrate all the aspects of visual identity with each other, and with the organisation's total communication program.

Probably the classic example of the use of visual identity is the way that the British royal family have mastered the art of creating images of splendour and tradition with a range of ceremonies and identity symbols.

End Notes

1 Landor Associates, *News Release*, Landor Associates, New York, 5 July 1988.

2 A. Ries & J. Trout, *Positioning: The Battle for Your Mind*, McGraw-Hill, New York, 1981.

3 E. Selame & J. Selame, *The Company Image*, John Wiley & Sons, New York, 1988.

4 W. Olins, *Corporate Identity*, Harvard Business School Press, Harvard, 1989.

5 D. Aaker, *Managing Brand Equity*, The Free Press, New York, 1991, Ch. 9.

6 B. Burrough & J. Helyar, *Barbarians at the Gate*, Arrow Books, London, 1990.

7 D. Heer, *Nestlé 125 Years 1866–1991*, Nestlé, Vevey, 1991.

8 W. Olins 1989.

9 J. McGuinness, 'Which bank? This bank!', *The Bulletin*, September, 1991, p. 35; L. Wright, 'A new logo puts Commonwealth's faith in the stars', *Sydney Morning Herald*, 31 August 1991, p. 32.

10 J.E. Miner, 'The colour of money', *Marketing*, December–January, 1992, pp. 8–10.

11 D.L. Masten, 'Logo's power depends on how well it communicates with target market', *Marketing News*, 5 December 1988, p. 20.

CHAPTER 8

Country, Industry and Brand Images: Where to Get Marketing Leverage

People often associate certain types of products with a particular country. For example, to many people Italian leather goods, French wine, Chinese food, Swiss watches, and US films are all special. Within these product categories brands like *Gucci* have helped enhance the image of other Italian leather manufacturers, and famous French champagne brands like *Moet & Chandon* have helped to promote the French wineries. This chapter focuses on the relationship between country, industry, company, and brand images. To illustrate the importance of understanding these relationships for your organisation, consider how two UK companies enhanced their corporate/brand images by linking them to their US parent company.

In the early 1980s, *General Motors* was manufacturing and selling cars and trucks in the UK and Europe under the names *Vauxhall* and *Bedford*. The *Vauxhall* and *Bedford* companies, like others in the *GM* family (such as *AC Spark Plug*, *Delco Products*), operated largely independently of each other. They did, however, cooperate through a group known as the Public Affairs Council (PAC). The PAC decided to investigate the potential for linking together companies like *Vauxhall* and *Bedford* by identifying them and their products with *General Motors*.[1]

It was not clear that such a clear identification with the giant US parent company would be beneficial to the various operating companies. Most people in the UK saw GM's various companies as solidly British. Would linking these companies to *General Motors* USA damage this parochial relationship? In effect, the PAC needed answers to the following questions:

- Would linking the companies to General Motors USA provide a greater sense of identity, cohesion, and purpose for the UK operations?
- Would there be any adverse effects of this strategy on customer preferences and loyalty?
- What were the relative strengths of the GM corporate image which could support such a communication strategy? What weaknesses needed to be avoided?
- What would be the overall effect of the strategy on the corporate standing of both GM and its individual operating companies?

A major research project was undertaken in the UK. It showed that there were considerable benefits to be gained from being known as a GM company. The PAC then used advertising, promotion, branding, and other communication strategies to build the GM association, and capitalise on this positive linkage. In effect, *Vauxhall* and *Bedford* were able to 'rent', or to use more formal terminology, to 'gain marketing leverage' from the *General Motors* name.

The aim of this chapter is to explore some ways to rent the positive associations of other images. In particular, how can your organisation get leverage from its high-profile brands (or vice versa); should it emphasise its links with a particular industry; and should it try to position itself using a nationalistic theme to trade on the parochial feelings of its stakeholders? While we see many examples of companies which use each of these strategies, there are few guidelines to help managers answer the questions posed above.

A Network of Images

Figure 1.2 (Chapter 1) shows that external stakeholders' images of an organisation can be affected by country, industry and brand images. That is, when most people think about an organisation, they do so within a relevant context. This context may be the industry in which the company operates or the brands it sells. For example, depending on what people know about *American Express*, they may think of it as a type of financial institution, or as a company involved in travel services. (When it originally started out in 1850 it did exactly what its name said— it was an express company which transported small parcels and cash throughout the east coast of the USA.) Hence, *American Express* belongs to an industry. Because some industries have more favourable images than others, a company like *American Express* could choose to associate itself with financial services and/or travel services.

The word *American* in the name *American Express* also automatically associates the company with the USA for most people. In this case, the image of America can be a positive or a negative attribute, depending on what people think of America, and the US finance and travel industries. If these linkages in people's minds are positive, they represent an important source of marketing leverage for a company such as *American Express*. If these linkages are negative, then the company must try to distance itself from its country of origin or its industry.

On the eve of the 1992 Barcelona summer Olympic Games, Spain launched one of the costliest public relations campaigns in history. This was aimed at changing the European stereotype of Hispanics as lazy, uneducated, corrupt, and cruel. This stereotype has its roots in the Black Legend, which was formed during the sixteenth century by the enemies of Spain. Their enemies could not defeat the Spanish armed forces, so they attacked Spain with words. The English, Dutch, Germans, Italians, French, and later the Americans accused Spain of atrocities during their conquest of the Americas, and in the conduct of the Inquisition. These charges were embellished and repeated so often over the next four centuries, that many Spaniards even believed them. To help repair Spain's global image, the country hosted a number of public relations events, such as the Barcelona Olympics and Expo '92 in Seville. It also became a full member of the European Community, embarked on a nationwide program to restore its museums and monuments, and started to actively promote Hispanic culture to the world.

It will take some time to tell whether these actions will change what people think about the country and its people. What we do know is that the image of countries like USA, Britain, and Spain can enhance or detract from the images people hold of their companies, industries, and brands. Research seems to indicate that these different types of images may exist in a network as shown in Figure 8.1. Each arrow represents a source of potential marketing leverage.

Arrow Number 1 in Figure 8.1 indicates that certain countries are known for their excellence in certain industries, namely, Australian Wool, Italian Sports Cars, Japanese Consumer Electronics, Saudi Oil, Scotch Whisky, Swiss (discreet) Banking and US Military Weapon Systems. Sometimes countries are also known for their expertise regarding a particular industrial process. For example, Finnish and Swedish design, French and Italian fashion, German engineering, Japanese production systems, and US advertising and finance. Often cities or areas may become associated with particular industrial activities. For example, Wall St (New York)—finance; Harley St (London)—medical specialists; Detroit (USA)—automobiles; Akron (USA)—tyres; Silicon Valley (California)—Computers; Hollywood (Los Angeles)—movies; Madison Avenue (New York)—advertising.

Large multinational companies have the opportunity to use the types of associations outlined above to help gain credibility for new product introductions. For example in Australia, *Mitsubishi Motors* advertise their *Pajero* Four-Wheel Drive recreational vehicles as manufactured in Japan (because Japanese cars are believed by Australians to be better designed,

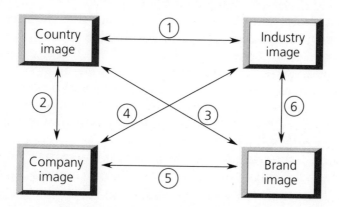

Figure 8.1   A Network of Images: Six Sources of Marketing Leverage

manufactured, and finished), but tested in the outback of Australia (which has an image as a rugged country). In contrast to this, *Ford Australia* decided to manufacture a small sports car (the *Capri*) for sale in Australia and export to the USA. Australians don't generally regard US auto companies as having special expertise in the design of small sports cars, nor would US buyers typically associate Australia with such cars. Hence, this decision by *Ford* gains no leverage from the image of either the US or Australian auto industries. (*Ford* now concedes that the car was a failure in both the US and Australian markets.[2]) Had Ford designed and built a four-wheel drive recreational vehicle in Australia, there would have been ample opportunity to use the image of the rugged Australian outback to add credibility to the brand image.

Relationship Number 2 in Figure 8.1 links country and company images. Many companies like to implicitly or explicitly associate themselves with their country of origin. A good example of a company which has tried to promote its country of origin is *Nestlé*. (*Nestlé* also has a policy of maintaining a majority of its share capital in the hands of Swiss citizens.[3]) This company–country association can be directly enhanced through the choice of the company name, as we saw with *American Express*. It can also be communicated with the tag-line or slogan with which many companies advertise their products and services, for example, *Qantas*—'The Spirit of Australia', *Lufthansa*—'German Airlines'. The perceived value of being associated with a particular country seems to fluctuate over time for some companies. For example, one of Australia's major domestic airlines started out being called *Trans Australia Airlines*. It then shortened its name to *TAA*, and later changed it to *Australian Airlines*. Its only major competitor, *Ansett*, could no longer resist not being associated with Australia, so it changed its name to *Ansett Australia*. This was not the most creative of name changes! For most companies however, any association with a country of origin is not readily apparent. For example, few people outside Britain know that the worldwide travel company *Thomas Cook* is British.

A look in any phonebook will illustrate that many companies believe that incorporating the name of their country, region, or city in their corporate name has marketing value. The interesting question to ponder when adopting such a naming strategy, however, is whether there is an order-of-entry limitation to using such a strategy. That is, does only the first company which uses the country/region/city name in an industry gain the advantage? Once *Australian Airlines* had adopted its new name, was it too late for *Ansett* to gain any leverage from the Australian connection? Do fliers believe that Australia can have only one *Australian* domestic airline? While there is no specific research on this topic in the public domain, it seems reasonable to believe that if customers already associate one company with a country/region/city, then the value for the later users of this naming convention will be diminished.

Like the first two arrows in Figure 8.1, arrow Number 3 is double headed. The double-headed arrows are used to indicate that either entity can rent the image of the other entity with which it is paired. In the case of the 'country image–brand image' connection (arrow Number 3), this two-way influence is a common occurrence. For example, on a grand scale, brand names such as *Apple, Boeing, Coca-Cola, Disney, Ford, IBM, Kodak, Levis, McDonald's,* and *Xerox* have helped shape the image of the USA. Also the USA's reputation as a fast moving business and consumer society, helps these brands to be successful outside the USA. Similarly, brands such as *Canon, Fuji, Honda, Mitsubishi, Nikon, Panasonic, Seiko, Sony, Suntory, Toshiba, Toyota,* and *Yamaha* help define the image of Japan, and are supported by Japan's reputation for quality products. On a smaller scale, it was the advertising of the international airline *KLM,* that helped shape the image of Amsterdam and Holland.

An interesting use of the country-of-origin of a brand has been as the basis for developing global brands. Traditional approaches to global branding emphasise selling more or less the same product, the same way in different countries. The assumption is that standardisation allows economies of scale and scope to be achieved, and lower prices for consumers.[4] The giant British advertising agency *Saatchi & Saatchi* has been a strong advocate of this approach. While there has been considerable argument about the pros and cons of global branding, one way in which it has been working successfully for some time is when a brand has a strong country heritage which consumers in other countries value. For example, one of the attributes of *Coca-Cola, Levis,* and *McDonald's,* is that they are US brands, and represent aspects of the US lifestyle which appeal to people in other countries. In a similar way, *Gucci* fashion and *Chanel* perfume have become global brands outside their country of origin, in part because they are associated with the elegance and *savoir-faire* of the Italians and French.

There has been little research on relationship Number 4 in Figure 8.1. The big Japanese Zaibatsu (diversified companies) like *Mitsui* and *Mitsubishi* seem to suffer no ill effects from being known to have interests in multiple industries. Many of these companies, and their US and European counterparts like *General Electric, Westinghouse, DuPont, Philips*, and *Volvo* use corporate advertising to inform (business)people about the range of industries in which they participate. The implicit assumption here is that there is value in explicitly promoting these associations—especially if these industries are driven by a core set of value enhancing activities like electronics, production expertise and research and development.

One way in which diversified companies can get marketing leverage for their products is to rent the image of making products in one industry to promote a product in a different industry. For example, the Swedish company *Saab*, occasionally advertises its cars using a reference to its origins as an aircraft manufacturer. A 1992 Australian advertisement showed a *Saab 9000 CS* parked in front of an aeroplane. The first sentence in the copy of the advertisement said: 'Saab's heritage is in the sky.'

Relationship Number 5 in Figure 8.1 reflects the common marketing strategy often referred to as 'umbrella' or 'family' branding. Some companies practise it, and some studiously avoid it. For example, *BMW* identifies its cars as *BMW*: 318, 320, 325, 520, 525, 535, 730, 735, 750, 850. Each *BMW* is positioned as 'The Ultimate Driving Machine'. (An 850 is just a bit more ultimate than a 318!) *Procter & Gamble* on the other hand, don't associate their brands with the company. For example, *P&G* make *Pert* shampoo, *Pampers* nappies, and *Tide, Cheer*, and *Bold* laundry detergents (in the USA). There is no common selling proposition among the three laundry detergents. The marketing strategy is to target them to segments of the market which value different attributes, and thus gain more market coverage.

In any single market, it is common to find competitors using different brand name strategies. Each have their advantages and disadvantages, which any good marketing text will elaborate.[5] The point here is that a company can give marketing leverage to its brands by linking them to the corporate name. In an interesting twist to this strategy the Australian company, *Amatil*, rented the world's best-known brand name to give marketing leverage to the company name—it changed its name to *Coca-Cola Amatil*. Another Australian company, *Elders IXL*, changed its name to the *Foster's Brewing Group* to gain the benefits associated with this well known brand of beer. In the USA, *Consolidated Foods Corporation* renamed itself *Sara Lee Corp*.

The last relationship in Figure 8.1 (arrow Number 6) reflects the influence that high profile brand names can have on the image of an industry. The images of *Coke* and *Pepsi* almost define the image of the soft drink industry. Similarly, the images of *McDonald's* and *Pizza Hut* help many people form their image of the fast food industry. Previously I labelled these as 'market driving' brands. That is, they influence the expectations of many people about how all the brands in the industry will perform. When the Taiwanese computer manufacturers wanted to enter the personal computer market they used the well-established image of *IBM* Personal Computers to help them legitimise their products. They called their new, cheaper personal computers '*IBM* Clones'.

Which of the relationships in Figure 8.1 will be more useful as a potential source of leverage for your organisation's image is best determined by research. There are few guidelines in this area because the value of a country, industry or brand image depends solely on how it is perceived by the particular stakeholder. Also, as Figure 8.1 indicates, two or more of these images may combine to affect your organisation's overall image.

Country Images

The discussion in the previous section identifies a country's image as a potential key frame of reference for an organisation's image. Because it is a potential source of marketing leverage, it is valuable to briefly review some of the major factors which may help shape the image of a country for a person who has not been there. (The images held by visitors and residents will tend to be shaped more by their personal experiences.) Figure 8.2 on p. 150 illustrates twelve such factors.

The Gulf War in 1991 focused attention on Iraq and Kuwait. The television pictures from this conflict probably did more to shape the image of these countries than any other single event in history. The news coverage also introduced many people to some of the cultural and religious aspects of life in this region of

Figure 8.2   Factors Which Shape a Country's Image

the world. In short, the power of the news media in shaping the images of countries can be significant, and often distorting. The mass media also distributes information about a country's business, culture, politics, and scientific and sporting achievements. The old 'East versus West' political alignments helped to typecast many countries. It also offered an opportunity for countries such as Switzerland to adopt a non-aligned position which its banking and ethical products industries have used to their advantage. To continue this theme, the USA–USSR 'space race', and other such mega-programs, helped to build a broad frame of reference within which people evaluated the potential for both countries to achieve their goals. The USA's achievements in space send a strong signal to the world that its companies can produce leading edge technology and systems. In contrast, the way the USSR organised and publicised its space program provided few spin-offs for its commercial enterprises.

A country's business leaders, multinational companies, global brands, sporting events, and promotions in a 'foreign' country are another important source of information which people use for forming an image of a country. For example, Brian Basham, who heads his own public relations company in Britain, says that the image of Australia in Europe is fifteen years behind the times. For many Europeans, Australia is a 'beaches-and-booze country'.[6] Its cultural exports (television soap operas, dramas, and films), international sports stars, cultural icons (kangaroos and koalas), tourist advertising, and direct consumer advertising (especially of beer and wine) reinforce this outdated image. Basham also suggests that many businesspeople in Britain think that Australia's high profile business leaders (like the 1980s beer barons, Alan Bond and John Elliott; and the media moguls, Kerry Packer and Rupert Murdoch) are perceived as more entrepreneurial than enlightened businessmen.

For Australian companies wishing to do business overseas, the image of Australia can often be a handicap. For example, do Europeans want to buy products produced by companies from a country known for its 'beaches and booze'? Or one that is also referred to as 'the land of the long weekend'? If these products are beer (wine) and swimwear (sportswear), the answer may well be yes. If it is a product such as high-technology medical equipment, it is best to try to gain marketing leverage from some of Australia's more modern image features, like its record for invention, and its tendency to rapidly adopt good new products. (The big Japanese companies often use Australia and New Zealand as a test market for their export products.) If we switch the problem to one of attracting foreign business investment, then the old image (beaches and booze) can be used to attract businesspeople 'down-under' for a holiday or convention. Many businesspeople like to invest in countries which are nice to visit.

A different type of image problem faces many Finnish companies. Outside Europe, Finland's next-door neighbour Sweden has a more established image as a country skilled in business. Companies such as *Saab* and *Volvo* have helped 'put Sweden on the (business) map'. Finland it seems, has both an awareness and an image problem. First, many (business)people know little about Finland or its major companies. Little knowledge in turn, generally leads to a weak image.

For a company interested in renting the image of its host country, it is important to understand the strength of the image of its country, the attributes on which the image is based, and whether any of these attributes help people favourably evaluate the company or its products. These attributes are the key to building associations in people's minds. They also suggest which industries may benefit from a country association. For example, if a target audience thinks that Australia is a 'lifestyle' country, then there is potentially more marketing leverage to be gained by industries (and companies) which are associated with this image, than say the elaborately transformed manufacturing industries. The only reliable way to uncover which attributes define a country's images is to use research. Talk to people who live in the place, and the people who visit the country. The research techniques outlined in Chapter 9 can also be used to profile country images. When you know what people think about your country, then it is relatively easy to decide whether or not to build an explicit country–industry–company linkage.

Guidelines

To summarise and coordinate the ideas presented in the two previous sections, Figure 8.3 presents a decision tree which describes the potential for using one image to enhance another type of image. This figure assumes that the target audience for

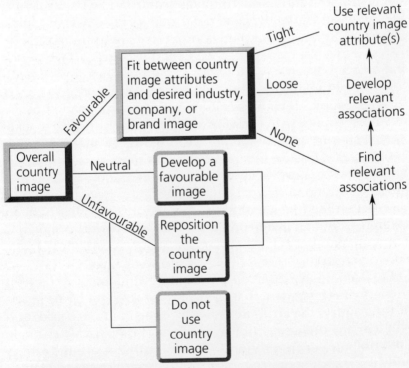

Figure 8.3   Routes to Potential Image Leverage

the communication is aware of the country being considered. Research is then needed to determine whether or not the overall image which people hold of the country is favourable or unfavourable.

This overall favourability of a country's image is important because research has shown that when consumers are not familiar with a country's products, country image may serve as a halo from which consumers infer a brand's (and company's) attributes.[7] That is, countries with a favourable image, will tend to be perceived to produce better products. This is one reason why emerging industrial countries such as Korea value hosting events such as the Olympic Games. It gives the country the chance to display its culture, products, and organisational ability to the world, that is, to create or reshape particular attributes of its image. This then becomes a platform to introduce its companies, products, and services to people in other countries.

When people become familiar with a country's products, country image may become a construct which summarises peoples' beliefs about its products, companies, industries, and skills. Thus, we may find consumers thinking that Germany makes the safest and best engineered cars, the USA makes the best aircraft, and Japan has the best consumer electronics. A country's image, as a summary of past success or failure, can then act as an entry barrier into new markets. For example, a Russian company would have a hard time trying to convince many people that it could design fashionable clothes.

When a country has a favourable image, it makes sense to search for attributes of the image which can be used to enhance the desired image of an industry, company, or brand. In Figure 8.3 this is referred to as finding a 'fit' between a particular attribute of the country, and the desired image. For example, the Australian beer *Foster's*, is advertised in Germany using the image of Australia as 'a sunburnt country'. The hot, dry landscape is an ideal backdrop for advertising the refreshing qualities of a cold beer. It also helps to substantiate the advertising claim that *Foster's* is a refreshing beer. (Using the Sydney Opera House in the advertisements would not be nearly as relevant.)

If a country has a neutral image, that is, there are no attributes which stand out and differentiate the country, then the first task is to develop the country's image. If a country has an unfavourable image, then the marketing task is to try to reposition the country's image. Developing or repositioning a country's image is not an easy task. It is generally attempted by advertising, and funded from the government coffers. For example, the Australian Tourism Commission invested $57 million in a five-year advertising campaign in the USA spearheaded by the famous 'Crocodile Dundee' (Paul Hogan) campaign. Qantas (Australia's government owned international airline) supported this campaign with its own advertising. Market research found that each dollar of the Tourist Commission's advertising generated between $19 to $32 of extra tourist dollar inflow.[8]

Figure 8.3 presents some guidelines for when to consider renting a country's image. The first issue to resolve, however, is whether the target audience for the communication is aware of linkages between a country and its industries, companies, and brands. If there is little or no recall or recognition of potentially beneficial associations, then these must be developed. The next section outlines some communication strategies which can be used to couple various types of image together.

Communication Strategies

The discussion in the previous sections of this chapter promotes the role of a country's image as a potential anchor point from which companies (industries and brands) can seek to gain marketing leverage. As Figure 8.3 indicates, however, the target audience for the communication must first be aware of the country–company linkage, and they must hold a (potentially) favourable image of the country. (Favourable in this case means that one or more attributes of the country will help people to favourably evaluate your company or its products.) Lack of awareness is a relatively simple problem to overcome. As we will see below, advertising agencies can use a number of different communication strategies to build a linkage between the image people hold of a country and a company. Often, however, the problem is to position a country in people's minds so that it can be used to springboard the image of the country's companies.

One of the founding fathers of modern advertising, David Ogilvy, and two famous, modern-day advertising consultants, Al Ries and Jack Trout, provide some useful advice on how to position a country in the prospect's mind.[9] Ries and Trout suggest that our minds see many cities and countries as 'mental picture postcards'. (Big countries may have more postcards than smaller countries.) Ogilvy argues that research can unlock the attributes which define these picture postcards. It is these mental images which a marketer must understand in order to see the potential for using the country's image as a source of marketing leverage. A country like Finland must understand what people think about it, before it can hope to compete with the favourable image of its Swedish neighbour.

To illustrate this idea, let's assume that research shows that most of our target audience know little about Finland, other than that it is next door (or close) to Sweden. Let's also assume that the images they hold of Sweden are favourable. How could advertising be used to (quickly) establish that Finland is a country worth visiting (for tourists), or doing business with. To borrow one of Ries and Trout's ideas, we might consider using the mental picture postcard of Sweden as the anchor for developing an image of Finland. The slogan: 'Finland—the country next door to Sweden' might begin the process of building an image. (Ries and Trout once suggested positioning Jamaica as the Hawaii of the Caribbean. Everybody knew about Hawaii, but few knew anything distinctive about Jamaica.) We could extend this idea by linking Finland to both its better-known neighbours: 'Finland—next door to Sweden, and the gateway to (St Petersburg or Russia)'. Now, it is unlikely that the people of Finland would be too enthusiastic about such a positioning, but the moral of the story here is that you have to start with what your target audience will give you. It costs a lot of money to try to build an image from scratch.

In the rest of this section, let's assume that the images people hold of the country you are thinking of using, have some positive attributes which your company can rent. The problem is: how do you signal an association between these attributes and the company? There are a number of possibilities. Let's start with the most obvious—advertising.

One approach is to explicitly tell people in the target audience about the association. For example, an advertisement for *Audi* cars in Australia started with the headline: 'Australia's Best German Luxury Car Value'. The advertisement ended with the tag-line '*Vorsprung durch technik*'. Another advertisement in the same newspaper had the headline: 'Sydney's Saab dealers offer Europe's best at prices to embarrass the Japanese'. A more subtle approach was used in an Australian television advertisement for a brand of jeans. It showed two people arguing about the jeans in French. Not a word of English was spoken. The advertisement implicitly rented the fashion image of France. The oil company *BP*, used a corporate advertising campaign called 'Britain at its Best' for a number of years. Many people had forgotten that *BP* stood for *British Petroleum*.

Corporate names are another important signalling device. It is not difficult to tell the country of origin of the following organisations: *American Airlines, Boston Consulting Group, British Airways, London Business School, London Fog Clothing Co., Singapore Airlines, Texas Instruments,* and *USAir.* It's a bit harder to tell where *these* brands originate, although many people can make a good guess: *Fuji, Heineken, Lowenbrau, Mercedes-Benz, Perrier, Pierre Cardin,* and *Volkswagen.* Sometimes when a company wants to signal its country of origin but its name cannot do the job, a tag-line or slogan may be used with the name. Two examples of this strategy have been referred to earlier: *Lufthansa*—German Airlines, and *Qantas*—The Spirit of Australia. (Qantas also uses a picture of a flying kangaroo as its logo.)

A third category of signalling devices is visual symbols. A variety of such symbols can be used to establish country-of-origin linkages. For example, a country's flag in an advertisement, or the major elements of the flag, can be an effective signalling device. Many people know the 'Stars and Stripes' of the USA, and the red maple leaf of Canada. An interesting twist to using a flag as a signal of a country occurred when Australia won the America's Cup yachting trophy. During this 'Campaign', waged specifically against the New York Yacht Club, the beer baron Alan Bond and his team unfurled their new flag. It was designed to serve the same purpose as the familiar pirate flag—the Skull & Crossbones. This one, however, was the 'Boxing Kangaroo'—a gold kangaroo standing on his hind legs, with red boxing gloves on his front legs, set on a green background. (Green and gold are the traditional Australian national sporting colours.) For a number of years after this sporting event, the boxing kangaroo flag came to symbolise Australian sporting achievement for nationals and many overseas people.

Each country typically has a number of cultural symbols. In

Australia the Sydney Opera House, kangaroos and koala bears are three of the favourites with overseas visitors. For Holland, their international airline *KLM* often uses pictures of wooden clogs, tulips, and canals. The Eiffel Tower of Paris, the Statue of Liberty of New York, Big Ben and the Tower of London are other well-known cultural symbols. These pictures can be worth a thousand words as signals of country and cultural linkages.

A final way to advertise a country connection is to use the words 'made in ...'. Research by David Head, an academic at the University of Bath in the UK, indicates that 'made-in' advertising slogans tend to fall into one of three categories.[10] The first category involves a direct appeal to the national pride of the target audience. As an example, of this strategy he cites the German bank *BfG*, which used the slogan '100 Years of Made in Germany'. In Europe, the Dutch company *Philips* is using its advertising to position itself as 'the European alternative (to the Japanese)'. Head's second strategy for using the made-in (country) connection represents the antidote to patriotism. It is characterised by drawing the attention of a foreign audience to positive, and usually stereotyped attributes of a country. The idea is to imbue the product or service originating from that country with these image-enhancing qualities. For example, *Swissair* printed this slogan over a full-page photograph of the workings of a (Swiss) pocket watch: 'Only the sum total of all the details shows how smoothly a Swiss airport operates'. The last strategy for this type of advertising derives from the allusion to a particular expertise which is associated with a foreign country. For example, outside Germany, German engineering is strongly associated with notions of workmanship, technology, and inventiveness. The electrical giant *AEG* used the following slogan in a British advertisement: 'AEG—ADVANCED ENGINEERING FROM GERMANY'.

Conclusion

This chapter outlines some of the principal avenues open for renting the image of other entities to enhance the marketing effectiveness of your company and its brands. While most of the discussion has focused on the images people hold of a company's (brand's) country of origin, managers must remember that these images are often only useful for particular industries. Research is the key to finding out which attributes of your country's image are linked to a particular industry, and which may be used to provide marketing leverage.

Nationalism and patriotism are powerful forces in many cultures. They are not, however, omnipotent in most advanced consumer markets. Yet this has not deterred some political and business leaders in countries like Australia, the UK and the USA from trying to use a 'made-in ...' advertising campaign to stimulate demand for domestically produced products. A good example of how such a campaign can be less successful than expected is in the US automotive industry. In the 1980s, many US auto brands were advertised using a primary or secondary theme of 'buy American'. Sales of Japanese cars were hardly affected. A large segment of US buyers were buying Japanese cars because they perceived them to be of superior quality. Had the CEOs of the US auto makers understood this, then more effort would have been directed to improving quality, as US auto manufacturers are now doing to catch up to the Japanese, rather than believing in the myth that more advertising can change consumer preferences. Advertising can help, but it has to be based on a thorough prior image investigation and a believable image proposition.

The guiding theme of this chapter is the need to do research to find out how your organisation's stakeholders link their country, industry, company and brand images. Opportunities exist to communicate linkages between two or more of these images to enhance the value of your corporate image. The search is for positive attributes in a country, industry or brand image which can be used to favourably differentiate your organisation in stakeholders' minds. Consider how successfully the USA has exported its 'culture' around the world through its sporting events, movies, and brands, and how this has provided many opportunities for its companies to follow.

End Notes

1 E. Fountain, I. Parker, & J. Samules, 'The contribution of research to General Motors' corporate communications strategy in the UK', *Journal of the Market Research Society*, vol. 28, no. 1, January, 1986, pp. 25–42.

2 B. Tuckey, 'Spring-clean gives Ford the edge', *Business Review Weekly*, 15 January 1993, pp. 26–7.

3 J. Heer, *Nestlé 125 Years 1866-1991*, Nestlé, Vevey, 1991.

4 T. Levitt, 'The globalization of markets', *Harvard Business Review*, May–June, 1983, pp. 92–102.

5 H. Davidson, *Offensive Marketing*, Penguin, 1987; P. Kotler, *Marketing Management*, Prentice-Hall, 1991.

6 T. Gray, 'A new image for Australia', *Business Review Weekly*, 7 April 1989, p. 73.

7 C. Min Han, 'Country image: halo or summary construct?', *Journal of Marketing Research*, vol. 26, May, 1989, pp. 222–9.

8 L. Moffet, 'Report backs Paul Hogan ads', *Financial Review*, 19 February 1991.

9 D. Ogilvy, *Ogilvy on Advertising*, Pan Books, London, 1983, Ch. 10; A. Ries and J. Trout, *Positioning: The Battle for Your Mind*, McGraw-Hill, New York, 1981, Ch. 15.

10 D. Head, 'Advertising slogans and the 'made-in' concept', *International Journal of Advertising*, vol. 7, 1988, pp. 237–52.

PART 3

Managing Your Desired Corporate Reputation

CHAPTER 9

Measuring Reputations: What Do Stakeholders Actually Think?

One thing that good marketing practitioners have taught all managers is that *the most dangerous place to look at their stakeholders is from behind their desks*. The simple truth of the matter is that the only way to accurately gauge what people think of an organisation is to ask them. This is easy to say, but often difficult to do. Why? Because it takes (valuable) time; it costs money which has no direct contribution to generating bottom-line profit in the period in which it is spent; most organisations will need to employ the services of an outside market research firm to help; and it is not intuitively obvious how one measures elusive concepts such as corporate image and corporate reputation. Any of these reasons is generally sufficient to kill the idea of measuring corporate reputations—especially year after year.

The problem for organisations that do not track the health of their reputations over time is that when a problem occurs, managers have to guess about the appropriate reaction strategy. A graphic example of this occurred for Australia's second largest retail bank, *Westpac*. A disgruntled employee 'leaked' confidential letters which showed that some of the advice given to customers about certain types of foreign currency loans was questionable. The bank reacted to this incident as if it were something which could be isolated from other aspects of the bank's activities. It called in the lawyers and tried to embargo any discussion in the press while a court case against the employee was pending. What it failed to realise was that customers and journalists saw this incident as impinging on the bank's integrity and trustworthiness. This crisis, which became known as 'the Westpac letters affair', escalated to the point where it contributed to the resignation of the then managing director of the bank.

Westpac's problem illustrates that the public affairs unit of the bank didn't fully understand that the legally correct course of action (hand the matter over to the lawyers) would have a negative impact on the reputations of the bank held by customers and journalists. The illegal action of an employee (the court finally ruled in favour of the bank against the employee's actions) highlighted how the bank's dealings with a small group of its customers could impact on its reputation with other groups (employees, other customers, journalists, and the general public). The adverse publicity surrounding this crisis was fuelled by a combination of factors. First, there was a series of inappropriate media responses by the bank (a topic covered in Chapter 11). Second, it seems that the bank didn't adequately appreciate how its actions were translated into a corporate reputation (the subject of Chapter 1). Finally, the bank had not been gathering adequate information about its reputations among various stakeholder groups which would allow it to estimate the potential impact of this incident across the various groups.

The 'bottom line' of the *Westpac* case is that *if you can't accurately measure your reputations, you can't manage them*. That is, if Westpac managers had a good measure of how important trust and integrity were to its corporate reputation, and how important a good reputation is to a bank, they would have reacted differently to the initial concerns of the stakeholder groups. The remaining sections of this chapter outline how such measures can be constructed. The discussion will not make you an expert on the subject, but it will equip you with an understanding of what the experts mean when they show you measures of your organisation's reputations held by various stakeholders.

What Are We Trying To Achieve?

The objectives of corporate reputation research are to provide managers with:

- a measure of the images and reputations of their organisation held by various stakeholder groups
- a measure of the images and reputations of competitive organisations
- an indication of the 'ideal' image of their organisation.

These measures must enable managers to change various aspects of the organisation's activities to build a better reputation. They also can be linked to what people think about the organisation's country of origin, the industry in which it operates, and to any high-profile 'brands' the organisation may control. Chapter 8 showed that it may be possible to use country, industry and/or brand associations to enhance an organisation's image and reputation. Alternatively, being linked too closely to an industry (such as forestry, nuclear power) or a particular product (such as plastic packaging, napalm) may be a distinct disadvantage. In either case, knowing how strongly your organisation is linked to these factors can be important.

This is a daunting set of objectives. Few organisations spend the time and effort required to achieve all of them. With this in mind, it is best to consider these objectives as a benchmark against which to compare your organisation's measures. What most organisations measure is the level of awareness of their company (and its major competitors), and some broad indicators of its advertising, products, prices, and customer service.

Chapter 6 outlined how to measure awareness. Recall that your organisation could be the 'dominant company', 'top of mind', 'recalled', 'recognised', or 'associated with the wrong industry'. Worse still, potential stakeholders may be completely unaware of it. (See Figure 6.2 on p. 112.) In essence then, your first problem is to determine if your company has an awareness or a (potential) reputation problem. Figure 9.1 on p. 166 outlines the nature of this decision.

There are two major types of research that can be used to measure your organisation's reputations. To achieve the objectives outlined above they both need to be used. The first technique is known as qualitative research, while the second is known as quantitative research. Use of either type of research

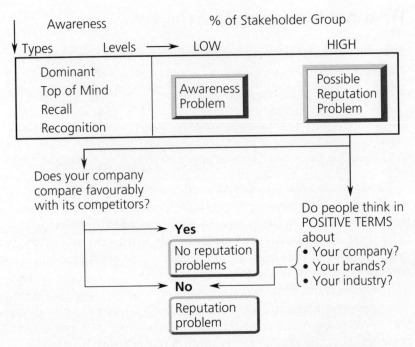

Figure 9.1   Does Your Organisation Have a Reputation Problem?

alone will often lead to a poor measure of the image and reputation constructs. In practice, however, many studies use only one type of research to measure the organisation's reputations. When this happens (usually because of budgetary or time constraints), managers or the researcher who designed the study must make a series of guesses about the missing pieces of information.

The next section outlines the contribution that qualitative and quantitative research make to measuring corporate images and reputations. Each type of research employs a number of techniques for measuring stakeholder reactions to organisations (brands, industries and countries), and for searching for insights into the hearts and minds of stakeholders. Most organisations employ the services of a market research firm to administer the techniques outlined in the next section. The major reason for this is to ensure that the findings from one technique are appropriately integrated with those derived from the other techniques. At the conclusion of this brief review, an extensive example is presented showing some measures of various organisations' reputations.

Research Techniques

The objectives of corporate reputation research are to identify the major characteristics of your organisation which stakeholders use to form their reputation about that organisation. It is also beneficial to search for characteristics that can be used to differentiate your organisation from its competitors. Before we start searching for these characteristics, it is worth the effort to pause and think about what types of characteristics might provide the best insight into how stakeholders think about various types of organisations. To guide this search, some of the foundation work of modern psychology is relevant.

In 1957, three US psychologists, Charles Osgood, George Suci and Percy Tannenbaum, published a pathbreaking book titled *The Measurement of Meaning*.[1] Their research focused on people's reactions to various objects of interest, and revealed that three basic dimensions explained most of the variance in these reactions. These three dimensions of meaning were:

1 an *evaluative* dimension, represented by adjective pairs such as: helpful—unhelpful, reliable—unreliable, trustworthy—untrustworthy
2 a *potency* dimension, represented by adjectives such as: strong—weak, powerful—powerless, experienced—inexperienced
3 an *activity* dimension, represented by adjectives such as: fast—slow, active—passive, responsive—unresponsive.

Marketing researchers have used these evaluative, potency and activity dimensions to generate lists of characteristics to describe the images and reputations of various types of organisations.

In the earlier chapters of this book, it was argued that organisations serve different functions for different groups of stakeholders. Attitude Theory and the Theory of Reasoned Action suggest that an organisation may help its stakeholders fulfil two main functions, namely:

• a *utilitarian* function where the organisation helps people to achieve desirable goals and avoid undesirable alternatives
• a *value-expressive* function where the organisation helps give positive expression to the individual's central values and self-concept.

For example, customers may only interact with a company by buying its branded products and watching its advertising. Employees on the other hand, make these products and receive a salary for their work. For both groups, the organisation fulfils a utilitarian function by providing goods and services to customers, and money for employees. In addition, the company's work practices may help employees give expression to their working life. The company's (lifestyle) advertising and high-profile brands may also help customers enhance their self-concept—the outcome of much *Coca-Cola* advertising.

Many groups also expect companies to carry out a stewardship function: of the environment by producing environmentally-friendly products, and of the countries in which they operate by contributing to their economic development. It is the role of qualitative research to uncover the range of stewardship, utilitarian and expressive functions a particular group of stakeholders expects of an organisation. Also, this type of research is ideal for uncovering the words and phrases a group of stakeholders use to characterise an organisation along the evaluative, potency and activity dimensions.

Qualitative Research—Understand Your Reputations

Qualitative research is the only research method capable of—but not assured of—uncovering the true characteristics people use to form their reputation of a company. There are many popular qualitative research methods for learning about how your stakeholders view your organisation. Three of these are:

1 management introspection
2 in-depth interviews with individual stakeholders
3 focus-group interviews with selected groups of stakeholders.

Each method has its merits. The method of choice depends on how much you already know about the characteristics which stakeholders use to define their perceptions of your organisation. (It is for this reason that market researchers sometimes call these exploratory research techniques.) The best approach is to use all three techniques. However, in practice management introspection and a few focus groups tend to be the most widely used combination.

When using in-depth interviews of stakeholders and focus groups, it is important to select carefully the people to interview.

They should be a broadly-based group so that they provide a wide range of characteristics. It is a good idea to include some people who are very familiar with the organisation and some who are not so familiar. The less familiar people often rely more than the very familiar people on country, industry and brand images to form their reputation. It can also be a good strategy to interview some people who hold a better reputation of your competitors than your company. These people are more likely to tell you what is wrong with the organisation than loyal supporters.

The validity of in-depth interviews and focus-group findings is largely dependent on the skills (psychological and marketing) of the interviewer—the moderator–analyst. The format of the interview typically starts off by asking the respondent(s) a few broad questions which are followed by more specific questions focusing on the organisations of interest. For example, the initial questions may ask people about the industry in which they think your organisation operates, and whether or not they think that organisations from various countries are better or worse at carrying out these operations. When these broad topics have been explored, questions become more focused onto competitors and then your organisation. For example, respondents can be asked about which companies operate in this industry, and what attributes make them seem to be similar and different from each other. The analogy of a funnel is a good one for thinking about the sequencing of these questions. Figure 9.2 illustrates how a typical interview might proceed.

In-depth interviews and focus groups are both designed to produce 'rich' insights into the way (different groups of) stakeholders think about organisations. (Producing generalisable findings is the province of quantitative surveys.) After a number of interviews or group sessions (often only five or six), the main company characteristics and the range of opinions about them will become clear. This is the point at which to terminate interviewing and compile the results. The moderator–analyst will describe the range of characteristics using the 'language' of the various stakeholder groups. Also, it may be possible to identify any distinct clusters of similar characteristics. Care should also be taken to search for linkages between your organisation and its country of origin, its industry, and high-profile brands.

A good moderator–analyst will also search for the benefits

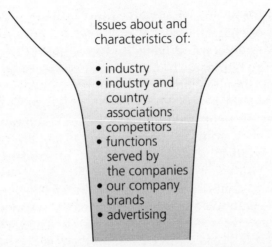

Issues about and
characteristics of:

- industry
- industry and
  country
  associations
- competitors
- functions
  served by
  the companies
- our company
- brands
- advertising

Figure 9.2   Sequencing Questions in Exploratory Interviews

that stakeholders feel are offered by the company, and the real
motivations that they use to form their reputation of the organisation. If these motivational 'triggers' are not found, then
qualitative research has not fulfilled its most valuable function.
In the terminology of Figure 1.1 (Chapter 1, p. 8), the moderator
must seek to understand how people evaluate the combination
of perceived characteristics (the corporate image) to form a
corporate reputation. A written report can then be compiled
which contains a rich description of the foundations of your
organisation's reputations, and a list of the characteristics which
are commonly used to describe them. There may also be some
attempt to prioritise these characteristics.

Quantitative Research—Describe Your Reputation

The addition of quantitative research to the prior qualitative
research can provide reliable estimates of the 'number' of stakeholders who have particular images and reputations. That
is, rather than obtaining subjective psychological inferences,
quantitative research attempts to:

- profile the relative contribution that the different characteristics
  make to the image of an organisation
- measure how important these characteristics are to each person
  (and thus how they affect the formation of their reputation)
- illustrate how (competing) companies differ on the set of
  characteristics.

The type of quantitative research described below is based on the use of highly structured questionnaires administered to representative samples of stakeholders. The aim of gathering data using this approach is to describe your organisation's reputations using the characteristics identified from the qualitative research techniques outlined above. Although thousands of these questionnaires are designed and administered each year, their design is still somewhat of an art rather than a science. We know more about the pitfalls associated with selecting respondents (sampling) and methods of administering questionnaires (by mail, phone and personal interview), than the biases caused by poorly-worded questions. When describing characteristics of organisations in questionnaires, the quantitative researcher must stay as close to the exact stakeholder language as possible. While survey research is a complex activity, it is worthwhile for managers who must interpret research findings, to develop a basic understanding of what is involved.

Let's start with sampling, that is, selecting a representative sample of people from each stakeholder group to interview. There are several ways of selecting a sample of stakeholders who are representative of the group from which they are drawn. The best (most representative) sample is one in which every stakeholder has a known and equal probability of being selected. This is known as a 'simple random sample'. Often, however, it is not a simple matter to select a random sample of particular types of stakeholders. For example, selecting a simple random sample of your employees is straightforward if the personnel department has an accurate and up-to-date list of employees. All employees' names are listed (or numbered) and then thoroughly mixed up. Using some type of lottery (random number) system, a number of names are drawn for inclusion in the sample.

Now consider trying to draw a simple random sample of customers. Do you have an accurate list of *all* your (potential) customers? The answer is probably no. Hence, any sample you draw won't be perfectly representative. The more difficult it is to get an accurate list of people from which to draw your sample, and the further you depart from using a random system for drawing the sample, the less representative it will be. Big sample sizes generally don't compensate for these problems. That is, if you are sampling an unrepresentative group of people, then it doesn't matter how many wrong people you talk to, they will still not constitute a representative group. (This is often the case for those huge phone-in television surveys.) There are a number of approaches market researchers and pollsters use to try to overcome this problem which need not be elaborated here.

Sample size is determined by how accurate your results need to be, and how confident you want to be about them. It has nothing to do with how many people are in a particular stakeholder group! This is a common misconception for many people who think that the bigger the stakeholder population, the bigger the sample needs to be. Sampling theory (which should be avoided by the faint-hearted) shows that if there are say 1000 people in the financial community who are crucial to survey, 5000 employees in the organisation, and 100 000 customers, then you would need a simple random sample of the same number of people from each group to be 95 per cent confident that your measure of the organisation's reputation was equally precise.[3] What sampling theory also shows is that there is a relationship between sample size and the degree of confidence or the level of accuracy of the survey results. For example, to double the precision of your measures of the organisation's reputation you need a simple random sample four times as large. Sample selection is probably the most technically difficult aspect of survey research. Hence, it is wise to seek professional help from a market research company.

The same advice is relevant for questionnaire design, and selecting the mode of administering the questionnaires. When surveying hundreds of stakeholders, preprinted questionnaires sent through the mail and telephone surveys are approaches commonly used by market research firms. Face-to-face interviews, which provide better quality data, are generally too expensive for most organisations. Often, combinations of these methods have proved to be successful in gaining respondent cooperation. For example, a good procedure is a phone call to potential respondents asking them to participate in the study (and sometimes offering a gift or monetary inducement), followed by a questionnaire sent by post, followed by a reminder letter or phone call. Each method, or combination of methods, has its advantages and disadvantages for gaining access to the selected sample of stakeholders, and getting them to provide an unbiased opinion about your organisation. Which method(s) to choose should be guided by an experienced researcher.

The mode of questioning and the topics covered in the questionnaires, play an important part in determining the response rate to a survey. It is a common observation that response rates overall are falling. While there are numerous reasons for this, one of the most common is the simple fact that most surveys are boring and uninteresting to many people! This pessimism notwithstanding, the question remains as to what is a reasonable response rate to expect? If your survey is administered to long-haul air travellers at 30 000 feet above sea level halfway between Sydney and Singapore, you would expect close to a 100 per cent response rate if passengers are asked to complete it at a sensible time during the flight. On the other hand, if a telephone survey is administered during mealtimes in a household, or late on a Friday afternoon to office workers, then you might be lucky to get a 10 per cent response rate. As a general rule of thumb, for the type of research discussed in this chapter, a response rate of less than 50 per cent would cause some concern. In any case, your research firm should report the response rate achieved, and some type of analysis of the reasons for nonresponse. You can then estimate how biased your respondents are likely to be.

The final issue to consider in this section is wording of the questions. It takes considerable skill and experience to compose an interesting questionnaire (from the respondent's point of view) which gathers the type of data that can be analysed to produce ratings of your organisation's reputation as it compares with that of other organisations. Most advice about designing questions comes in the form of admonitions: 'Don't ask leading questions' and 'Don't ask ambiguous questions'. This advice is easy to give, but more difficult to follow—even for the professionals. So what happens in practice is that each questionnaire is pretested with a focus group or a small sample of stakeholders before it is administered to the larger sample. This pretesting is crucial to ensure that respondents understand the questions (and think that they are sensible), and that their responses show enough variation to facilitate subsequent statistical analysis.

In general, the simpler a rating scale question is for a person to answer (for example, a 'yes' or 'no' answer versus 'rank order the following seven items'), the more sophisticated the statistical data analysis will need to be to extract the maximum amount of information from the data gathered. Again the researcher must make tradeoffs, and these can have a significant impact on the quality of the data collected, and the types of analysis which can be conducted. In order to illustrate the nature of some of these tradeoffs, it is useful to briefly outline four of the major issues which a researcher must consider when designing a questionnaire:

1 What amount of information is to be sought? (How many organisations and how many stakeholder groups are to be surveyed?) What types of information will be collected? (Awareness, characteristics of the organisation, linkages between the organisation and its country-of-origin and/or high-profile brands, etc.)

2 How will data be collected? (Via the phone, personal interview, mail. This will be contingent on how much data needs to be collected, and the most convenient time and place to interview respondents. For example, it is difficult to keep people answering questions on the phone for more than ten minutes.)

3 How will the individual questions be phrased? (Will open-ended questions be used, or multichotomous questions, or are rating scales preferred; in what sequence will the questions be asked. The method of data collection in 2, and the amount of data needed in 1 will both affect these choices.)

4 How will the data be analysed and reported to management? (If sophisticated statistical procedures are to be used, then this will generally require the use of some type of rating scale question format. Alternatively, if managers want verbatim comments about the organisation's reputations, then open-ended questions will be necessary.)

Figure 9.3 summarises the overall research methodology outlined above. You start with an analysis of past research and management experience, and then proceed with exploratory research to gain a rich understanding of the characteristics which stakeholders use to form their reputations about your organisation. You then use descriptive research to produce robust measures of these reputations which reflect the perceptions of each stakeholder group. The figure shows two feedback loops. The first (solid) loop suggests that a periodic monitoring of these reputations be conducted (say every six months—or more often during a crisis). The second (dashed) loop indicates that further qualitative research may sometimes be needed to help clarify unexpected or ambiguous survey findings. The figure also provides an outline for the example described in the next section.

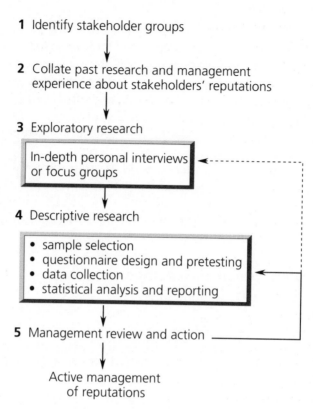

Figure 9.3 How to Measure Your Organisation's Reputations

Measuring the Reputations of Some of Australia's Biggest Organisations

The following example is based on an actual study conducted by a market research firm. It has been selected because country-of-origin and brand issues were not relevant (to simplify the presentation), and to illustrate some of the issues discussed above. I have also disguised some of the findings to protect the innocent and the guilty. This example is not presented as the one and only, nor as the best way to conduct this type of research. It is used to illustrate some novel aspects of reputation research, which produce more insightful results than many commercial studies such as the Image Power research referred to in Chapter 7. However, this study has two shortcomings—the major one being that it measures only corporate image and not corporate reputation.

Background

The research was undertaken in the late 1980s to track the effects of a corporate identity change on the perceptions of various groups of current and potential customers. The corporate identity program incorporated a new logo and a new advertising campaign. One part of the research study focused on the corporate images of some of Australia's biggest organisations. Prior to the launch of the new identity, the company commissioned a benchmark study to measure what customers thought of the organisation and other organisations of similar size and standing in the community. Six months after the launch of the new identity campaign, a second measurement of these organisations' images was conducted.

Research Design and Methods

A total of 2000 telephone interviews were conducted in the five mainland state capital cities. Respondents were selected using what is known as systematic random sampling, where every 'nth' name from the telephone directory was contacted. The person over eighteen who last had a birthday was selected for interview, and two callbacks were used to minimise sample bias. The response rate was 65 per cent, and the demographic profile of the 2000 respondents closely matched that derived from census data published by the *Australian Bureau of Statistics*.

Of the 2000 total interviews, 300 responses were received from business users of the sponsoring company's products and services. Each of these respondents evaluated up to six organisations, which always included the sponsoring company, on a list of eighteen characteristics such as: a company 'whose products and services are expensive', 'that is technology-driven', 'well managed', 'an industry leader'. Each respondent was asked whether or not each characteristic described the organisation. A 'yes' or 'no' response was all that was required, and respondents only evaluated organisations they were aware of. (For a respondent who evaluated all six organisations, this would require a big effort.) For this sample of 300, we could be 95 per cent confident that the overall percentage of yes/no ratings would be accurate to + or – 6 per cent.

The eighteen characteristics on which each organisation was evaluated were derived from the market research company's past research experience. This research company 'introspection' was supplemented with a series of in-depth personal interviews with the sponsoring company's managers. (In effect, the questionnaire was pretested using previous clients' research studies, and the in-depth interviews were used as an 'insurance policy' so that no important organisational characteristics were omitted. This is not uncommon practice.)

Findings

Table 9.1 shows the percentages of business respondents who said that each characteristic described the sponsoring company before and after the new identity campaign. (These are two different samples of approximately 300 people.) Percentages in boxes are statistically significantly different at the 95 per cent level of confidence. We see that for 10 out of 18 characteristics (or 56 per cent), the two groups had different evaluations. In most cases, the direction of change is in a favourable direction. One exception is that after the advertising campaign, businesspeople thought that the company's products and services were more expensive! (Are Australian businesspeople really this astute?)

The research firm presented another interesting finding from this survey—the number of characteristics used by each person to describe the company. These are shown at the base of Table 9.1. They indicate that six months after the identity campaign, businesspeople were using three more (of these eighteen) characteristics to describe the company. In effect, the new logo and the new advertising campaign had stimulated businesspeople to think about the company using twelve rather than nine characteristics. (For this conclusion to hold, it is necessary to assume that there was no significant change in the company's services, and that publicity or some other factor did not change people's perceptions.) This type of analysis leads naturally to the question about which of these characteristics discriminate between this company and other major Australian organisations.

Figure 9.4 shows a perceptual map which helps answer this question. These maps show the set of characteristics (the arrows) which discriminate among eight of the organisations evaluated by respondents. The closer two organisations are to each other, the more similar they are perceived to be on the set of characteristics evaluated. For example, Qantas (Australia's international airline) and Esso (an oil company) are the two most similar organisations, and Australia Post and IBM, the least similar. If

Table 9.1

Pre/Post Advertising Changes in Evaluations

% Business people who agree that company is:

Characteristic	Pre-campaign	Post-campaign
1 large	54	62
2 highly profitable	47	51
3 wide range of products/services	49	55
4 products/services are expensive	35	44
5 stable, dependable	58	58
6 technology-driven	71	77
7 truly international	57	64
8 interested in customer needs	49	60
9 a necessary part of Australian life	60	66
10 customer-oriented	42	49
11 well-managed/progressive	37	49
12 at the forefront of technological change	58	71
13 aggressively seeks new business	33	48
14 an industry leader with innovative products	34	41
15 market-driven	33	47
16 important for Australia	68	68
17 efficient in comparison with Australian companies	35	34
18 efficient in comparison with overseas competitors	36	40
Average number of characteristics used by each person to describe the company	9	12

two organisations lie at 90 degrees to each other (for example, *BHP* and the *Commonwealth Bank*), they are regarded as not being in any way similar or dissimilar to each other on the characteristics used to derive the perceptual map. Longer arrows indicate more powerful discriminating ability of the characteristics. In effect, these arrows are statistically derived measures of the relative importance of each characteristic. The vertical and horizontal axes show that 41 per cent of the variance in respondents' evaluations occurs in a North–South direction, while 21 per cent occurs in the East–West direction. (The remaining 38 per cent is not explained by this map.)

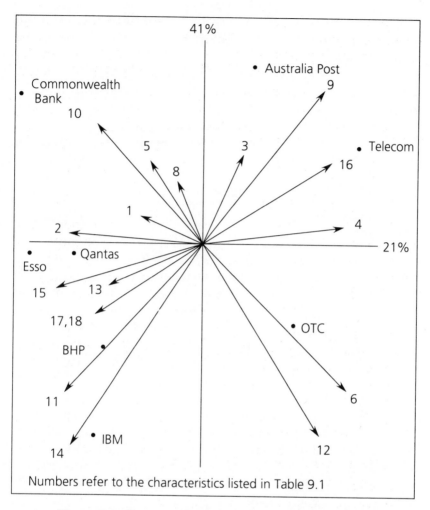

Numbers refer to the characteristics listed in Table 9.1

Figure 9.4   Perceptual Map of Australian Organisations

Perceptual maps are a powerful way to summarise a vast amount of data once you learn how to interpret them. Some managers find that a less mentally taxing way to review this type of data is to calculate the average level of response to each characteristic for each organisation, and then to use these averages to rank order each organisation beside each characteristic. For example, we would use each organisation's average pre- or post-campaign score to produce a row of eight organisations beside each characteristic ordered from lowest score to highest score. The rank ordered position then illustrates which organisations are perceived as better or worse on each characteristic.[5]

Having briefly reviewed an actual case study, it is useful to make some comments about the strengths and weaknesses of the approach described. The perspective taken is that of a manager rather than a professional market researcher. You need to know what types of research results are useful so that you can brief researchers to supply useable information. It is not uncommon for managers to read research findings which are interesting, but which give few clues about how to use them to manage the organisation's reputations.

Critically Evaluating the Findings

The sampling and data collection procedures described above are typical of this type of commercial research. The more time and money you can afford, normally the better your sampling and data collection will be. The main shortcomings of (Australian) commercial research tend not to be in the areas of sampling and questionnaire administration, but rather in the areas of question design and data analysis. The main reason for this is that there is no 'theory' of reputation formation and use (like the one outlined in Chapter 1) which guides the development of measures and the statistical analysis of the data collected.

Table 9.1 listed eighteen characteristics which were used to describe the eight organisations profiled in Figure 9.4. It is informative to compare them (in hindsight) against the criteria developed in Chapter 1 and the previous sections of this chapter. Chapter 1 identified four major factors (in addition to country, industry and brand factors which are not relevant in this case study) which combine to help stakeholders form their images and reputations of an organisation. These were Vision, Formal Policies (which includes strategy), Organisational Culture, and Marketing Communications and Product/Service offerings. Content analysing the characteristics in Table 9.1 indicates that there are no characteristics which focus on vision, five focus on strategy (numbers 6, 7, 12, 13, 15), three on organisational culture (numbers 8, 10, 11), and two on products/services (numbers 3, 4). Of the additional characteristics, six focus on what can be called 'outcomes' (numbers 1, 2, 5, 14, 17, 18), and two on the organisation's social role (numbers 9, 16). In summary, there is an imbalance of characteristics across the major determinants of image formation.

If we now turn our focus to the three dimensions which people use to ascribe meaning to organisations, content analysis again shows an imbalance across the characteristics. For example, there are 13 evaluative characteristics (numbers 3, 4, 6, 7, 8, 9, 10, 11, 14, 15, 16, 17, 18), two potency characteristics (numbers 1, 2), and three activity characteristics (numbers 5, 12, 13). A similar outcome occurs when the characteristics are related to the three primary functions the organisation can fulfil for a stakeholder. The utilitarian function is represented by six characteristics (numbers 3, 4, 8, 10, 14, 15), the stewardship function by two (numbers 9, 16), and the value-expressive function by none.

These theoretical imbalances across the descriptive characteristics signal that important aspects of the organisation's images may have gone unmeasured. If the initial in-depth interviews showed that these aspects were unimportant, then the type of imbalance revealed above may be of little concern. However, in this case study, only internal company managers were surveyed to help generate the list of characteristics. My guess is that a more balanced set of characteristics could have been developed had the researchers used the criteria outlined above, and conducted some focus groups with external stakeholders.

The major shortcoming of this research, however, is that an important piece of information was not measured. The missing information relates to the respondents' ratings of how important each characteristic was to their overall evaluation of the organisation. In effect, the research methodology measured how each organisation performed across a set of characteristics, but not how important these were to respondents. According to the definitions outlined in Chapter 1 (Figure 1.1), this study measured corporate image rather than corporate reputation. It is the importance of a particular characteristic which reflects a person's values and which creates the linkage between image and reputation.

Had this piece of information been gathered, then an importance–performance matrix like the one shown in Figure 9.5 could have been constructed. Without importance measures, all a manager can do is use Figure 9.4 to find out which characteristics need to be changed to move the company's overall image towards, or away from, one of the other organisations. However, there is no information available to suggest which of these organisations the respondents considered to have the best reputation. In other words, Figure 9.4 doesn't show the reader a target at which to aim.

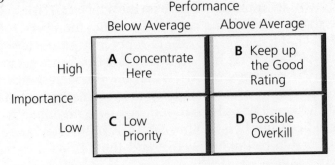

Figure 9.5   Importance–Performance Matrix

Source: Martilla, J. & James, J., 'Importance–performance analysis', *Journal of Marketing*, January, 1977 pp. 77–9.

Measuring the importance of the characteristics which describe organisations is a relatively straightforward task. It can be done directly in the questionnaire by asking respondents to rate the importance of each characteristic on a scale (for example, How important to you is it that this company be involved in international operations? On a scale of 1 to 7 with No Importance at 1 and Extremely Important at 7). Alternatively, importance can be derived from the image ratings of the characteristics using different statistical techniques. (One needs to exercise care here, because different statistical procedures make a different set of assumptions to derive a set of importance weights for the characteristics.) Regardless of the technique chosen, however, measuring the reputation of your organisation held by a group of stakeholders requires some measure of importance.

The findings from this case study, as illustrated in Figure 9.4, fail what I call the 'So What' test. That is, they are interesting as a measure of this group of stakeholders' perceptions, but they do not present a clear guide to managers concerning what they should do to improve or reposition their company in the minds of stakeholders. For example, assume you are the CEO of the *Commonwealth Bank*. What would you do to improve the image and reputation of the bank? One option is to make improvements on the characteristics in the bottom left quadrant of Figure 9.4, that is, become more efficient, better managed, more innovative, aggressive, and market driven. You would not have the resources to do all of these, so which factor are you going to change first? It isn't obvious without more information. It does become easier, however, if you have the information to plot each characteristic on an Importance–Performance matrix such as illustrated in Figure 9.5.

Conclusion

This chapter integrates the theoretical framework outlined in Chapter 1 with the types of research necessary to measure your organisation's images and reputations. When these research techniques are linked in the fashion suggested in Figure 9.3, it is possible to derive a good measure of a stakeholder group's reputation of your organisation. If measures of both the import- ance *and* performance of a set of descriptive characteristics are obtained, then you can see which factors are crucial to manage and change your organisation's reputations.

The case study outlined in the previous section is typical of many commercial studies of corporate image. It is presented precisely for this reason. It is also used to demonstrate that it only requires a little bit more work to upgrade the potential contribution that such research can make to an understanding of corporate reputations.

The crucial points to consider when measuring reputations are:

- use a professional market research firm
- use exploratory research and the theoretical guidelines out- lined in this chapter to develop a broad list of descriptive characteristics of your organisation
- measure both the importance and performance of each characteristic
- for external stakeholder groups, measure the reputations of a number of relevant organisations (to provide an absolute and a relative measure of the organisation's reputations).

Each stakeholder group will use a different set of character- istics to evaluate your organisation. Hence typically, a number of research studies are needed to fully profile the images and reputations held by all stakeholders. To get the full value from these studies, it is advisable to use a small core set of descriptive characteristics in each study. These characteristics can then be used to provide a partial comparison of the reputations of the various groups.

End Notes

1   C. Osgood, G. Suci & P. Tannenbaum, *The Measurement of Meaning*, University of Illinois Press, Urbana, Ill., 1957.

2   L.W. Rodger, *Statistics for Marketing*, McGraw-Hill, London, 1984. Also, most market research books will cover these topics, for example, G.A. Churchill, *Marketing Research*, Dryden Press, Hinsdale, Ill., 1990.

3   The statistical purist will note that I have assumed that the variance of each group's responses to the measurement scales is the same when making this statement.

4   G.R. Dowling, 'Measuring corporate images', *Journal of Business Research*, vol. 17, no. 1, 1988, pp. 27–34.

5   While this type of simple tabulation looks easier to interpret, it is easy to draw incorrect inferences from such data. For example, unless the data are weighted in some way to indicate the relative importance of the characteristics, a company may appear to 'lead' its competitors on a number of characteristics—but these may be the less important ones.

CHAPTER 10

Managing and Changing Corporate Images: It Can Be Done

We have now reached the moment of truth. Is it possible to actively manage the information stakeholders use to form their images and reputations of your organisation? As the title of this chapter suggests, the short answer is yes. The title also suggests that you try to change the images people hold of your organisation, not their reputations. The reason for this is that it is unlikely you can change people's basic values. (Recall the definitions of image and reputation in Figure 1.1 which said that an individual's reputation of your organisation is how he/she values his/her image of it.) Hence, in this chapter the focus is more on corporate image than corporate reputation.

This chapter outlines some alternative approaches to managing and changing your organisation's desired image. Each approach will work, and the choice of one depends on two factors. First, how much information is currently available about your organisation's current images, and second, how decisions regarding change are usually implemented within your organisation.

Chapter 2 proposed that the best way to analyse your

organisation's activities is from the stakeholders' point of view, that is, what needs does your organisation help its stakeholders fulfil. Chapter 6 built on this framework by examining how organisations communicate that they can fulfil stakeholders' needs. In essence, this discussion focused on communicating what we call your organisation's 'value proposition'.

Value propositions are what organisations offer to their stakeholders. For example, in the 1960s and 1970s *IBM*'s value proposition for its mainframe computers was 'superior reliability of your data processing system'. In contrast, one of the key factors for the *Apple* computer company's success was that it designed a computer for individuals who wanted the value proposition: 'easier access to applications software', that is, a friendly personal computer. These people were prepared to trade off computer speed, processing power, and price to achieve this. This 'personal computer' position was so successful that it established a completely new category of computers—'personal' as opposed to 'small' computers. It was also developed by Apple into one which focused on enhancing the user's productivity, so that by the early 1990s, *Apple* PCs were advertised using the tag-line: 'The power to be your best'.

Value propositions differentiate one organisation from another, and play an important role in shaping stakeholder images and reputations. An outdated value proposition, strongly held by customers, can be the prime stimulus for an organisation to change its advertising and/or identity symbols. For example, in the late 1960s *Continental Airlines* was the USA's fifth largest airline. It was well regarded by both customers and employees for its efforts to live up to its advertising slogan: 'the proud bird with the golden tail'. After deregulation of the US airline industry, *Continental* was acquired by Frank Lorenzo and got into financial difficulties. It also developed an image as a no-frills airline for the masses. By 1990 however, *Continental* was offering better service than its no-frills image implied, and management wanted to move the airline's image upmarket. In came the identity consultants (*Lippincott & Margulies*) who set out to realign traveller perceptions with the airline's new customer service-based strengths.[1]

The *Continental Airlines* example could imply that using an outside consultant to help change an organisation's desired image is common practice. It is for large corporations which have (substantial) funds available. Even in this case, however, the executive responsible for managing his/her organisation's desired image should think about all the options available before bringing in a full-service consultant.

The next section briefly outlines four approaches that the CEO can·adopt to build a desired image. Following this, a three-step approach to choosing among alternative desired images is outlined. The topic of how to position the organisation against its competitors is then discussed. The chapter concludes with some suggestions about how CEOs can lead the required change in their organisations.

Building a Desired Image

The strategic management literature has identified a variety of approaches to implementing strategy.[2] Four of these represent possible candidates for CEOs to use to integrate their organisation's internal activities, and to coordinate these with its external communications to project a desired image. These 'Pathfinder', 'Commander', 'Change', and 'Vision' models are summarised in Table 10.1. The selection of a particular approach will be contingent on the history and size of the organisation, and the personal decision-making style of the CEO. It should be no surprise to discover that my favourite approach is based on the vision model. (Recall Figure 1.2 in Chapter 1.)

The Pathfinder Model

Pathfinders in business are often entrepreneurs, company founders, or company reorganisers. Some (in)famous examples are Alan Bond of the old *Bond Brewing* and America's Cup fame; Bill Gates who co-founded *Microsoft*; Steve Jobs, one of the founders of the *Apple Computer* company; Anita Roddick, founder of the *Body Shop*; Maurice and Charles Saatchi, *Saatchi & Saatchi* advertising; Jan Carlson, who rejuvenated *SAS Airlines*; Akio Morita, co-founder of *Sony*; and Thomas Watson, founder of *IBM*. The emotion, conviction and public profile of these leaders helped ensure that employees, customers, other stakeholders, and the general public knew where the company wanted to go, and what it stood for. The role of pathfinder CEOs is to convince other people that their dream is worthwhile following.

Table 10.1

Approaches to Building a Desired Corporate Image

Model	CEO's Question	CEO's Role
1 Pathfinder	'How do I create an organisation to fulfil my dreams?'	Leader
2 Commander	'How do I create the optimum image?'	Rational Analyst
3 Change	'I have a different image in mind, how do I implement it?'	Architect
4 Vision	a 'How do I get the top management team to commit to a shared vision and then a desired corporate image?'	Coordinator
	b 'How do I involve the whole organisation in implementation?'	Mentor

Adapted from: Bourgeois, J. & Brodwin, D. 1984, 'Strategic implementation: five approaches to an elusive phenomenon', *Strategic Management Journal*, vol. 5, pp. 241–64.

The Commander Model

The commander model defines the role of the CEO as a rational analyst. Extensive analysis of the environment, market conditions, and competitors is undertaken before any action is taken to change the desired image of the organisation. Environmental scanning and market research provide information which is used as input into some type of formal decision procedure to guide the choice of the projected ideal image. Robert S. McNamara (Harvard MBA, *Ford Motor Company* senior executive, one-time Secretary of the US Department of Defense) is a person who had a personal reputation for being the archetype rational analyst. He could reportedly absorb and process vast amounts of information about the most rational course of action to follow. Harold Geneen of International Telephone and Telegraph Corporation (*ITT*) was another domineering commander. His amazingly accurate memory, speed reading ability, and capacity to absorb large amounts of information, allowed him to intellectually dominate most of his subordinates. During his era he used these skills to mould *ITT* into one of the world's largest companies.[3]

The Change Model

This model is an extension of the commander model. Here the CEO is an architect who uses the resources and control mechanisms of the organisation to establish a taskforce to examine its current images and to recommend a course of action for change. These types of CEOs, like the rational analyst commanders, imbed the corporate image building program within the formal strategic planning process. Here, the inherent control mechanisms which are built into the organisation's planning cycle ensure that budgets are allocated, timeframes set, and implementation procedures employed. Lee Iacocca of *Chrysler Corporation*, Lord King of *British Airways*, James Strong of *Australian Airlines*, and John Scully of *Apple Computer* have been stereotyped as architects of corporate image change.

The Vision Model

The vision model is a shared decision making version of the pathfinder model. The first stage of the image-building process occurs when the CEO brings together a group of top executives to design a vision for the organisation. The vision statement summarises the purpose and basic values of the organisation. As such, it guides the creation of value for both employees and customers. A good vision statement should also ensure that the organisation fulfils the needs of most other types of stakeholders. Chapter 3 provided an extensive overview of the contents and role of a vision statement. As a catalyst for building an organisation's desired reputation, the vision statement must be 'sold' throughout the organisation by the CEO.

The four approaches outlined above and summarised in Table 10.1, differ mainly in how CEOs use the organisation's culture and formal procedures to design a desired image, and how they acquire the commitment of managers and employees. The demarcation lines between these four approaches are often blurred. In most cases, CEOs will adopt a hybrid approach to image design and management. As illustrated later in this chapter, the particular blend of pathfinder, commander, change, and vision depends on the resources the CEO can call on to obtain the required information to make a quality decision. This, however, begs the question of what is a quality decision regarding the design of a desired image?

Choosing a Desired Image

Chapter 9 provided an important part of the framework to answer the question of what is a 'quality desired image'. It outlined how to measure what stakeholders currently think of your organisation, and how these perceptions differ from those of other organisations. Hence, your organisation's desired image should a) include the set of desired characteristics for an organisation operating in your country and your industry, and b) differentiate your organisation from other similar organisations on one or more characteristics important to stakeholders.

The characteristics which define an organisation as a good member of a country and industry are easy to discover. They will be based on the value and belief systems of the general community about the way organisations should operate. Market and social research firms regularly measure values such as the perceived stability, dependability, trustworthiness, reliability and environmental concern of organisations. For example, stakeholders generally require that banks be reliable and trustworthy. Banks should not make too many mistakes with other people's money, and they have to be trusted.

The communication of one, or a cluster of related characteristics is what differentiates one organisation from another. This communication can also add value to the relationship that stakeholders have with the organisation. These characteristics define the strategic position, or desired image of the organisation, relative to its competitors. George Day, a noted corporate strategy thinker, argues that the organisation's positioning theme is the critical link in the chain of activities needed to gain a competitive advantage.[4] His simple three-link chain is:

1 choose a generic strategy as outlined in Chapter 4

2 favourably distinguish the business from competitors

3 devise a marketing strategy to support the positioning theme.

Day's approach to searching for a (new) positioning theme around which strategy can be hinged is a three-step process:

Step 1 Identify alternative positioning themes.

Step 2 Screen each alternative according to whether it is

    a valuable to customers (and other external stakeholders)

    b feasible given the organisation's distinctive competencies and customer perceptions of what it is capable of achieving

    c competitive—superior or unique relative to competitors, and difficult for them to match or exceed

    d helps meet long-term performance objectives.

Step 3 Choose the position that best meets the criteria in Step 2, and which generates the most enthusiasm and commitment within the organisation.

The key step in this process which can have a significant impact on the quality of the desired image adopted, is not Step 2, but rather Step 1. Researchers studying the quality of decision making have discovered that better decisions result from the choice among a number of good alternatives, rather than assessing the strengths and weaknesses of just one or two alternatives.[5] The best decision-making approach is to generate four or five desirable image positions which CEOs and their top management teams can evaluate. The decision then becomes which one of these to choose using the criteria outlined in Step 2. Before implementing the chosen position, the organisation should commission research to measure customer, and other stakeholder reactions to this theme.

While many CEOs ignore the issue of competitive positioning, it is a problem with which their brand managers and advertising agencies continually grapple for the company's brands and new product introductions. It is also at the brand level that most research has been conducted to understand how consumers react to different positioning strategies. At the corporate (or country) level there are fewer guidelines readily available. Hence, the next section borrows from the highly competitive world of advertising and brand management to present some ideas about positioning strategies appropriate for organisations.

Positioning the Organisation in Stakeholders' Minds

Having emphasised the need to develop a variety of alternative positioning themes, we now need to consider what alternatives are available. These will form the building blocks for your organisation's desired image. While twenty or more alternatives can be identified, only a handful will be feasible given the screening criteria outlined in Step 2 above. These positioning alternatives may, or may not, be grounded in objective reality. It is what stakeholders come to believe about an organisation that is important. This was the prime reason *Continental Airlines* attempted to change the perceptions of its customers.

Positioning Guidelines

When choosing a desired position, you need to answer two basic questions.

1 How should the organisation be positioned with regard to the industry?
2 Should your position be defined by the characteristics of the organisation or by its relationship to your stakeholders?

Answering the first question should precede answering the second. In the 1994 edition of his new advertising text, my colleague John Rossiter offers the following advice regarding Question 1.

With regard to its industry, a company has two options. Either adopt a 'central' (or 'prototypic member') position or a differentiated position. Companies which should choose a central position are those which are:

a the successful pioneer in the industry, eg., *Cray* in super-computers, *IBM* in mainframes, *Apple* in personal computers, and *Compaq* in portable computers, or
b the market leader in the industry, eg., *Intel* in computer chips, *Microsoft* in personal computer software, or
c pursuing a 'me-too' strategy to emulate the successful pioneer and/or the market leader, eg., the '*IBM* clone' personal computer companies.

In all other cases, companies should choose a differentiated position.

Before outlining some differentiation options, a couple of points about these three 'rules' need to be made. First, the 'me-too' imitator strategy/position will generally only work if the company/product performance is easy to assess by the user, and the price is significantly lower. That is, the company is offering better (objective) value.

The second point refers to what I call the 'Club' position. In some industries, the big companies all seem to be pursuing a similar strategy. One of these organisations is the market leader, and one or two of them have pioneered many developments in the industry. Customers typically perceive that these companies are quite similar to each other. Under these circumstances, this group of big organisations often become known as the 'Big 3' or the 'Big 6' or whatever the number is. For example, we have the Big 6 accounting firms, the Big 3 US auto manufacturers, and the Big 4 Australian retail banks. Being a member of the Big Club is often (more) important to managers and employees (than customers).

The three 'rules' outlined above imply that most organisations should try to differentiate themselves from other industry participants. As Question 2 above suggests, this can be done in two broad ways:

- by defining the organisation in terms of one or two of its principal characteristics
- by linking the organisation directly to its stakeholders.

The second strategy can be operationalised by linking the organisation to a particular group of stakeholders (usually a specific market segment) or a customer benefit. For example, *SAS Airlines* links itself to business travellers with its advertising tag-line: 'The business airline of Europe', while *Caterpillar* offers a valuable benefit to some of its customers: '24 hour parts and service anywhere in the world'. The next section outlines some alternative differentiating themes.

Differentiating Positioning Themes

Table 10.2 lists seven major themes an organisation can use to differentiate itself from its competitors.[7] Within each of these major themes are a number of alternative positions. In total, Table 10.2 lists more than twenty generic positioning strategies. Most of the alternatives have a straightforward interpretation.

Table 10.2

Alternative Positioning Themes

Organisational Attributes
- size (large or small)
- technology leadership (first to develop new technology)
- innovation (new product leadership)
- people (best employees)
- flexibility (adaptable to customer requests)

Customer/Stakeholder Benefits
- rational appeals (based on organisational attributes)
- psychological appeals (a consequence of using or being associated with the organisation)
- environment-oriented
- community-oriented

Price
- bargain (lowest price)
- value (best price/performance)
- prestige (high price–high quality)

Competitors
- market leadership (biggest market share)
- challenger (firms which aspire to become the market leader)
- follower (firms which imitate the strategies of leaders or challengers)
- niche marketer (firms which serve parts of the market where they avoid clashes with the major firms)
- exclusive club (the Top 3, the Big 6, etc.)

Use/Application
- full or restricted range of products/services
- level of relationship/commitment to customer

Customer/Stakeholder Group
- heavy, medium, light user
- particular industry sectors
- particular sized customers

Geographic
- regional versus global scope

For example, if an organisation is big, and being big is valued by stakeholders, then this is an easy position to communicate. During the 1980s, the Australian steel and resource company *BHP*, called itself 'The Big Australian'. Its management, employees, and shareholders liked being associated with Australia's biggest company. Also, the company's public relations group thought that reminding the politicians and public servants that *BHP* was a big contributor to the country's economy was a good idea. For customers of the company's steel products however, being reminded that *BHP* was the Big Australian was not highly valued. It just reminded them of the power the company used when allocating its steel production to subservient customers.[8]

Two of the major positioning themes in Table 10.2 need some explanation. The first is labelled 'Customer/Stakeholder Benefits'. Here, the effectiveness of the two options—rational and psychological appeals—has been researched. Rational appeals to stakeholders will usually be based on an easily identifiable attribute of the organisation such as market leadership, the size of the organisation and its product range. These attributes provide easily recognised 'rational' benefits to stakeholders. For example, a big accounting firm means that there will be more expertise available to handle a customer's business. This benefit follows logically from the fact that big accounting firms have more qualified accountants. Psychological appeals on the other hand, are inferred by the stakeholder. For example, customers using a big accounting firm may think that the partner handling their business is well-trained and successful. This in turn may help customers reduce their level of perceived risk.

For consumer products, research indicates that rational appeals are better than psychological appeals, *but* a combination of one rational and one psychological appeal was the best.[9] The message is clear; when stakeholders can personally identify with a benefit the organisation offers to them, then this is likely to be a better basis for a positioning strategy than relying solely on hard-nosed rational claims. Recall the discussion in Chapter 6 about those awful corporate advertisements—the ones with the weighty, sombre tone and the abstract images. This is another reason they are so ineffective. Most of these don't even offer a rational appeal, let alone invite the reader to become emotionally involved with the company's products and/or services!

The second positioning theme needing further elaboration is that labelled 'Competitors'. Whether a company is a market leader, challenger, follower, or a niche marketer (a company serving a narrow market segment) will inhibit its ability to select some of the other positioning options. For example, 'follower' companies generally can't lay claim to either the technology leadership or product innovation positions. If they could, then why are they a market follower rather than the market leader or a company challenging for the leadership position? As the previous section noted, what a follower could credibly claim is an 'imitative' position, and/or a 'bargain' or 'value pricing' position—like all those companies which made *IBM clone* personal computers. Market leaders and challengers will also have more positioning options open to them than followers and nichers. This follows simply from the fact that they have more credibility because they are already successful.

It is important to use research to find out what stakeholders think are the attributes which attach to your organisation's size and market standing, and to your competitors. Good positioning strategies start with what stakeholders already believe. The idea is to build on your organisation's perceived strengths, rather than argue against a perceived weakness. More good advice from those masters of strategic positioning, Al Ries and Jack Trout, is not to choose a position based on your aspirations.[10] The famous *Avis* position of 'We're number 2—We try harder' is much better than *Avis* saying that they want to displace *Hertz* and become number 1 in car rentals. It is a believable proposition for customers that the market challenger will offer better service in order to become the market leader. This is also an example of how a potential weakness (being number 2) can be transformed into a strength by insightful market research and creative thinking on the part of the advertising agency.

There are two common positioning themes which are difficult to establish. The first is the people theme. Many organisations argue in their corporate advertising that they have the best people, or offer the best people-based customer service. There are a couple of problems with such a claim. One is that many people believe that only the market leader has the credibility to claim this position. That is, the best companies attract the best people to work for them. If you are not the market leader, and you try to position the organisation as having the best employees, then you will need to provide a credible explanation of why your people are better than those who work for the leader. It can be done, but it is often difficult.

A second problem with using your employees to position the organisation is shown in many airline television advertisements. In the USA and Australia, it is not uncommon to see a group of airline employees lined up in front of a plane smiling and singing about how they are here to serve customers. The advertisements typically end with a tag-line such as 'we're here to serve you' or 'the way we do the things we do'. I once saw an account executive from the giant advertising agency *Saatchi & Saatchi* show two such television advertisements for US airlines with the soundtracks reversed. The problem was that the audience didn't realise the words of the singing employees belonged to the other airline commercial! The real problem, however, with employees in corporate advertisements saying that they want to provide excellent service is that customers take this as given—or why would they be employed? Many times the true target audience for these types of advertisements is the employees themselves. The advertisements are trying to tell employees what standards of service to provide by using the implied threat of telling customers what to expect at the same time.

The second positioning theme which is hard to use successfully is a diversification theme. The giant *Shell* and *Westinghouse* corporations have run corporate advertisements which show the range of industries in which they are involved. One Westinghouse advertisement ended with the tag-line: 'The Best-Known Unknown Company in America'. This advertisement publicly admits the failure of its communication strategy! Ries and Trout (and common sense) argue that this type of conglomerate diversification and positioning are opposite ideas. It is difficult for people to form an image and/or a reputation of an organisation that tries to be all things to all people. Even politicians are (slowly) coming to realise that they have to take a stand on some issues.

Repositioning the Organisation

Sometimes organisations change and sometimes change is forced on an organisation by competitors or new market needs. When this happens, two options are available. One is to change the organisation and try to reposition it in stakeholders' minds. The other is to create, or buy a new organisation that has a better fit with the new market. Both options can be effective, and the choice of option usually depends on whether there is a (loyal) group of customers who value the products and services of the 'old' organisation.

When an organisation tries to reposition itself, it usually does so by changing its products/service and/or its name. For example, *Kentucky Fried Chicken* changed its name to *KFC* to move away from the unhealthy associations of 'fried' food. The *Amatil* cigarette company got out of cigarettes and into soft drinks and snack foods, and changed its name to *Coca-Cola Amatil*. *Minnesota Mining and Manufacturing* changed its name to *3M* to break the position described by its name. When the computer companies *Burroughs* and *Sperry* merged they changed their name to *UNISYS*, and used the tag-line 'The Power of 2'.

Charles and Maurice Saatchi used the acquisition strategy to expand their business empire and offer integrated advertising, consulting, design, marketing and promotion services to their clients. (They also acquired a number of independent advertising agencies to increase their coverage of the advertising market.) The accounting firm *Arthur Andersen* used a similar strategy to the Saatchi brothers. It expanded into management consulting by forming the (semi-independent) company *Andersen Consulting*.

A good example of what not to do when repositioning an organisation is illustrated by the giant oil company *BP*.[11] In 1989, *BP* ended one of Australia's longest-running corporate advertising success stories: 'The Quiet Achiever' campaign. This campaign drew an analogy between the Australian characteristic of quiet achievement and *BP*'s hidden technological achievements and low-profile customer service. The campaign was started in 1981, and by 1988 the company claimed that the advertising had positioned *BP* as the most responsible oil company in Australia.[12] In the UK the theme of the domestic campaign was 'Britain At Its Best'. Market research in the UK showed that this campaign successfully positioned the company as British, and a provider of quality products. Both these campaigns relied for their success on being parochial.

By the late 1980s, it was argued by *BP*'s UK management and its advertising agency *Saatchi & Saatchi*, that the company and the world had moved on. The time was appropriate to update people's perceptions of the company using a new advertising campaign. The new campaign was to be used around the world. It was based on the theme 'For All Our Tomorrows', and incorporated three messages: environmental concern, community help, and research-based product development. There is nothing wrong with arguing that *BP*'s desired corporate image should be based on these three characteristics. In fact, it is difficult to think of any oil company the community would like not to embrace these goals. And this represents *BP*'s positioning blunder. They threw away a successful and powerful parochial position in stakeholders' minds, for an untried position that competitors like *Chevron* and *Shell* could also claim.

BP is not the only multinational company to walk away from a successful position because it got sick of it. Remember Coke's great position—'It's The Real Thing'. Coke seems to change its advertising tag-lines (positioning statements) fairly regularly. 'Coke Adds Life' and 'Just For The Taste Of It' are two tag-lines which followed 'It's The Real Thing' position. While I was writing this chapter, I saw an Australian television advertisement with the tag-line 'Can't Beat The Real Thing'. Maybe Coke managers have a memory after all!

Choosing a Positioning Theme

Having outlined some alternative positioning themes, the task now switches to choosing one of these. To help this decision process, Thomas Kosnik (of the Stanford Business School) advises using the CRUD test to screen any feasible positioning alternatives.[13] The CRUD acronym stands for: is the position Credible, Relevant, Unique, and Durable.

The CRUD criteria are self explanatory and complement those advocated by George Day which were outlined earlier in this chapter. They are useful, however, because they elaborate Day's Step 2a by focusing explicitly on what is important to stake-holders. A short example for the Australian international airline *Qantas* illustrates how the CRUD criteria can be used to choose a good positioning theme.

Qantas has (at least) three credible positioning alternatives. One was broadcast to the world by Dustin Hoffman in the movie Rainman—'the world's safest airline'. (*Qantas* has a perfect safety record.) The second is to position *Qantas* as *the* specialist long-haul airline. The basis for this position is that it is a long way to Australia regardless of which country you come from. The third position is the parochial theme summarised by the *Qantas* kangaroo logo and the tag-line 'The Spirit of Australia'. All three positions pass the first of the CRUD criteria.

Each is credible to travellers and other stakeholders. The safety theme is relevant to all air travellers, while the long-haul specialist and Australian themes are valued by many Australian travellers and overseas visitors. Two of the themes are unique to *Qantas*, namely, safety and Australian. The parochial theme, however, seems to be the most durable of the three, and also the one which *Qantas* can exploit more easily. For example, airlines don't explicitly advertise their comparative safety records, nor do they tend to advertise that it takes a long time to reach your destination. Also, few travellers would fly on any long-haul airline if they considered it was unsafe. Hence, the Australian position gets the best overall rating on the CRUD criteria. (It is also the one which has been used most often by *Qantas*. Their latest tag-line is 'The Australian Airline'.)

Changing Your Organisation's Images

The previous sections of this chapter outline various approaches to building an image (Table 10.1), and a range of alternative desired images (positions) to consider (Table 10.2). This section outlines a five-step approach to coordinate changing the organisation's images:

1 internal evaluation
2 stakeholder research
3 design and implementation
4 internal and external marketing
5 audit.

While the direction of this change program will be the primary responsibility of the organisation's CEO, its implementation will often be delegated to a committee of senior managers. Candidates for inclusion in this committee are the CEO (as chairperson), and the senior managers responsible for marketing and publicity, production or operations, strategic planning, customer research, human resources, and a 'project officer' to get the other managers organised. I label this group the Image Management Team (IMT). Calling this group a 'team' rather than a committee is a deliberate attempt to emphasise the cooperation needed to reshape an organisation's desired image.

1 *Internal Evaluation*
Figure 1.2 in Chapter 1 shows how the organisation's vision

statement, formal policies, and culture are crucial in shaping the images and reputations of any organisation. Hence, a good place to start evaluating the driving forces behind the development of your organisation's images and reputations is an audit of these three factors. Questions such as the following can guide an assessment of the degree of fit or misfit among vision, formal policies, and organisational culture.

- Does the organisation have a formal vision statement (credo or mission statement)? Does this statement incorporate all the elements outlined in Chapter 3? Is it widely accepted throughout the organisation?
- Is there a tight internal fit between the organisation's business strategy, organisational design, and management control processes? Is there a tight external fit between the organisation's market environment and its resources and competencies? (Chapter 4).
- Does the organisation have a homogeneous culture or a set of complementary subcultures? Do these cultures support translating the values outlined in the vision statement into employee behaviour? (Chapter 5).

During this evaluation stage, two other topics need consideration from the IMT. The first was covered in the previous section, and refers to choosing a desired image position. The second topic was outlined in Chapter 2, and relates to identifying the organisation's key stakeholder groups. Each organisation can identify a set of stakeholder groups of primary and secondary importance to its operations. The IMT needs to explicitly decide which stakeholders are more/less important so as to facilitate the choice of a desired image position. It is unlikely that a desired image will perfectly fit the expectations of every type of stakeholder. Hence, a tradeoff will be necessary in favour of the more important groups.

2 *Stakeholder Research*

Chapter 9 outlined how to research the images and reputations which stakeholders hold of your organisation. Few organisations, however, seem to collect data about how different groups regard an organisation and its competitors on a regular basis, for example, annually. The IMT can create a budget for this activity and thereby imbed it into the formal policies of the organisation. The research design (data collection and analysis) is best contracted out to a market research firm. As noted in the previous subsection, a key factor when doing stakeholder research is to collect data from those groups who are most important to the organisation. When analysing the data gathered from these stakeholders, it is also crucial to compare the organisation's images and reputations across different groups, and across different organisations for the same group. This type of comparative analysis can often reveal sources of potential trouble for the organisation. For example, if the reputations held by journalists are less favourable than those held by other stakeholders, then the media reports of this group could change the opinions of other groups. This is a popular complaint of most organisations battling a media crisis. (See Chapter 11).

3 *Design and Implementation*

Stage 3 focuses on integrating all the factors in Chapters 3 to 8. In effect, the IMT takes on the role of an architect. Like a good architect, it must be multiskilled so that vision, formal policies, organisational culture, communication, and identity can be integrated to form a mould to create the organisation's desired image. If the IMT feels uncomfortable with the complexity of the task, it can use the services of an external consultant to adopt the role of 'project officer' for the IMT. As will be clear from the previous discussion in this book, a design consultant, advertising agency, public relations firm, or a market research firm are not recommended for this role. Their skill base tends to be too limited around their primary function. If a consultant is invited to work with the IMT, then that consultant needs to be multi-skilled in order to ensure that the factors which shape an organisation's reputation are kept in balance. This person can also advise on the selection of an advertising agency, market research firm, graphic design firm or other specialists to supply information to the IMT.

Knowing if and when to call outside assistance is a critical factor in the successful design of your organisation's images. In order to help you think through this problem, Figure 10.1 presents seven questions structured in the form of a decision tree. Tables 10.3 and 10.4 then describe eight options (or decision problems) to which the yes/no answers to these questions lead. Each option is identified by a circled number in Figure 10.1. Table 10.3 lists a set of decision strategies which are appropriate for each of these decision problems, and Table 10.4 describes each of these decision strategies. The rationale behind each decision strategy is fully described in the original research which led to this decision tree.[14] Working through Figure 10.1 is worth the effort. It is based on what is known as the Vroom–Yetton model of leadership which is probably the most useful piece of management research I have ever seen. CEOs or other managers responsible for actually deciding on a particular desired image position will welcome the clarity of the advice incorporated in this figure and its accompanying tables.

4 *Internal and External Marketing*

The fourth step in the change process involves *selling* the (new) image position first to employees, and then to external stake-holders. You may (or may not be) surprised to be told that the internal marketing of why the organisation is trying to reposition itself is often overlooked by change managers. It is not uncommon for the IMT to work in isolation from most other managers and all other employees. Often, the first time front-line employees hear about the whole idea of image management is when they see a new advertisement for their organisation or when the CEO announces that the organisation will have a new name TOMORROW! The IMT can usually come up with some good reasons for not sharing their ideas with employees. The usual ones are that they don't want to signal the organisation's future plans to competitors, or that they couldn't involve every-one in the decision process because they could never reach a decision. Either way, it's insulting to many employees to find out about their organisation's new direction in the media, and it can reinforce feelings that senior management does not trust the people who work in the organisation.

The chapter on organisational culture suggests that it may take considerable time to get all employees enthusiastic about contributing to their organisation's (new) ideal image. Also, this chapter argues that an organisation will have real trouble projecting any type of clear image if employees don't feel that it is in their best interest to do so. Hence, internal marketing and gaining the commitment of employees *must* precede any attempt to signal a new direction to external stakeholders. Customers and other external stakeholders become very cynical of an organisation which says in its corporate advertising that it has improved its service, product quality, or whatever, when in fact it is merely *trying* to do so. Ask the customers of Australian

Manager's Questions

A	B	C	D	E	F	G
Do I know what information I need?	Do I have sufficient information to make a quality decision?	Do other managers have additional information?	Is acceptance of my decision critical to its effective implementation	If I make the decision myself, is it certain that it would be accepted by others?	Can other managers be trusted to base solutions on organisational considerations?	Is conflict among other people likely for my preferred solution?

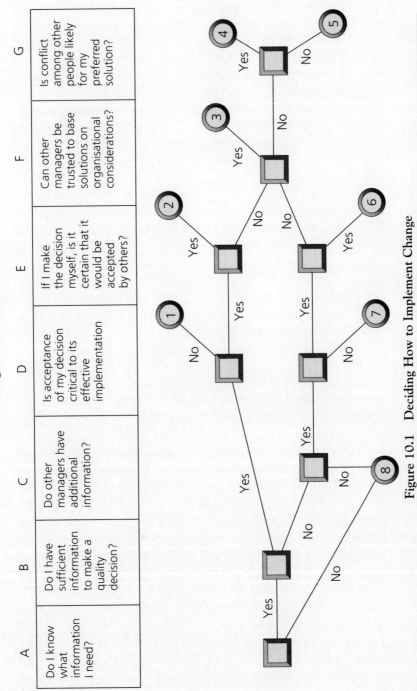

Figure 10.1 Deciding How to Implement Change

Source: Vroom, V. & Yetton, P. 1973, *Leadership and Decision Making*, Pittsburgh Press, Pittsburgh.

Table 10.3

Recommended Set of Leadership Styles

Decision Type	Recommended Methods
1	A1, A2, C1, C2, G*
2	A1, A2, C1, C2, G*
3	G
4	C1 or C2+
5	C1 or C2
6	A2, C1, C2, G*
7	A2, C1, C2, G*
8	Bring in a consultant

*   G is recommended only if the answer to Question F is yes
\+   If the leader can cope with (i.e. legitimise) conflict use C1, otherwise use C2

Source: Vroom, V. & Yetton, P. 1973, *Leadership and Decision Making*, Pittsburgh Press, Pittsburgh.

Table 10.4

Alternative Decision Strategies

'A' stands for autocratic ' C' for consultative, 'G' for group

A1   You make the decision yourself, using information available to you at the time.

A2   You obtain the necessary information from subordinates and other managers, then make the decision yourself. You may or may not tell other people what the problem is in getting the information from them. The role played by other people is one of providing the necessary information to you, rather than generating or evaluating alternative solutions.

C1   You share the problem with relevant managers and subordinates individually, getting their ideas and suggestions without bringing them together as a group. Then you make the decision, which may or may not reflect the other people's influence.

C2   You share the problem with relevant managers and subordinates as a group collectively obtaining their ideas and suggestions. Then you make the decision, which may or may not reflect the other people's influence.

G   You share the problem with relevant managers and subordinates as a group. Together you generate and evaluate alternatives and attempt to reach agreement (consensus) on a solution.

Source: Vroom, V. & Yetton, P. 1973, *Leadership and Decision Making*, Pittsburgh Press, Pittsburgh.

banks what they thought of the advertising claims that said 'You can trust your bank' and then saw their government appoint a bank ombudsman. Ask the customers of the US car maker that said 'Quality is Number 1', and then a couple of years later this company confessed that their quality standards had just reached those of their Japanese competitors.

5 *Audit*

Many organisations go through the fist four steps of the image change process and then STOP. A feeling often develops among members of the IMT that 'we've now fixed up the organisation's image and reputation problems and it's time to move on to something else'. Reputation management, however, is an ongoing process. These reputations take a long time to form, and they can be damaged quickly in the event of a crisis as we will see in the next chapter. Also, the actions of competitors will have an impact on the organisation's relative position in stakeholders' minds. Hence, the organisation's current reputations need continual monitoring to detect changes in stakeholder perceptions, and in the factors which combine to form them (Figure 1.2 in Chapter 1).

Keeping track of the organisation's reputations over time usually requires an annual, or sometimes a bi-annual survey of stakeholder perceptions. It is also recommended that an annual organisational culture survey be undertaken. The collection of these two pieces of information should be budgeted for in the annual planning process. The IMT should then meet once or twice a year to integrate this new information into its database, and to review the organisation's overall reputations and their fit with the strategic objectives for this marketing asset. If a crisis occurs, the IMT can provide important information to the crisis management team about its potential effects on particular aspects of the organisation's reputations. This is crucial information for formulating an appropriate response to the media.

Conclusion

This chapter outlines a number of different approaches to building a desired image and reputation. What they all have in common is that they try to position the organisation to offer value to its various stakeholder groups. The pathfinder, commander, change, and vision models are alternative ways to implement change. In practice, elements of each approach are often combined to achieve the desired change. Forming an IMT is an effective way to manage the data collection necessary to profile your organisation's current reputations and develop a desired image.

The single most important point made in this chapter is that the senior management team must become actively involved in designing a desired image for their organisation. This positioning theme is the critical link in the chain of activities needed to gain a competitive advantage. If managers don't know what the organisation wants to stand for, then it is unlikely that employees can communicate a desired position for the organisation to customers and other stakeholders. In a competitive market, no clear image and value proposition usually means that the organisation's reputations will be of less use as a strategic marketing asset.

End Notes

1 C. Chajet, 'A new image for Continental Airlines', *Design Management Journal*, Winter, 1992, pp. 71–5.

2 J. Bourgeois & D. Brodwin, 'Strategic implementation: five approaches to an elusive phenomenon', *Strategic Management Journal*, vol. 5, 1984, pp. 241–64.

3 R.T. Pascale & A.G. Athos, *The Art of Japanese Management*, Simon and Schuster, New York, 1981.

4 G.S. Day, *Market Driven Strategy: Processes for Creating Value*, The Free Press, New York, 1990, Ch. 7.

5 J. Edward Russo & P.J.H. Schoemaker, *Decision Traps*, Simon & Schuster, New York, 1989.

6 J. Rossiter & L. Percy, *Advertising and Promotion Management*, McGraw-Hill, New York, 1987.

7 This table is based on: D. Aaker, *Managing Brand Equity*, The Free Press, New York, 1991, Ch. 5; and T.J. Kosnik, 'Designing and building a corporate reputation', *Design Management Journal*, vol. 2, no. 2, 1991, pp. 10–16.

8 During the 1970s and early 1980s, BHP was often accused by some of its customers of giving preferential treatment to its 'mates'. This was done by adjusting its steel rolling cycles to fit the requirements of favoured customers.

9 Aaker, op. cit., p. 119.

10 A. Ries & J. Trout, *Positioning: The Battle for Your Mind*, McGraw-Hill, New York, 1986.

11 G.R. Dowling, 'BP catches the global brand fad', *Australian Institute of Management Magazine*, February, 1991, NSW Edition, pp. 7–8.

12 N. Shoebridge, 'Goodbye quiet achiever, hello global togetherness', *Business Review Weekly*, 27 October 1989, pp. 94–5, 97.

13 T.J. Kosnik, 'Designing and building a corporate reputation', *Design Management Journal*, Winter, 1991, pp. 10–16.

14 V.H. Vroom & P. Yetton, *Leadership and Decision Making*, Pittsburgh Press, Pittsburgh, 1973. Summaries of this research can also be found in most good textbooks on leadership and decision making.

CHAPTER 11

The Crisis: Communication Strategies to Protect Your Reputation

The Chinese characters for crisis denote two words—danger and opportunity. From the point of view of your organisation's desired reputation, it is the danger component which is the focus of this chapter. While opportunities may arise as the result of a crisis, the short-term effects on your image and reputation are almost always negative.

Business organisations encounter a wide range of unforeseen circumstances which have the potential to damage their desired reputations. Some of these are totally unexpected and outside the control of management (such as an earthquake), while others may be directly or indirectly caused by management actions (such as a management scandal, hostile takeover, industrial relations dispute, customer service problems, contaminated or faulty products, incorrect waste disposal, chemical spills and leakages or factory fire). A crisis where management can be implicated provides fertile ground for investigative media reporting. For example, *Nestlé* faced an eleven-year controversy over infant feeding in the Third World.

Unfortunately, there is a natural tendency for many managers to think that a major crisis 'can't happen to our company'. Hence, many companies fail to adequately plan how to respond to a crisis. In fact, some managers state that the phrase 'planning for a crisis' is itself an oxymoron. Bob Berzok, Director of Corporate Communications at *Union Carbide* noted that nobody at the company could have dreamt that a disaster like the chemical leak at Bhopal in India was even remotely possible.[1]

Sometimes a lack of crisis planning, or the failure to implement existing plans, results from management overconfidence. For example, we know that space travel is a risky activity. As *NASA*'s successes in space travel and exploration became legendary, in part due to their effective self-promotion, they started live television coverage of their operations. One example of this was the coverage of space shuttle lift-offs and landings. However, when the explosion of the space shuttle Challenger was broadcast live to millions of people on 28 January 1986, *NASA* responded badly.[2] While they did have an emergency public relations crisis plan, the years of promoting their successes made them complacent. They were caught off guard. Also, at the time of the Challenger disaster, their new acting chief administrator had been on the job for only a week.

The facts are that the media is reporting more and more 'disasters' involving the activities of specific organisations. In many cases, this publicity has damaging effects on the organisation's reputations among customers, the financial community, public policy-makers and the general public. The aim of this chapter is to outline some of the communications options available to your organisation when responding to a crisis. These options are suitable for organisations which have conducted an audit of their activities and developed a crisis plan, as well as those which do not have any formal crisis reaction contingency plan.

Knowing the range of communication options available in a crisis situation is crucial for the senior managers and public relations experts which have to deal with the media during such an event. They need to choose an appropriate overall theme for their media presentations which is appropriate for the crisis at hand. They also need to do this quickly as discussed in the following section. The careful selection of an appropriate communication strategy can help to minimise the adverse effects of the public's perception of the organisation, and its products and services.

If external stakeholders have a good reputation of your organisation then this is one of your most powerful marketing assets. The enhancement and defence of this asset is therefore a primary concern for the senior management of any organisation. In recent years the media, special interest groups, and politicians have increased their scrutiny of business, and have questioned the ethics of certain business practices (such as legal tax minimisation, high interest rates), the morality of some management practices (for example, the size of executive compensation packages), the effectiveness of business (for example, levels of exporting, the degree of competition), and the social cost of pollution, waste disposal and accident rehabilitation. As mentioned in Chapter 1, it is not an uncommon claim that the overall reputation of business has declined over the past decade.

When a crisis occurs, how should your organisation respond to the media to minimise the potential damage to its reputations? Before outlining some of the options available, it is necessary to identify areas of potential risk because the type of crisis you face will impact on the types of communication strategies which are suitable for your 'defence'.

The remainder of this chapter is organised as follows. First, a risk analysis technique is proposed which can help you identify high, medium and low risk crisis areas. Second, a four stage communication response model is presented. Then a number of alternative responses are presented from which your organisation can select to communicate its concern about, and remorse for the crisis. Some type of contingency planning can and should be undertaken to develop broad guidelines for action in the unlikely event that a crisis occurs. This planning can commence with an analysis of the likely areas in which a crisis may occur, and the impact of such a crisis on the reputations held by various groups.

Risk Analysis

Each organisation relies on the goodwill and support of a wide variety of people in order to fulfil its mission. Chapter 2 suggests that the two primary groups are employees and customers. Other casualties of a crisis may include shareholders, distributors, service agents (such as the advertising agency), local authorities, and the financial community. Also, there are other groups which may take special interest in the misfortunes of your organisation, such as politicians, government agencies, environmentalists, and journalists. Management needs to identify a set of disasters which could have an unfavourable impact on the reputations each of these groups hold of your organisation. These disasters should reflect the range of activities carried out by your organisation, and the impact each could have on the reputations people hold of the organisation.

A disaster scenario can be written for each high risk area of the business. It can be as simple as a description of the effects of publicity after the occurrence of say the (accidental) death of a senior manager, or it can be as detailed as an action plan to be implemented after a fire in a chemical plant. In the first example, the main target audiences interested in the crisis may be other managers and employees, the financial community, and share-holders. Journalists and the broader public may show little interest in this incident unless the person has or had a high public profile (such as a sports star). In the second example, all the groups identified previously may take an interest in the crisis.

A number of potential disasters should be identified, and their likely impact on the organisation's operations and the reputations held by various groups should be prioritised. Risk analysis is a formal procedure for identifying potential crises and their negative effects on stakeholders and the organisation. Typically, crises are caused by two interacting sets of failures.[3] RIP failures in the organisation's operating environment (Regulatory, Infrastructure and Preparedness) interact with the HOT factors inside the organisation (Human, Organisational and Technolog-

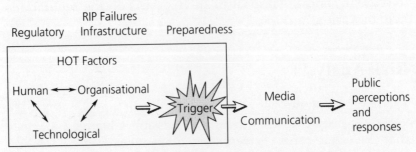

Figure 11.1   The Anatomy of an Industrial Crisis

Source: Adapted from Weick, K., 'The vulnerable system: an analysis of the Tenerife air disaster', *Journal of Management*, vol. 16, no. 3, 1990, pp. 571–93.

ical). This is illustrated in Figure 11.1. Often these two sets of potential failure points are triggered by the occurrence of a number of low probability events that become linked and amplified in ways that are incomprehensible and unpredictable.[4]

The matrix outlined in Figure 11.2 suggests how to profile the negative effects of a crisis on your corporation's reputations. It is a simple cross-tabulation of corporate stakeholders against the potential impact of a crisis. In the cells of the matrix are five hypothetical disaster scenarios (DS_1 to DS_5) reflecting how they might impact on each group. Plotting various scenarios on an impact matrix such as this provides an overview of the organisation's risk profile. It is also a useful first step in stimulating the development of crisis contingency plans for those scenarios which will have a moderate or high impact on the organisation's reputations. To be able to prioritise a set of scenarios requires identifying the various target audiences affected by the crisis (relatively easy), and estimating the likely impact of such a crisis on the organisation's 'bottom line', and reputation (more difficult).

Figure 11.2

Corporate Reputation Crisis Impact Matrix

Organisational Stakeholders	*Negative Effects on Corporate Reputation*		
	Low	Medium	High
Customers		DS_2	
Employees	DS_3 DS_4	DS_2	DS_1 DS_5
Distributors	DS_2		
Service agents	DS_2		
Financial community	DS_1		
Government agencies			
Local authorities			DS_3
Special interest groups		DS_4	

DS_1 to DS_5 are potential Disaster Scenarios

Any major crisis should always be reported to employees—
hence the inclusion of all five scenarios in Figure 11.2 in the
employee row of the matrix. Also, employees should always be
told the truth, and they should be contacted (just) before any
statements are made to the media. The fullness of this disclosure
is a matter for management discretion and should be guided by
the principle of trust. It is good to remember that

- it is this group which has to carry the burden of recovery
- employees have most to lose in the long run from a poor
  corporate reputation (namely, their jobs)
- talking to employees is more likely to limit speculation and
  gossip
- it is insulting to employees to be informed about their company
  by a media report.

Another requirement is to inform distributors and independent service agents if a crisis will have any marked effect on
customers. The other groups to be informed, and how this
should be done (covered later in this chapter) will depend on the
particular nature of the crisis.

The impact of a crisis on the reputation a particular group
holds of an organisation is a function of three factors. The first is
how favourable or unfavourable their current reputation is, the
second is the magnitude and type of crisis, and the third is the
amount and tone of media publicity. While the second and third
factors are problematic, the first can be measured quite easily as
we saw in Chapter 9. To date, published scientific studies of how
a crisis (adversely) affects a company's image and/or reputation
are rare.[5] However many managers believe that a good corporate
reputation acts as a type of insurance policy the first time the
company faces a serious crisis. Here are three examples:

> Mr Justice Mars-Jones said that the penalty would have been
> substantially greater if Shell had not had an outstanding
> record for conservation and for generous support for the arts
> and other worthwhile causes.
>
> (Daily Telegraph report on Shell's £1 million fine for the Mersey oil spillage.[6])

> We had a good reputation before Bhopal and we did not lose
> a single customer afterwards.
>
> (Bob Berzok, Director of Corporate Communications, Union Carbide.[7])

...the reputation of the corporation, which has been carefully built over 90 years, provided a reservoir of goodwill among the public, the people in the regulatory agencies, and the media, which was of incalculable value in helping to restore the brand.

(Jim Burke, Chairman of Johnson & Johnson speaking about the Tylenol poisonings.[8])

The final issue to be addressed in this section relates to how your organisation can plan to respond to a potential crisis. The safest option is to develop a full contingency plan which would deal with all facets of disaster recovery.[9] Such a plan generally includes a strategy for:

- isolating the crisis area from the rest of the organisation
- forming teams to contain and rectify the problem and to investigate causes and propose future changes
- procedures for selecting a company spokesperson to liaise with the media
- the development of a specific media strategy.

Full crisis contingency planning is appropriate for scenarios classified as potentially highly damaging to the organisation's reputations.

A less-detailed crisis plan might cover only a broad media strategy. Here the organisation outlines:

- the timing of its response to the media
- the type(s) of information to be released
- the method of its response to employees, the media and other relevant parties (such as local authorities).

Crises of moderate importance warrant this type of planning. The minimum amount of communication that should be made after a crisis is some type of verbal or written statement by a senior manager to the interested groups. The reason for this is that it is better for management to control the timing and content of the information flow than to have to react to (unanticipated) questions at some undetermined future time (like the small shareholder who asks a difficult question during the annual general meeting).

The aim of risk analysis is to identify the potential impact of a serious crisis on the corporate reputations held by various groups. The organisation can then think about how it should communicate with interested and affected groups.

Communication Strategies for Responding to a Crisis

In this section, a simple four-stage crisis reaction plan is presented. It is designed to help your organisation a) gain time to formulate a comprehensive communication response, and b) select a strategy that helps the organisation to express its concern about the crisis and demonstrate suitable remorse for any part it played in causing it. Managers who have been involved in an industrial crisis are quick to point out that there is no single communication procedure which is appropriate in all circumstances. (See [10] for a more extensive set of crisis handling steps.) This advice is well taken. Consequently, here a simple, yet flexible approach is outlined which can be adapted to a wide range of situations. The overall aim of this strategy is to restrict the potential damage to your organisation's reputations.

Crisis communication should address both the cognitive needs (for facts and analysis) and emotional needs (for reassurance, sympathy) of affected stakeholders. It should also reinforce the organisational culture and procedures which keep the company operating.[11] Within this framework, responding to a crisis requires three sequential actions:

1 the immediate communication response
2 answering the three basic media questions
3 demonstrating remorse.

The first action is designed to gain time so that when a spokesperson talks to the media (action 2), this more detailed response is an informed and credible one. If the first two actions are carried out well then the organisation can implement a program of corporate reputation damage control (action 3). In some cases it may even be possible for an organisation to enhance its reputation if the three actions are implemented appropriately.

The Immediate Communication Response

Immediately after a crisis or even during one like a factory fire, is the time when the media (especially television reporters) are at their most active (and potentially lethal). At this stage of a crisis 'facts' are scarce, and there is often speculation about the cause and effects of the crisis on the people involved and the general public. The 'game' some reporters play is to find a company spokesperson and ask a series of speculative and sometimes intrusive questions in the hope of obtaining a sensational/newsworthy story. While the journalism profession frequently denies these allegations, the nightly news and current affairs programs often show behaviour which seems to support such claims. From your organisation's point-of-view it is best to be prepared for the 'worst' type of media questioning. The decision about the type of statement to make about the crisis at this time is crucial.

If the organisation is not ready to talk to the media immediately this can lead to two outcomes:

- management is perceived as confused, incompetent, or as withholding information, and/or
- the media will find someone else to interview such as an eyewitness or an independent 'expert'.

In the second case, management has let the agenda for the next round of communications be set by an external party. Its next response will be reactive rather than proactive because the spokesperson will have to respond to the issues raised in the first media coverage. A better option is to have someone immediately available to show that the organisation is in control. Such a strategy provides the tactical advantage of setting the crisis in the relevant context, and establishing the agenda and the timetable for future reports.

Implementing this proactive strategy requires answers to two questions:

- Who should be selected as the company spokesperson?
- What should he/she say?

Answers to both questions are fairly straightforward. First, the spokesperson should be a (very) senior manager who has functional expertise in the area involving the crisis, for example, the Director of Finance for budgetary, accounting, taxation issues or the Regional General Manager for a crisis involving a local facility. Another equally good alternative is to have the CEO as the spokesperson—especially if that person already has the trust and respect of the general public (such as Lee Iacocca of *Chrysler*). If at all possible, journalists recommend against using someone from the public relations department, or the claim that your lawyers have advised that 'no comment' would be an appropriate response. Both these options are likely to have negative source credibility effects.

Whoever is chosen for this most demanding assignment should:

- have received media presentation training (or be a 'natural presenter'), and
- remain as the spokesperson for the duration of the media coverage.

This person should also be part of any crisis management team that is set up (to ensure they are fully informed), and they could also take the lead role in communicating with employees (to ensure that one consistent story is presented to everybody).

What should the company spokesperson say at this initial media encounter? Given the twin aims of a) establishing the context and agenda for the information to be presented, and b) trying to ensure that the way the crisis is reported cannot further damage your organisation's reputations, then if the facts surrounding the crisis are not completely clear make a statement to the effect that:

- everything possible is being done at present to contain the damage, or minimise the effects of the crisis
- the spokesperson doesn't know all the relevant details at this time, so any statement now may be misleading
- (preliminary) investigations are underway
- the spokesperson will be available to the media at a certain place and time with detailed information
- the organisation is extremely concerned about this issue.

At this point, the company spokesperson should leave the reporters and say that his/her time is best spent managing the crisis and gathering more information. In essence, this is how *Occidental International* responded when an explosion and fire occurred on their Piper Alpha oil drilling platform in the North Sea.[12]

The time interval for the spokesperson to be available with detailed information cannot be too long otherwise it will lead to suspicion and speculation. On the other hand, it has to be long enough so that a clear picture emerges about the cause and possible effects of the crisis. Employees should be informed at this point if this has not already occurred. The time interval chosen is a 'judgement call' and some advice from the public relations department or a friendly journalist can help here.

Where management perceives that a crisis has the potential to expose damaging information about the organisation, there is often a tendency for them to talk to the lawyers before making any public statement. Advice from this source, however, is often a two-edged sword. Lawyers are accustomed to studying matters thoroughly before making an opinion. Also, their opinions tend to err on the side of caution. Waiting for, and then relying on such advice is likely to make it difficult for the spokesperson to take the initiative in any ensuing media dialogue.

This first response to a crisis can be critical. For example Dr Jean-Jacques Saltzmann, head of corporate safety and environmental protection for the Swiss chemical manufacturer *Sandoz* said that after his company polluted the Rhine river with water used to put out a chemical fire, the company handled the media poorly. The company, local authorities, and the government all made statements prematurely because of a lack of information. This degraded the reputation of the company, the effects of which outweighed the material damage to the plant. The result was a loss of confidence for both *Sandoz* and the chemical industry.[13]

What to Tell the Media

In a crisis situation the media generally have three basic questions:[14]

- What happened?
- Why?
- What are you going to do about it?

Answering the 'what happened' and 'why' questions can be a factual recount of cause and effect. These 'facts', however, should be of the 'unshakeable variety' so that there is little chance that they will have to be modified at a later time. The way this information is presented should lead naturally into the organisation's answer to the third question. A good discipline is to prepare a carefully worded written statement(s) for distribution to employees and the media. Then insist that the media read the statement before they ask questions. If their subsequent questions can be answered by reference to the written statement then refer them to it. The urge to answer a question by rewording what is already stated should be avoided as this encourages reporters to continue this line of questioning and to make their own interpretation of the spokesperson's written response. In this exchange with the media, the spokesperson must endeavour not to lose control of the situation. Such 'trial by media' can easily lead to the potentially damaging strategy of calling an embarrassed halt to the interview when reporters are being filmed queuing up to ask more questions.

Public relations experts (either in-house or from a separate agency) can play a vital role during this stage of your organisation's response to the media. Their understanding of media deadlines, the temperament of particular reporters, and their drafting skills for media releases can make an important contribution to the clear reporting of your organisation's actions to resolve the crisis. They can also play a useful role in keeping the media away from all senior managers, and arranging times for the release of press statements and interviews with the spokesperson. If the crisis generates long-term interest, the public relations group can monitor all the media coverage, and draft responses to any initial speculation or unfounded allegations. This is likely to occur when media interest shifts from wanting facts about the crisis to gathering 'human interest' stories.[15]

Strategies for Demonstrating Remorse and Salvaging the Corporate Reputation

This subsection outlines some ideas for answering the media's third basic question: 'What are you going to do to make amends for the crisis?' While there is no single foolproof communication strategy here are some options:

1 **Call in the lawyers** This is a strategy which is sometimes used when the company is being attacked by hostile outsiders (for example, during a takeover), or when an employee leaks highly damaging confidential information. In 1991 the Australian bank *Westpac* used such a strategy to try to limit exposure of confidential correspondence from its solicitors regarding foreign currency loans made by one of its subsidiary companies. The bank's lawyers issued injunctions against various individuals and the media to inhibit publication of the damaging material. One effect of this legal action was that the crisis migrated from the business press to the front pages of the popular newspapers and the television news. 'Human

interest' stories kept this crisis in the media for many months and gave it the name 'The Westpac Letters Affair'.

2 **Product recall** When *Perrier* found traces of benzene in its mineral water and when *Heinz* found pieces of glass in its baby food, both companies recalled their products. The strong image of both brands and the quick reaction by the companies reduced the negative effects on both corporate reputations. (*Perrier*'s initial responses to the media, however, were made before they had all the facts about the cause of the contamination.[16])

3 **Product recall and relaunch with a significant product modification** Probably the best known example of this strategy was *Johnson & Johnson*'s relaunch of their *Tylenol* brand of pain relief product. *Tylenol* packages were found to have been opened, contaminated with cyanide, and resealed. The company withdrew the product until a tamper-proof package was developed. Consumer loyalty to this brand was such that it was relaunched under the same brand name and regained its market leadership.

4 **Public sacrifice of the guilty** A good example of this strategy occurred after the *British Midlands Airways* plane crash on the M1 motorway in Britain. After an exhaustive public inquiry where pilot error was established as the major cause of the crash, the two surviving pilots were publicly dismissed from the airline. Another example occurred when the Chairman of *British Airways*, Lord King prematurely resigned in 1993 after BA was found guilty of conducting a 'dirty tricks' campaign against one of its small competitors, *Virgin Airlines*. Sir Colin Marshall, King's CEO, whom many people thought was as much to blame as King, then took control of the airline.[17]

5 **Build a monument** The following example could be fact or fiction—I have never been able to verify its accuracy. It does, however, provide a good illustration of this strategy.

A person with a gun entered a *McDonald's* restaurant in the USA and killed and wounded a number of innocent people. This was one of those unfortunate random incidents that occurs. No blame could be ascribed to the *McDonald's* corporation. A major element of the company's reputation repair response was to demolish the restaurant, turn the area into a small park in memory of the victims, and open a new restaurant nearby.

6 **'Take-it-on-the-chin'** When the Piper Alpha drilling platform exploded in the UK's North Sea oil fields killing 167 men, the *Occidental* company chairman pledged fair and prompt compensation, and put £100 million in a fund to back up his intention. (A good description of how the company managed this crisis can be found in R. David's article.[18])

7 **Blame someone else** In many crises the actions of another person, company or local authority may play a (significant) part in causing the crisis. When this strategy is adopted, the company states its case along the lines that: 'it followed all the regulations and guidelines, however, they turned out to be inadequate' or 'the crisis was caused by the actions of other people outside its control', or 'it was really the victims' fault for letting themselves be exposed to a situation where harm could come to them', etc. The risk of using this strategy is that it often stimulates a savage reaction from the accused party. Also, if the accusations are incorrect then the company's credibility can be damaged when the full facts of the crisis emerge. Such a situation happened to the *London Transport Authority* after a major fire in the King's Cross underground railway station. The transport authority speculated that the fire's severity may have been due to the use of a particular type of paint. Subsequent investigations established that this was a highly unlikely contributing factor to the spreading of the fire. Another example had *Audi* blaming US car drivers for poor driving technique when some of their *Audi 5000* cars were alleged to have a 'sudden acceleration' problem.

8 **Withdraw from the market** This is the fate of many faulty childrens' toys, unhealthy food products, and people in high profile occupations who get caught in personality scandals. While it is one of the more drastic strategies to adopt, it is often a logical outcome of the isolate and containment procedures used during the management of a crisis. Sometimes this strategy is adopted because post crisis investigations show that the potential rewards from an area of business do not offset the inherent risks. In other cases, the decision may be forced on the company by adverse consumer reaction. This happened to the US airline *Pan Am* after the sabotage and crash of one of its planes over the Scottish city of Lockerbie. Passenger numbers on *Pan Am*'s flights from the USA to London fell to such an extent that they sold this air route to *United Airlines*.

9 **'Give us another chance'** Here the CEO publicly accepts all

the responsibility for the crisis and asks that the company be given another chance. The apology may or may not be accompanied by the CEO's resignation as happened when *Japan Airlines* President Yasumoto Takagi resigned immediately after the crash of one of its planes; and *Solomon Brothers* chief executives resigned after the securities firm was found to have broken several laws regarding bond trading. This strategy is often adopted by political parties where the president, prime minister or a cabinet minister accepts responsibility for a mistake. The psychology behind such a strategy is interesting. The bigger the crisis, the more senior a person needs to be to accept ultimate responsibility in order for the public to think the sacrifice is appropriate. In large corporations where it is commonly accepted that a CEO cannot know about (or be really held responsible for) the actions of people well away from the centre of control, use of this type of strategy can demonstrate concern, imply that changes will be made, and give the company another chance.

10 **Referral to a higher authority** This strategy is based on the fact that the fallout from many crises will also contaminate the reputations of other related organisations. For example, the nuclear reactor accidents at Three Mile Island in the USA and Chernobyl in the former Soviet Union, affected the reputation of the whole nuclear industry. The Exxon Valdez oil spill in Alaska had a negative impact on the reputations of all the oil companies. Implementation of this strategy involves getting an industry association, a government body, an independent scientist, or some person with relevant expertise to lend their public support to the company in its time of crisis.

11 **'We were just unlucky'** This is sometimes known as the 'Act of God' strategy. It is designed to appeal to the target audience's sense of fatalism or bad luck. For example, when *Pan Am* lost an aircraft in New Orleans in the early 1980s, they suspected freak weather conditions were the cause. To substantiate this claim, they brought in independent meteorological experts to verify their suspicions (referral to a higher authority). The experts' reports were publicised to inform people that the cause of the crash was a unique weather condition, beyond anyone's control.[19] This strategy could also be implemented by the company citing examples of similar crises occurring in their (or other) industry, or convincing people that when a company works at the leading edge of

technology (in order to make advances for society) some problems are inevitable. If there really is a realistic chance that something dramatic can go wrong, then it is probably wise not to have live television coverage of the organisation's operations as *NASA* did during the Challenger disaster.

12 **'Keep your head down'** This approach calls for saying as little as possible and waiting (hoping) that the media's interest will be diverted to something else. A second aspect to this strategy may be to let the apportionment of blame for the crisis be determined by an independent body such as a public inquiry or a court of law. Taken to the extreme, this approach is the classic 'no comment' strategy and relies for its (potential) success on the assumption that a lower perceived involvement with the crisis will minimise the damage to the company's reputations. However, if the crisis involves a loss of life and the media develops a human interest theme, then the company will be vulnerable to receiving negative media publicity while the victims are seeking due compensation. Also, if the findings of the independent body turn out to be perceived as 'unjust' for some reason, then the media may criticise the company (again) for its part in the crisis, and seek a public statement about how it will compensate the victims. An interesting example of this scenario occurred after *P&O*'s car ferry, the *Herald of Free Enterprise* sank in the English Channel. The bow doors of the ferry were left open as it sailed from port which caused it to sink. The English courts, however, acquitted the crew on charges of negligence, and for legal reasons could not charge the company with manslaughter. The victim's relatives and the media then publicly criticised the company and the legal system for their inability to apportion blame for the accident.

13 **'Counter and Disarm'** This is a variation of the advocacy advertising carried out by some large corporations. The company involved in the crisis uses publicity and advertising to counter the claims made by another party and to state its own case. This strategy is sometimes used during an 'ongoing crisis' such as an industrial relations dispute. For example, during the long-running 1989/1990 Australian domestic airline pilot's dispute, both the major airlines took out full page newspaper advertisements to criticise the pilot's union for withdrawing their services, and to apologise to the travelling public. The media attack by *Suzuki* against the *US Consumer*

Reports magazine's article that its *Samurai* 4-wheel drive car had a tendency to tip over is another example.[20]

These thirteen communication strategies are presented to reflect a range of options open to a company and to stimulate further thought. They are not presented as an exhaustive list, nor is it advisable to try to 'pick the best one' for all crisis situations. The idea is to evaluate the strengths and weaknesses of each approach, and then use elements from various strategies to design a suitable media strategy. In effect, these thirteen strategies present the raw materials for the design of your company's media response.

Choosing an Appropriate Strategy

Choosing an appropriate media strategy is simple in theory but more difficult in application, and will generally require the help of a public relations expert. It involves using the communication strategies outlined above to design a broad media crisis response for each of the disaster scenarios developed during the organisation's risk analysis evaluation. These can take the form of a short plan outlining the timing and sequence of actions to be taken in the event of a particular type of crisis, such as

- form a disaster team
- isolate and contain the crisis
- brief the public relation's team
- select and brief a company spokesperson.

The media strategy part of each crisis plan should be extracted and written as a 'concept statement' understandable to a member of the general public or the particular target audience for the communication. In fact, a number of alternative media strategies should be developed into concept statements for each major disaster scenario. Market research techniques can then be employed to determine the target audience's reaction to each one. This idea of 'concept testing' is common in the field of advertising when a new campaign is being developed. A short stylised example of such a concept statement is shown in Table 11.1.

A number of market research techniques could be used to evaluate the target audience's response to such a scenario. In-depth interviews and focus groups (discussed in Chapter 9) with members of the target audience would be used to uncover

Table 11.1

Sample Concept Statement for Audience Evaluation

Possible Disaster
Fire on the XYZ offshore rig with loss of life

A Company's Initial Media Response
Chief Manager Operations issues a short press release stating:
a   cause of fire (not) known at this stage
b   deaths and/or injuries have occurred but numbers unknown
c   disaster recovery team being assembled
d   company is very concerned about what is happening
e   will be available for further comment at 0900 hours the following day.
The Chief Manager will not answer any reporter's questions at this time.

B Next Media Response
a   state known facts of case
b   if cause known then state this; otherwise state that investigation team is currently working to discover the cause
c   state how company will address the concerns of employees, public and other affected parties
d   will be available for further comment at xxxx hours.

(un)favourable reactions to this and other scenarios. Responses from these interviews would be content analysed to provide feedback on the media response outlined in the scenarios. This type of information is essential to supplement the opinions of senior managers and public relations specialists, and should form the basis of the final media strategy for each type of disaster scenario.

Conclusion

The reputations of your organisation held by various stakeholders are fragile constructs. They are a measure of the overall health of the company, and at the same time they act as facilitators for its success. These reputations also generally take far more time to establish than to damage, as the *Exxon*

Corporation discovered after its tanker the Exxon Valdez disgorged approximately 10 million gallons of oil into Alaska's Prince William Sound. It was not the oil spill so much as the company's poor handling of the ensuing crisis which changed their overall reputation from 'the parade horse of the American oil industry' to a company with 'a giant black eye which will take years to get rid of'.[21] Its response to the crisis was the typical strategy of an organisation uncomfortable with the press and unprepared for a crisis: denial; playing down the incident; adopting the 'keep your head down' strategy, and consequently losing the initiative to the press and other interest groups. Finally *Exxon* responded to mounting public concern with an apology which was too little and too late. This sequence of events cemented hostile relations with the media.

The variety of industrial crises noted in this chapter adequately demonstrate the risks organisations must seek to avoid. They also sound a warning that corporations should not become complacent about what can happen to their reputations if a crisis occurs. The overall planning framework outlined in this chapter is a simple one, namely, conduct a risk analysis, and then plan a reaction strategy based on the nature of the potential crisis, and an understanding of how the organisation's reputations are formed. In the first few hours or days of a crisis, management generally sets the 'tone' of how the crisis will be handled, and hence the potential negative impact on its reputations. Damage to an organisation's reputation after a crisis generally occurs because of media scrutiny and speculation. In fact, public relations people say that it is the media which often escalates an incident into a crisis![22]

End Notes

1   T. Nash, 'Tales of the unexpected', *Director*, March, 1990, pp. 52–5.

2   D. ten Berge, *The First 24 Hours*, Basil Blackwell, Oxford, 1988.

3   P. Shrivastava, I. Mitroff, D. Miller & A. Miglani, 'Understanding industrial crises', *Journal of Management Studies*, vol. 25, July, 1988, pp. 285–303.

4   K. Weick, 'The vulnerable system: an analysis of the Tenerife air disaster', *Journal of Management*, vol. 16, no. 3, 1990, pp. 571–93.

5   M. Sullivan, 'Measuring image spillovers in umbrella-branded products', *Journal of Business*, vol. 63, July, 1990, pp. 309–29.

6   R. David, 'Damage limitation', *Business*, April, 1990, pp. 88–91.

7   Nash, loc. cit.

8   ten Berge, 1988.

 9 ibid.

10 G. Meyers, with J. Holusha, *When It Hits the Fan: Managing the Nine Crises of Business*, Unwin Hyman, London, 1986.

11 R. Kanter, 'Note on management of crisis', *Harvard Business School*, 9-389-054, 1988.

12 David, loc. cit.

13 Nash, loc. cit.

14 ibid; David, loc. cit.

15 David, loc. cit.

16 Staff Reporter, 'When the bubble burst', *The Economist*, vol 320, 3 August 1991, pp. 61–2.

17 Staff Reporter, 'Qantas in bed with a bully?' *Australian Business Monthly*, March, 1993, pp. 42–4.

18 David, loc. cit.

19 ten Berge, 1988.

20 D. Kiley, 'How Suzuki swerved to avoid a marketing disaster', *Adweek's Marketing Week*, 28 October 1988, pp. 27–8.

21 ten Berge, 1988.

22 Nash, loc. cit.

Index